The First Royal Media War

Edward VIII, the Abdication and the Press

Adrian Phillips

PEN & SWORD
HISTORY

First published in Great Britain in 2023 by
Pen & Sword History
An imprint of Pen & Sword Books Limited
Yorkshire – Philadelphia

ISBN 978 1 39906 541 2

A CIP catalogue record for this book is
available from the British Library

Typeset by Mac Style
Printed in the UK by CPI Group (UK) Ltd, Croydon, CR0 4YY.

Pen & Sword Books Limited incorporates the imprints of After the
Battle, Atlas, Archaeology, Aviation, Discovery, Family History,
Fiction, History, Maritime, Military, Military Classics, Politics,
Select, Transport, True Crime, Air World, Frontline Publishing,
Leo Cooper, Remember When, Seaforth Publishing, The Praetorian
Press, Wharncliffe Local History, Wharncliffe Transport,
Wharncliffe True Crime and White Owl.

For a complete list of Pen & Sword titles please contact

PEN & SWORD BOOKS LIMITED
47 Church Street, Barnsley, South Yorkshire, S70 2AS, England
E-mail: enquiries@pen-and-sword.co.uk
Website: www.pen-and-sword.co.uk
or
PEN AND SWORD BOOKS
1950 Lawrence Rd, Havertown, PA 19083, USA
E-mail: Uspen-and-sword@casematepublishers.com
Website: www.penandswordbooks.com

For my brother David

Contents

Introduction: The First Celebrity Monarch

King Edward VIII was the first celebrity monarch. He grew up as the modern media came of age when cinema and radio followed mass-circulation newspapers and magazines in creating a world where the projection of royal image began to take over from power politics as the dominant aspect of the institution. With his good looks, charm and active lifestyle, Edward was perfect for the job. Not the least of his appeal was that he was a bachelor and publicly unattached, so he became one of the world's biggest male sex objects, naturally by the chaste standards of the day.

The media was respectful if not downright reverential towards the monarchy. Their private lives were a no-go area so Edward's love-life escaped scrutiny until the crisis over his relationship with American divorcee Wallis Simpson tested this discretion to the limit in 1936. Discretion revived for a brief period afterwards as the wholesome family life of his brother, by then King George VI, and wartime solidarity held sway but the system was broken. The determination of the by-then Duke of Windsor to fight out the grievances of the crisis and its aftermath put the final nail in the coffin.

In the traditional narrative of the abdication crisis the British media is only given a brief and uninfluential part. The true action played out behind closed doors, hidden from the vast bulk of the public as the newspapers observed a freakish silence over the scandal of the King's relationship with an American divorcee which mutated into a national crisis when he informed the prime minister that he wanted to marry her. The King's negotiations with the government over the marriage were reaching deadlock and abdication looked almost certain when, probably by accident, the press silence broke. For a few frantic days some newspapers supported the King's right to marry whom he chose and others opposed it, above all *The Times*, mouthpiece of the conservative establishment. This was true but, as the greatest novel of the 1930s and perhaps all journalism, Evelyn Waugh's *Scoop*, put it, only 'Up to a point Lord Copper.' The two sides had been fighting a cold war in the press that briefly flared into open conflict well before the scandal broke.

The old media way of covering royalty had ended but the new world had not fully come into being. It was a more innocent age. The media war of the crisis and after was fought on an amateur basis. Edward applied a strictly do-it-yourself approach. Today's legions of ever-vigilant advisers were entirely absent which brings an accidental benefit to anyone trying to understand events and personalities. The picture that the active players tried to project showed their true feelings rather than a calculated assessment of what would boost their image. Like everyone, they saw some things wrongly but their errors of fact can tell us quite as much as their accurate testimony. It is not just true perceptions of reality that make people think what they do about others. Illusion is often more powerful than truth.

Edward's most important adviser during the crisis and afterwards, Walter Monckton, was first and foremost a man of the establishment and a lawyer. His preferred option was the same absolute silence that the royal family wanted.

In the 1930s the media was still a national phenomenon so Edward's affair with Mrs. Simpson was news in every corner of the world except in Britain. Coverage in American newspapers figures as a peripheral factor in accounts of the crisis but this should not mask the fact that Edward and Mrs Simpson were fully aware of the importance of US coverage. The first media tycoon to become actively involved was the American William Randolph Hearst. Even before Edward acceded to the throne he had used a Hearst journalist to issue a manifesto for his kingship that declared his thinking and intentions with great frankness. Hearst is famous for his willingness to influence great events and certainly hoped to put Mrs. Simpson on the throne but he was also a businessman who saw the commercial possibilities of the 'love story of the century' and wanted to exploit them to the full.

The media and celebrity royalty have always been bound by a mixture of money and information management. Hearst's motivation was mainly money but the British pressmen most deeply involved in the crisis were far less motivated by money or the imperative to inform. Above all, Lord Beaverbrook, the Anglo-Canadian newspaper baron, was driven overwhelmingly by his personal political agenda: hatred of prime minister Stanley Baldwin that dominated his actions during the crisis and his attempts to influence how history recorded it afterwards. Esmond Harmsworth, whose family owned the *Daily Mail*, was a friend of Edward and wanted to help him. Geoffrey Dawson, editor of *The Times*, saw himself as a statesman and public servant and this still shapes the way he is perceived, but the coverage in *The Daily Telegaph*, the newspaper that Baldwin made his mouthpiece, escapes attention.

The British government mounted unprecedented intelligence operations during the crisis. The stakes were so great that these were seen as legitimate and necessary to protect national stability. Beaverbrook – and the King's one serious political supporter, Winston Churchill – were the prime targets but Hearst's organization did not escape and the product from this part of the operation deeply influenced government perceptions of Mrs. Simpson and her intentions.

Afterwards the battle over the memory of the crisis was fought out by book publishers and lawyers. Here we come close to what happens today. The memoirs by the couple were bestsellers but less than accurate. Even if they sold well at the time, the books by unavowed literary proxies for either side have generally disappeared from view, but this does not diminish their value as a means of knowing what the players directly involved wanted to be believed.

What was the reality behind the spin?

With very few exceptions, everyone in government or the court thought that Mrs. Simpson was unacceptable as the King's wife. Her divorces were undeniable and a matter of public record, but that was not all that there was to hold against her. These other complaints were powerful factors in swinging opinion against her, but they could not be disclosed. A police investigation in 1935 had reported that she was not merely cuckolding her husband with the Prince of Wales, but being unfaithful to both with a car salesman. As the crisis got properly under way in 1936, Mrs. Simpson was known to be working with Hearst to promote the plan of marrying the King; she was on his payroll as well.

The ultra-establishment newspaper *The Times* wrote of Mrs. Simpson bearing the 'brand of unfitness for the Queen's throne'. Almost no one in power had any doubts that she deserved this, either before the abdication or afterwards. Days after the abdication the prime minister, Stanley Baldwin, engineered a broadcast by the country's highest ethical authority, the Archbishop of Canterbury, that pressed the brand firmly on Mrs. Simpson and, by extension, the ex-king.

Supporters of the Duke of Windsor argued that Mrs. Simpson had provided a handy pretext to force him off the throne. Baldwin had long held doubts about Edward, but it cannot be argued that he acted positively to drive him to abdicate. Baldwin was an astute politician and knew that the government would not be forgiven if it did not give the King every opportunity to remain on the throne. But that is different to working actively to keep him there. When Edward thought that Baldwin would back down in the face of his popularity and told him that he would abdicate if he were not allowed to marry Mrs. Simpson, Baldwin did not blink and told the King, 'Sir, that is most grievous news.'

1

The House of Windsor Enters the Age of Media

The abdication crisis of 1936 coincided with the time when press deference towards the British monarchy was at its height. The British monarchy's greatest sex scandal was not manufactured by the media. The British media made no mention of even the basic facts until the very last moment. The press had become exceedingly docile over the preceding century and a half. In part this was a reaction to the practices of the eighteenth century when the press had taken advantage of relatively relaxed controls compared to its European counterparts to deliver brutal and often near-pornographic criticism of the royal family. By the middle of the twentieth century this was part of a distant past and other forces ruled in a radically changed environment.

Press criticism of the British monarchy had been most extreme in the second half of the eighteenth century. The House of Hanover had been installed on the British throne by Parliament but its kings were anything but puppets. They played an active role in the politics of the day and were sucked into all aspects of political debate, including the battle for public opinion through the press. The notion that somehow monarchy should enjoy a sacred standing above criticism was never going to survive the second change in dynasty in a generation, forced through by a coalition of the aristocracy and a Parliament that could claim to represent the country as a whole. The most powerful media commentators on the Georgian monarchy were cartoonists. The savage lampoons of James Gillray, Isaac Cruikshank and Thomas Rowlandson still shape the historical image of the later Hanoverian monarchs as inept voluptuaries. The personal lives of the royals were irresistible targets for criticism. The relationship of the Prince of Wales (later Prince Regent and King George IV) with a Catholic, Mrs. Fitzherbert, was an especially fruitful topic which blended protestant religious prejudice with sexual morality and the recurrent enmity between Hanoverian kings and their heirs. The revelation that his brother the Duke of York's mistress had taken payments to obtain army commissions was a heaven-sent opportunity for adverse observation. The violent death of the valet of another brother, the much-hated Duke of Cumberland, provoked a flood of insinuations. Cartoonists did not just attack the royals; they attacked journalists who went too far in supporting the royal house. Some of the press lavished fawning and vacuous flattery on one royal, so extreme that it has been compared to the media adulation of Princess Diana.[1] The Duke of York's wife was extravagantly praised for her supposedly dainty feet, which inspired Gillray's cartoon 'Fashionable Contrasts' showing only the feet of the couple having sex while Cruikshank mocked society ladies attempting to force their large feet into the Duchess's size of shoe in 'Getting the Length of the Duchess's Foot' with an image that could have inspired Cinderella's ugly sisters.

When Queen Victoria came to the throne in 1837, she turned the leaf from the sordid days of her 'wicked uncles'. She was an attractive innocent teenager who became a model wife and mother. She offered hope of political and moral reform for the nation. As a teenager, it was inevitable that her political activities would start from a limited base, which shielded her from the policy debates of her day. When she married Albert, the political influence of the royal couple was further restrained because she intentionally limited her husband's standing to that of Prince Consort. She wanted to keep tight hold on her status as a sovereign. As a foreigner Albert had to overcome nationalist instinct amongst politicians and the public as well. Albert's most notable contribution to public life was to master-mind the Great Exhibition of 1851, often seen as a high-water mark of Britain's achievement. As she matured, Victoria's own direct political influence focused chiefly on the choice of prime ministers, but it was far from decisive. She was a powerful ally of the Conservative Benjamin Disraeli who was prime minister for two terms but she was unable to keep the Liberals Palmerstone and Gladstone, whom she actively disliked, out of office. She supposedly claimed that Gladstone spoke to her 'as though she was a public meeting'. Republicanism was a noticeable force but it was essentially a press campaign only; it had no worthwhile political backing. It was only after the death of Albert that Victoria drew any open personal criticism and that was extremely mild compared to the savagery meted out to the Hanoverians. Her reclusiveness in widowhood was seen as obsessive and a neglect of her duties as monarch. Her relationship with her Scottish servant John Brown was viewed unfavourably, but it is hard to find specific press items. The only hostile cartoon that it was possible to trace appeared in a French newspaper.

The private lives of Victoria and Albert were blameless but her son and heir, the future King Edward VII, provided ample potential material for salacious comment with his gluttony, philandering and gambling; however, by the end of the nineteenth century the British press had lost its appetite for this kind of thing. There is no single precise reason for this. The nature of the press had changed radically. It had generally become more staid and less prone to violent attacks on those in power. Newspaper circulation had soared from the eighteenth century. Growing public investment in education meant that literacy levels had increased dramatically, so potential newspaper readership grew far beyond the small educated – and by extension politically conscious – section of the population of the previous century. Rising income levels allowed people to buy what had once been luxury items such as newspapers and the new advertising that aimed to shape their purchases of other goods brought more money into the newspaper business in a virtuous circle; at least from the press proprietors' point of view. The advent of mass newspapers may have worked to tone down content, as their proprietors attempted to avoid upsetting their readers with anything that they might have found offensive. As the political role of the royals had dwindled, press coverage of their personal lives would have been intrusive and sensationalist. As Prince of Wales, Edward did twice face serious threats of appearing at the centre of public scandals – the Tranby Croft gambling affair and the Mordaunt divorce – but a combination of astute handling by the establishment and a spontaneous lack of enthusiasm on the part of editors to pursue the stories meant that public attention lasted only briefly.

The first British monarch of the modern media age was George V who reigned from a few years before the First World War to a few years before the Second World War. Mass-circulation newspapers were already well established when he came to the throne and their reach and influence grew during his reign. As their circulation continued to grow, the opinions of their readers now mattered to the politicians. The arrival of near universal suffrage gave the opinion of the masses an entirely new political and constitutional dimension. The ability of the newspapers to help shape or channel this opinion became a potent force in the land. The press went through the same process of expansion and concentration into a small number of vast companies observed in almost every sector of the economy. The press magnates were members of the fabulously wealthy industrial plutocracy and a number of them tried to parlay the power of their newspapers into political influence. Their wealth brought them seats in the House of Lords which gave them a direct voice in national politics, serving as the basis for political careers for themselves or their sons. The political positioning of their newspapers could match their demographic positioning as advertising media. The First World War may also have contributed towards press docility. Almost every aspect of national life was subordinated to the war effort including the press. On one side it was subjected to draconian government censorship, but on the active side of the ledger, it contributed to the national struggle by spontaneously and willingly working to sustain public morale. Anti-German nationalism also sold papers.

In the second half of George V's reign two new phenomena transformed the media landscape. Radio – or wireless in the word of the times – arrived as a source of near instant news and comment, which reached into practically every household in the country. Even if the ownership of wireless sets was far from universal in the early days, ownership did spread rapidly enough for the contents of broadcasts to be disseminated rapidly and comprehensively. The affluent middle class told what they heard to their then numerous servants who then spread it in shops, the streets or the pubs. In Britain the potentially revolutionary aspect of wireless was dampened by the BBC's monopoly of wireless guided by the deferential, conservative and determinedly uncontroversial figure of Sir John Reith. Wireless's peculiar status in Britain gave it an extra degree of authority, which reinforced its standing as part of the establishment.

Cinema began to displace live theatre or music as the primary source of popular entertainment, especially once technological advances added sound to the medium's offering, 'the talkies'. As well as entertainment, cinema featured news and current affairs through the now almost-forgotten feature of the newsreels which were part of almost all cinema programmes between the wars.* Newsreels had almost the same impact

---

* The author can remember in the 1960s watching the last newsreels ever made which were shown in a rolling programme of cartoons and shorts at the cinema by the side entrance to Birmingham New Street Station.

as television in its early days as a source of news and current affairs in visual form. Whilst British newsreels were not as deeply embedded in the conservative establishment as wireless, they were part of a whole-heartedly money-making industry which aimed to tap a consensus in public taste and interest. Unlike newspapers, cinemas offered news as a subsidiary part of an entertainment product and distinctive political stances might have alienated consumers. Self-censorship was the order of the day. Cinema was never remotely as lucrative as newspapers so its proprietors were under an even greater imperative to make decisions for commercial and not political reasons.

By some measures George V's reign was a long rear-guard action against the modern world. He was well aware of these changes in the media landscape and how they might change the standing of the monarchy. At its worst, public opinion could trigger revolutions such as had overthrown the monarchies of eastern Europe in the wake of the First World War, depriving two of his first cousins of their thrones and one of them the lives of him and his family as well. George V bitterly resented the erosion of royal constitutional authority and fought a long defensive battle to preserve as much as he could. His reign had opened in the midst of Britain's most dangerous constitutional crisis ever. The fight over Lloyd George's 'people's budget' of 1911 had threatened to reduce the King to the servant of an elected government, instructed to create peers in their hundreds to defeat entrenched aristocratic opposition to the budget. The King had been spared that humiliation but it was merely the first of many moves to encroach on his authority.

George V bowed to the inevitable with the maximum grace possible but the picture was not entirely bleak; the new world held opportunity as well as threat. Long before Buckingham Palace saw any need to engage routinely with the printed media, George V engaged with broadcast media. Under the joint urging of his trusted and long-serving private secretary, Lord Stamfordham, and Sir John Reith, he overcame his instinctive reluctance and opened the series of royal broadcasts at Christmas on the BBC which has continued ever since. Royal visits to his subjects were a regular staple of newsreels. The BBC's resolutely establishment stance under Reith and the newsreels' respectful depiction of the royal family's doings as an unarguably positive aspect of national life provided ideal forums. The primitive technology of early cinema positively worked to the advantage of the establishment. Set-pieces such as royal occasions which allowed cameras to be placed in advance at the best locations provided perfect content. George V's industrial visits fed and fed off newsreels. They were part of his strategy to demonstrate a monarchy in touch with the modern world. They can fairly be described as Britain's first media events.

The European tradition of monarchy has always featured public displays. The magnificence of coronations or weddings and events such as tournaments have all served to proclaim the standing, wealth and potency of royal rulers. George V was doing no more than updating this practice. There is a fine line between the noble practice of receiving the accolades of one's subjects and the demeaning exercise of going out to court this adoration. George V had little doubt that he was staying firmly on the right side of the line. His reign was a succession of public events that ranged from the immense splendour of the lavish Durbar that served to proclaim his imperial status in India in 1911 to his tours of Britain, little different to the programmes undertaken by today's royals. A visit to one steel-works in Wales in 1912 had a fateful echo nearly a quarter of a century later.

Almost from the start George V's sons, above all his heir, were called on to do their share of this work. Edward was too young to attend his father's coronation in the robes of a peer, but he was rapidly elevated to a Knighthood of the Garter which meant that he could be suitably and lavishly attired. Edward's investiture as Prince of Wales in 1911 created the opportunity for a show all of his own. As this was the first such ceremony in three centuries much of the proceedings, including the extravagant robes that he wore, were entirely invented. The event was covered by a very early newsreel. It is entitled *The Boy Prince* and he is the star, dominating the image whilst all the newsreel of his father's coronation the previous year had showed of George V was the outside of the state coach.

Edward's serious work for the public face of the monarchy began after the First World War. Most of the 1920s were occupied by a succession of gruelling tours of the Empire; the endplates of his memoirs showed the routes he took. The formal constitutional ties that bound the newly autonomous dominions to the mother country had weakened to vanishing point so personal loyalty to the monarchy took over as the essential glue of the British Empire. In the days before easy air travel, a senior royal who could be absent from the country for the long periods that shipborne tours of distant lands required, offered an ideal solution. The immense Royal

Navy of the day could provide the ships required. Edward was almost invariably rapturously received by the inhabitants of the dominions; his youth, good looks and personal charm were crucial assets. Edward was the first true celebrity royal.

The overall result was well up to his father's expectations but flaws did appear. Inevitably Edward's performance sometimes fell short of perfection; all too often his off-handed, unpunctual behaviour became obvious. In today's media environment he would have been immediately and savagely punished, but in those deferential days with a far narrower media world, it was only amongst his inner circle and those directly involved that this grated. The demands of these royal tours helped foster what was to become a damaging and perhaps ultimately fatal mindset. Edward began to split his life into the official duties of 'princing' (his word) and a private life of which he became ever more protective in which he was the sole master. The notion that royalty was an inescapable, all-consuming state – albeit one with major material and status compensations – which imposed an iron rule of duty gave way to the ethics of a salaried worker who provides given service for a specific reward.

George V was also to be disappointed in other aspects of his heir's approach to life. He failed to conform to established practice by marrying a suitably well-born lady and begetting the next royal generation. Edward was content with a string of discreetly married upper-class girlfriends and ample casual sex. This had taken a turn for the worse in 1934 when he began an affair with a lady of the utmost obscurity, a Mrs. Wallis Simpson. His personal friendships were concentrated on social lightweights who counted for nothing in the establishment. His taste for innovations in clothing was a permanent source of tension. None of his father's attempts to bend Edward to his will worked and when George V died at the comparatively early age of 70 in January 1936, he had almost abandoned hope that Edward would allow himself to be fitted into the mould of what he hoped for in his successor. Perhaps fittingly for his position as the first monarch of the media age, George V's life came to an end in the ultimate piece of news management. His doctor, Lord Dawson of Penn, composed an official bulletin stating that the 'King's life is moving peacefully towards its close' as he lay in a coma before euthanizing him with a fatal dose of morphine at around midnight. This ensured that the news of his death appeared 'in the morning papers rather than the less appropriate evening journals'.[2]

2

No Minister Will Dare to
Go Against This Force

It was in the course of one of Edward's tours that he did something mildly unusual. Just as his great-grandmother, Queen Victoria, had bought Balmoral Castle in the Scottish Highlands as a personal possession, thereby establishing the modern, essentially fake Scottishness of the royal family, Edward bought a ranch in the remote west of Canada. He paid the very large sum of £10,000 (skilled workers then earned about £150–200 per year) for what he renamed the EP (Edward Prince) ranch in the Eden Valley in the Rocky Mountains. It offered a glimpse of the simple unadorned life of a back-country settler. He never explained how he planned to use his new property. It was never a practical proposition for Edward to adopt this life full time and in the days before easy air travel even occasional visits would have absorbed an enormous amount of time. Buying the ranch gives a hint that he yearned for somewhere that offered seclusion and complete control of his doings and company. A few years later he was to acquire a home that gave him most of these desiderata but easily accessible to London, Fort Belvedere in Windsor Great Park, the shelter and symbol of an entirely private life.

It was the purchase of the EP Ranch that introduced Edward to the immense possibilities and perils of close personal contact with high-profile media. One of his neighbours there was one of the day's leading American journalists. Frazier Hunt had made his name as a war correspondent covering the US Army on the Western Front in the First World War and, crucially, the infinitely smaller but far more contentious participation of American troops in the doomed and futile western intervention in the Russian Civil War on behalf of the Tsarist side. What Hunt saw in Russia made him deeply suspicious of British imperialist motives in the affair and deeply hostile to the 'woof-woof, what-what' senior British officers he encountered.[1] His trenchant articles denouncing the American presence in Russia struck a chord in Washington and helped trigger the withdrawal of troops. He then spent three years in London, much of it in American expatriate circles, but this did not soften his loathing of the British. Hunt's stance was music to the ears of America's most powerful press proprietor, William Randolph Hearst, who personally inducted him into the cadre of journalists bound to him personally, the well-paid elite of a press machine that reached everywhere in the US. Hunt became the European representative for all of Hearst's magazine interests, notionally subordinate to Ray Long, one of the organisation's highest-spending executives. Hunt covered the Irish Civil War and secured scoop interviews with Lenin, Hitler, Stalin, the Mexican revolutionary leader Pancho Villa and Gandhi among others. His work for Hearst went beyond simple journalism and he was sent to Mexico, where Hearst owned a huge cattle ranch and which was something of a personal obsession for him, on 'a small gumshoeing job' in the late 1920s. This appears to have involved obtaining government support from the president and agriculture minister of Mexico in exchange for favourable coverage.

Hunt was a thoroughly professional journalist and his loathing of the British did not prevent him from cultivating a potentially magnificent source of news. He developed a convivial friendship with his royal neighbour, cemented by a relish for the game of poker dice which Hunt taught Edward to play. The friendship survived a specimen of the Prince's already marked tendency toward inconsiderateness, when he telephoned Hunt late one night to demand another game of dice to give him the opportunity to win back the $50 that he had just lost to Hunt.

The Prince and the journalist remained in touch, meeting when Edward visited Canada again in 1927 and then in London in 1928. Hunt was on good enough terms with him to get away with teasing him on his inability to roll his Rs, which made him claim to be a 'wrancher'. Edward spoke extensively and freely to Hunt, explaining how he intended to act when he became king. In the mid-1930s Hunt's friendship with Edward took a professional turn when Hunt spent some time while in London, apparently with the sole purpose of researching the Prince's life and views. The result was a biography of Edward that appeared in April 1935 under the title *The Bachelor Prince*. It is little more than an extended interview with him taken at Edward's dictation and is gushing and wholly uncritical. Hunt was at pains to flag up his closeness to Edward. He subtitled the book 'An informal biography of H.R.H. The Prince of Wales by his neighbor in Canada'. The physical description of Edward's quarters in York House, St James's Palace, together with Hunt's reference to his own flat nearby whilst he was researching the book, implies that he was a regular visitor. When Hunt's book was serialized after Edward's accession to the throne, the newspaper boasted that no writer knew him more intimately. The close ties between the two men were clear to another senior Hearst journalist when she arrived in London early in 1936.[2] *The Bachelor Prince* had little literary merit and was light on solid biographical fact; its interest lies in the open and candid discussion of Edward's ideas of his royal status and his plans for kingship. Hunt had written Edward's manifesto for kingship by proxy.

The balance of evidence suggests that the Hearst organization was not directly involved in Hunt's book, which received no more than routine coverage. When Edward acceded to the throne in 1936, the book was serialized in newspapers but the Hearst titles profiled the new King with pieces by a recognized historian, Willem van Loon. Hunt's professional association with Hearst seems to have ended in 1930; his autobiography is unspecific on the point. By then Hunt was more interested in a career in broadcasting. He was also a strong supporter of President Franklin Roosevelt which would not have endeared him to Hearst in 1936.

The picture painted of Edward's intentions and attitudes did not flinch from controversy; practically everything in his plans involved a radical departure from the ways of the past. The dominant theme was Edward's sympathy for the working classes which recurred throughout the book. In one of the book's most debatable claims, Edward was described as visiting working men's clubs to unwind after a hard day of duty. He might even be called the 'Socialist King' once he ascended the throne. This might all have been calculated to terrify and offend conservative politicians.

Edward's claim to sympathy with the majority of his subjects was not idle. He had directly experienced more of what millions of his less fortunate contemporaries had to bear than any of his predecessors. As a young man he had served near the front line in France, although to his fury his father and the generals refused to let him share the dangers and misery of the combat soldiers with whom he felt an enormous affinity. Even before the Great Slump struck in its full vigour during the early 1930s, he had toured the poor areas of Britain, notably those where coal was mined in conditions that had scarcely improved from the preceding century. His sympathy for the miners and anger at the lives they had to bear prompted him to speak publicly against their 'perfectly damnable' conditions early in 1929.[3] This provoked some outraged harrumphing, notably from Lord Londonderry, an immensely rich hereditary aristocrat, owner of coal mines and sometime government minister, who complained – on no evidence at all – that the scenes of squalor that the Prince had witnessed had been stage-managed and that his remarks would be exploited in wage negotiations. There is no doubt that Edward's concern for his subjects was genuine and heartfelt. Five years later he tried to persuade Neville Chamberlain, then Chancellor of the Exchequer, to take seriously the issue of poor housing conditions. He had chosen a singularly unpromising target. Chamberlain was a passionate advocate of sound money and a small state. Even though Chamberlain, as a former Minister of Health, was fully aware of the slum conditions in which many people lived, he treated the idea with withering condescension and distrust of anyone who tried to recruit royalty for the cause of social reform: 'He [Edward] is himself very earnest about it but he has been got at by sentimentalists who know very little of the subject and it was a delicate task to damp down the ideas expressed while showing a proper appreciation of the spirit.'[4]

Conservatives might have been alarmed at Edward's social views, but it was in his claims for his constitutional position that he went far beyond anything a British monarch had aspired to since the Hanoverians. He was proposing to rejig Britain's unwritten constitution to create a novel and more powerful monarchy.

Fearlessly he has carved out his own different and individual career as Prince of Wales. He will unquestionably do the same as King of England.

He will find his own way of doing this, just as he discovered his own method of being a different Prince of Wales.

England, with her two million unemployed, her ten million over-population, her housing problems, her losses in trade, her vast discouragement and deep though silent unrest, trusts this slender forty-year-old Prince more than she trusts any other single individual in the world. He has won the heart of England. He IS England.

And so it is that when this Bachelor Prince becomes the Bachelor King he will have in his strong athletic hands a power greater than any King of England has had for more than a hundred years. ...

Quietly he will go about his business of helping save England and the British Empire – and all the world. He will not mix in politics or interfere with the orderly process of elective government, but behind the machinery will be this heroic figure of a man whom England loves and trusts.

His influence on his ministers, on the elected men who make up the Government, will be greater than any constitution-monarch has ever had, *because his influence on the masses of people will be greater.* [italics in original]

No minister, no premier, will dare to go against this force. It will exercise the pressure born out of the changing mood of millions.[5]

The lesson that Edward had taken from the adoring crowds on his tours and the unremittingly flattering press coverage was that he enjoyed a unique popularity which gave him the power and right to decide how the country should be run. He thought it gave him a more valid and potent authority than that of elected politicians. Like so many celebrities he had fallen into the trap of believing that his public standing was permanent, all-embracing and untarnishable. He made a distinction between the workings of parliamentary democracy and the actual work of deciding policy. His distant predecessors had claimed the divine right of kings; he was claiming the divine right of celebrity. Edward imagined that he held a mandate directly from the people and that he would be able to use it to solve all the nation's problems. There is no sign that anyone in the British government was aware of Edward's messianic megalomania, but he was already giving proof of his intention to influence political events directly.

Just as Hunt was working on Edward's pitch for populist constitutional power, Edward was already trying to influence government policy by outspoken public comments in the summer of 1935. In the space of forty-eight hours, he contrived to make two highly contentious speeches. The first was the more controversial. He had told thousands of members of the Royal British Legion at their annual meeting in the Albert Hall that their organization was the ideal body to stretch out the 'hand of friendship' to Germany, against which most of those present had fought during the First World War. As ex-servicemen and veterans of the First World War they were his natural constituency. The laudable desire to bury the hatchet and embrace former foes was somewhat diluted by the fact that Germany had been ruled for two years by Adolf Hitler, who was rather more interested in restoring her pre-war power and glory. This speech came at an extremely embarrassing moment for the government as the recently negotiated Naval Treaty with Germany limiting the size of the Kriegsmarine had been greeted with the deepest concern in France, which suspected Britain of protecting its imperial interests at the expense of France. The suspicions would, of course, be fed by any indication that Britain was seeking a wider rapprochement with Germany. As if to balance any imputation of being overly peace-loving, Edward had compounded the offence by speaking out at Berkhamstead School in barely veiled criticism of pacifist measures ordained by the Labour-controlled Greater London Council. As well as sounding provocatively militaristic, Edward had strayed squarely into the realm of a domestic political controversy, attracting fire from Labour pacifists.

Edward's speeches were such flagrant breaches of the constitutional custom that forbids the monarch (and by extension near relatives) from any political speeches other than as avowed mouthpieces of the elected government, that measures had to be taken. It fell to Prime Minister Stanley Baldwin, who had recently returned to 10 Downing Street for the third and final time, to do the job. He got approval from the Cabinet for King George V to show to the Prince the minutes of the meeting which had discussed his transgressions as clear proof of the concern and embarrassment that his actions had caused. George V told his son firmly that, 'You must never speak on such controversial matters without consulting the government.'6 The Prince obeyed his father's order and there was no repetition in his remaining months as Prince and his first months as King were conducted – as regards politics – with full decorum. But Edward had not reformed. He and his father were stuck in a futile cycle they had pursued since Edward's early adulthood. George V would try to impose paternal authority on his son and Edward would resist. Edward would push against the boundaries of authority and rules, then retreat into resentful and only superficial acquiescence when called to order.

Edward's true feelings were unchanged. He believed that he had a right to intervene in public policy. Through arrogance or stupidity, he believed that he was able to identify unerringly what was the right thing to do and to push for it to be done. Days after the Albert Hall speech he compounded his indiscretion and spoke unrepentantly to Leopold von Hoesch, the German ambassador to Britain, complaining that:

> his utterances had been misinterpreted in many quarters. In making his pronouncement he had not ... wished to get involved in the maelstrom of political events but had only expressed, entirely on his own initiative, an idea which had seemed right to him and useful and of whose expediency he was as convinced as ever. Comment which tried to construe his words as a political declaration were mistaken. He believed, however, that the timidity and hesitation which, as is well known, were characteristic of politicians, were much slower in achieving results than a frank word spoken at the right moment, even though it might exceed the bounds of reserve normally maintained.[7]

This and similar utterances helped feed the dangerous delusion of Joachim von Ribbentrop, the Nazi foreign policy specialist, who was to succeed von Hoesch as ambassador to London and later became foreign minister, that Edward was a friend to his regime and that he would be able to swing British policy away from a supposedly anti-German stance. Ribbentrop later claimed that Edward had been forced to abdicate precisely because the establishment rejected the 'Führer-will of the young king'.[8] After he had become king, Edward also shared his ambitions to influence policy with the ambassador of Fascist Italy, 'Although under a parliamentary regime the King does not control the Government, he would continue to attempt what appeared to him possible and necessary.'[9]

Edward knew that he had overstepped convention but he came up with the pretext that this was justified in order to short-circuit what he believed was the weakness of normal political process. He was writing himself a specification for how he saw his job as a constitutional monarch that he held to until almost the end.

When Edward acceded to the throne on the death of his father in January 1936, he was still full of the conviction that he would be able to claw back constitutional power. Once again, he chose to share this conviction with a senior German representative, this time a convinced

Nazi as well. Amongst the mourners at the funeral was Edward's distant cousin, the Duke of Saxe-Coburg Gotha, who had abdicated as sovereign and switched to ardent support for the new regime. Saxe-Coburg asked the new king whether a discussion between the British prime minister and the Führer would help relations between their countries. He was curtly told that this was a question for him and not for Baldwin, 'Who is King here? Baldwin or I? I myself wish to talk to Hitler, and will do so here or in Germany. Tell him that please.'[10]

Hunt also set out Edward's agenda for his personal life in *The Bachelor Prince*. He was presented as a rebel against the desire of the court and the government to marry him off to some suitable European princess in a traditional dynastic union, and he was not going to take the line of least resistance and fall in with this programme. It is an open question whether Edward was ever seriously pressurized by the court to make a dynastic marriage, but his belief that he had been and the hostility towards the idea remained a running obsession for the rest of his life. However, Hunt was behind the times on the question of how much an alternative long-term relationship might figure in Edward's plans. Hunt quoted Edward claiming that he had more important things to do and that he was too busy to get married as the book's title emphasized. Hunt wrote of Edward becoming 'the Bachelor King'. The image of a ruler solely dedicated to his people's well-being and willing to sacrifice a domestic life in order to work for it was strong and appealing to many. It was also the image that Adolf Hitler sought to project.

The only hint that Hunt's book contained of Edward's affair with the American socialite Wallis Simpson, which had begun in earnest in 1934, was his rejection of the shackles of social convention in the choice of female companions. It recounted the story of an evening in Panama when the Prince had been warned off dancing with an attractive girl who had particularly caught his eye because she was merely a shop assistant. The only possible source for the tale is Edward himself and in it he coldly rebuffed the suggestion that his choice of dance partner should be dictated by social considerations and not physical attraction. The following year Hunt's assertion that Edward was determined to remain single proved to be spectacularly inaccurate which might help explain why the book faded so rapidly from view despite the glaring light that it shone on Edward's plans to use his royal power. Hunt's one-time patron, Hearst, enthusiastically adopted the idea that Edward might marry an American woman was a major news story.

In the time-honoured style of celebrities attempting to manipulate the media to suit their own goals, Edward pretended to despise press coverage. He said he was 'bitterly opposed to publicity'. He insisted that many of his serious activities be kept out of the papers.[11] He was implying that as well as the official duties listed publicly in the Court Circular he was doing extensive important work behind the scenes, which presumably contributed to his being too busy to marry. Like his purported visits to working men's clubs, this has left no trace in the record if it ever existed at all.

3

Unnatural Silence

Edward began his reign as he meant to go on with a series of assaults on the outworn habits of monarchy as he saw them. His first target was a purely family and domestic quirk. His father had instituted a practice under which the clocks at his personal home, Sandringham in Norfolk, were set half an hour early to give extra time for his adored hobby of shooting. This had clearly irked his son and the clocks were reset to normal time the morning after George V's death with no notice or discussion.

The first of the archaic traditions of British royalty that Edward set out to affront was one of the most arbitrary and pointless. Inexplicable tradition dictates that the new monarch should not watch his own formal proclamation. It still rules today and, most recently, Charles III respected it. Edward did not and viewed the ceremony from a room overlooking the courtyard in St James's Palace where it takes place. A newsreel camera was in position to make a permanent record of this transgression, although there was naturally no chance that it would have been shown at the time. Even open-minded and modernistic friends of the new king like Duff Cooper, the government minister and world-class womanizer, thought that he was making a mistake by not respecting the convention, however inexplicable it might be. Edward compounded the rebellion against the established rule by being accompanied by Mrs. Simpson, which was similarly caught on camera and was similarly suppressed. There was no rule or practice barring a new sovereign's lover from the event, but the public was not going to be exposed to a combination of the two challenges to habit. A media time-bomb had been set ticking.

Handled otherwise, few would have questioned Edward's refusal to enslave himself to the dead hand of antique tradition, but somehow he chose ways to do this that caused the maximum offence to the bodies and individuals concerned for no gain to his reputation or stature. It was the sovereign's prerogative to change many things at will, but a wiser and more considerate man might have held back from Edward's peremptory approach of presenting the changes as faits accomplis with no prior warning. These ran from his insistence that a clutch of privileged bodies with the ancient right of presenting a loyal address should be given a single royal reply in a group and not one each. It was established practice to alternate the profile of the sovereign's head used on coins and postage stamps – left profile for one sovereign then right profile for his or her successor. In Edward's case this would have meant using his right profile but he felt it was less flattering and insisted his left profile be used. Edward VIII stamps carried the left profile but no coins were ever circulated. More justifiably Edward and his brothers opposed a plan by the Archbishop of Canterbury to commemorate George V by creating a new plaza between the Palace of Westminster and Westminster Cathedral, which would also have been an architectural glorification of the Church of England. The brothers preferred to support a national network of playing fields, many of which still exist.

The dispute over the memorial to King George V set the seal on the new king's poor relationship with the Archbishop that had begun badly in the early days of his reign. Cosmo Gordon Lang was a conservative and unappealingly unctuous clergyman, a good friend to George V who had shared his worries about his heir with him. Fatally, a few days after the accession, Lang chose to tell Edward that he had talked about him to his father. Edward was furious and instantly changed the subject. He had the greatest contempt for his father's reservations about his behaviour and friends and found it highly offensive that anyone should bring this up now that he was king. In Edward's mind Lang's intervention was emblematic of the forces of conservatism in the establishment that he imagined were fanatically opposed to his modernizing instincts because they threatened their comfortable existence. The scene was set for one of the most obsessive, one-sided and delusional feuds of Edward's life. After this initial rebuff Lang did not repeat the error and gave the monarch a wide berth for the remainder of his reign. This did not weaken Edward's grievance which grew to immense size during the abdication crisis. Even though Lang's part in the crisis was peripheral, Edward was convinced that he had been one of the major forces that conspired to force him from the throne.

None of these squabbles were ever made public, although people deeply versed in royal etiquette and alert for evidence that it was not being respected, might have spotted the innovations mandated by Edward VIII. Curiously the only body sufficiently affronted by Edward's discourtesy to break the strict law of silence was the senior regiment of the Brigade of Guards, usually the home of the strictest discipline and loyalty to the Crown. Here attachment to the age-old customs of military precedence trumped discretion. The senior regiment was the Grenadier Guards and they had naturally expected to be honoured by the first royal review of the reign in keeping with ancient practice, but Edward reviewed the Welsh Guards – a mere fifth in seniority – two days before them in what even *The Times* noted was an unheralded move.[1] *The Times* rubbed in the sense of affront when it reported the Grenadiers' disappointment when the King finally got round to paying them their due. The offence was great but only comprehensible to connoisseurs of military arcana. The breach of press restraint was tiny but an omen of things to come.

Edward was hyper-sensitive about his press coverage and was inclined to build up imaginary conspiracies surrounding it. Even the most trivial incident could provide fuel. When a newspaper carried a photograph of him walking down St James's holding his own umbrella to protect from the rain, Mrs. Simpson told him that a senior MP and confidant of Prime Minister Stanley Baldwin had told her at a dinner party that this had compromised the dignity of the monarchy. Neither he or she ever gave the name of the MP (assuming she had even known it) so it is impossible to verify the story. No one else was worried. When the King's friend and long-term adviser Walter Monckton was asked about the tale long afterwards, he thought the notion that Baldwin had objected was 'absurd'.[2] It does not feature in any of the litanies of complaint at Edward's behaviour that circulated amongst the establishment, so most likely Mrs. Simpson had simply seized on a passing social remark which Edward amplified into significant criticism of him which he resented deeply for the rest of his life.

As well as assaulting the antique and irrelevant, Edward also set out to give a more positive expression to his view of modern monarchy. Edward's willingness to reach out to all classes had been clear when he was Prince of Wales and was the source of much of the widespread enthusiasm with which his accession was greeted. His father had inspired reverence and respect as monarch. He had made populist gestures, such as introducing royal broadcasts at Christmas, but they had been carefully calibrated so as not to detract from the formal dignity of the Crown. His son's apparent openness to direct contact with all of his people was another facet of the refreshing modernity which his new subjects detected in him. Edward was later to mock the style of royal visits conducted by his grandfather, Edward VII, in which the royal carriage would arrive somewhere for the King to deliver an address, cut a ribbon and then depart for dinner at some grand house, all without leaving the carriage.[3] Edward was determined to change this. It was soon put on display when he went to Glasgow on a visit that featured both ends of the spectrum of royal duties in the shape of two very different queens. The immediate purpose was to inspect the new Cunard ocean liner the *Queen Mary*, which was soon to take her place as the pride of Britain's merchant fleet; her name alone gave direct proof of the mystic status of the royal family. But the King did not merely visit the John Brown shipyard and its directors' lunch room; he also toured the parts of the city where ordinary people lived, beginning with a new housing development but ending up in one of Glasgow's notoriously squalid tenements.[4] There he called on a Mr. Thomas Queen, who had been blind for thirty years. Even though it was the humblest dwelling imaginable, the King made one of his trademark gestures of respect, personally knocking at the door and asking for permission to enter. When Mr. Queen asked him who it was, he replied simply 'I am your King' and gave him a firm handshake.

With the apparently sole exception of the Grenadier Guards' umbrage, the reign of Edward VIII played out in eerie and unnatural media silence in the UK apart from respectful coverage of the set-piece events detailed in the Court Circular, the daily official bulletin. As far as anyone in Britain without access to inside gossip would have known, there was nothing at all exceptional about the new king. The closest he came to public rebellion was at the British Industries Fair where he advised men to wear stay-up socks with elasticated tops instead of the traditional sock suspenders. A tiny handful of the unaware general public might have wondered about the guest list in the Court Circular for the first formal dinner given after strict mourning for George V ended that the King gave at York House, St James's Palace: amongst otherwise august company they would have seen Mr. and Mrs. Ernest Simpson. Diligent research might have found that Mr. Simpson was a minor shipbroker. A few weeks later Mrs. Simpson on her own was listed as a dinner guest. Insiders were appalled that the King should publicly be pushing his mistress as a pawn up the visible social chessboard, but the true significance of these invitations remained hidden to anyone else.

The British media silence became all the more unreal as the King's behaviour became ever more flagrant. The first major threshold he crossed was to take Mrs. Simpson – without her husband – on holiday with him. They cruised the eastern Mediterranean on a luxury yacht, the *Nahlin*. This was in theory a purely private and informal occasion, unreported in the Court Circular, but it involved high-profile political contacts, notably with the Turkish leader Mustafa Kemal whom the King invited to a state visit to Britain entirely on his own initiative. The Foreign Office was left with the delicate task of rowing back on this invitation. The cruise offered almost no scope for concealment or discretion. No attempt was made to hide Mrs. Simpson's presence and the non-British press of the world had a field day with extensive coverage of the romance, featuring photographs of the couple together.

Of far less interest to the international press but possibly even more outrageous to British conservatives was the King's next assault on the decencies. He invited Mrs. Simpson to join him for the quasi-mandatory late summer stay at Balmoral Castle in the Scottish Highlands, the heart of the House of Windsor's invented and largely fake Scottishness, which had become an immutable fixture in the royal calendar. Traditionally the great and good of the land are asked. But Edward's guests were the couple's usual lightweight friends from London. Unlike the *Nahlin* cruise, this was reported in the Court Circular. Like the York House dinners the names of guests were reported without comment in the Court Circular but a powerful bush telegraph swiftly broadcast news of a further gratuitous insult to Scottish sentiments: the King had been due to open a new wing at the Aberdeen Infirmary fifty miles from Balmoral but had delegated the task to his oldest brother, the Duke of York, on the flimsy pretext that he was still in mourning for his father. Instead, he personally drove to Aberdeen station to collect Mrs. Simpson off the train from London, where he was easily recognized. The scandal spread by word of mouth and soon graffiti was urging, 'Down with the American whore.'

Amongst the other guests at Balmoral was one of the King's few personal friends who had any standing in the wider world. Esmond Harmsworth was not there for purely social reasons. To a great extent, Edward avoided the company of the great and the good of the land, preferring the company of undemanding social lightweights. He had few friends who counted for much in the broader life of the country but one of them was Esmond Harmsworth, scion of a family of press barons which owned amongst other titles the *Daily Mail,* one of the most powerful national newspapers of the era. Esmond was very much in the mould of Edward: young, a keen sportsman and a fixture in café society. Unlike his father Lord Rothermere and his late uncle Lord Northcliffe, he had no grand political ambitions. His two older brothers had been killed in the First World War to the permanent grief of their father who had obtained a seat in the House of Commons for Esmond at the extraordinarily early age of 19 and had even, ludicrously, tried to get him a seat in Cabinet three years later. Rothermere's hopes that Esmond would continue the family's tradition of high-level politics were disappointed and Esmond abandoned his seat in 1929. He devoted his time to the family newspapers, albeit focused on the business rather than the journalistic side. By 1934, he had become Chairman of the Newspaper Proprietors' Association, the trade body whose chief job was to represent the provincial press.

The British media had shown itself helpfully docile and respectful in limiting its coverage of the King's doings to the uncontroversial and formal aspects, but this was about to face a possibly decisive challenge and the King knew that he had to make his preparations. In deep secrecy before she had left for the *Nahlin* cruise, Mrs. Simpson had filed a divorce case against her husband. The King was determined to marry her which exposed her to the risk of publicity from a court case. In those days divorce cases were far less common and were routinely reported in the national newspapers, albeit under tight legal restraints. Having sheltered their relationship from public attention in Britain, the King was concerned that his name might be linked to Mrs. Simpson's when the divorce case became publicly known. The King's first priority was to ensure that the British press continued to keep the story of his affair with Mrs. Simpson quiet despite the obvious temptation for them to use the divorce case as a peg on which to hang the far larger story of the royal romance.[5] There was no thought to spin the story in any particular direction, but simply to suppress it entirely. The King and Harmsworth were alert to the possibility of further ramifications that might involve the government and discussed political personalities. The King told Harmsworth how much he disliked Sir John Simon, the Home Secretary, who had had to come to Balmoral on Privy Council business. Simon was a highly successful lawyer but was almost universally disliked; he was to emerge as one of the most active hard-line ministers as the crisis unfolded.

4

Friday's Job

The King was right to make plans ahead of Mrs. Simpson's divorce court case. It would present the newspapers with a temptingly hard domestic news item, and even the vaguest public mention of the King in connection with it would be too horrible to contemplate. Inevitably the story that the case was coming up before the courts began to leak. One of the most formidable predators of the British political and media jungles sensed vulnerable prey and began to stalk. On Monday, 12 October, Theodore Goddard, Mrs Simpson's solicitor, received a telephone call from the press magnate, Lord Beaverbrook, warning him that one of his newspapers, the *Evening Standard*, had the story of the divorce case and intended to publish it.[1] Goddard tried to persuade Beaverbrook to give his client privacy, but he received a studiedly non-committal reply.

Beaverbrook was one of the great troublemakers of his time. He had built a fortune in his native Canada as a financier by deals that many had thought scandalous before moving to Britain where he launched a career in politics and built a press empire around the *Daily Express*, one of the country's two bestselling newspapers. He soon tired of a conventional political career but delighted in operating behind the scenes and using his newspapers as a tool. One of his happiest moments came as a player in the series of intrigues that removed Herbert Asquith from power in 1916 and replaced him with David Lloyd George, as a resolute war leader. Ever afterwards Beaverbrook believed that he had been the dominant force in the conspiracy. He took an impish delight in manipulating men and events from behind the scenes. The Harmsworths' *Daily Mail* and Beaverbrook's *Daily Express* stood together as the great popular newspapers of their day, reviled by conservative politicians; their owners tried to translate their huge circulations into political influence.

Beaverbrook now began a discreet auction for his assistance in keeping the press quiet about the Mrs. Simpson divorce. There had long been an uneasy stand-off between him and Edward, who, like any celebrity, understood something of the dangers of getting too close to the media. In 1928, Edward played golf with Robert Bruce Lockhart, the former British secret agent and now one of the star journalists in the Beaverbrook empire, who noted in his diary that 'The Prince does not like Beaverbrook, says he wants to get everyone under his thumb and, if he cannot get them, he tries to down them'.[2] In 1929, Beaverbrook had opened one potential channel of communication to Edward by hiring as a senior executive in his organization Mike Wardell, a close friend of the Prince, despite his only very modest business qualifications. Whilst this helped establish Beaverbrook firmly in the same social set as Edward, direct contact was modest. In his memoir of the abdication Beaverbrook is ambiguous as to how actively he had sought Edward's friendship. He did invite him to dinner, but claimed that the other guests 'were made up of my own group of friends and had not been gathered for the purpose of entertaining the Prince of Wales. Dean Inge and his wife were among them.'[3] The 'gloomy Dean's' blend of intellectual Christianity and social conservatism might have been calculated to repel Edward. However, when Edward became King, Beaverbrook saw the prospect of a 'new outlook in public life'. He broke his habit of not participating in formal functions and attended Edward's Accession Council, making great play of what he presented as the great sacrifice of donning his, admittedly uncomfortable, Privy Councillor's uniform.

Beaverbrook did not have to think for a long time as to how to follow up his first call to Goddard. Edward showed how desperate he was to shield Mrs Simpson from publicity by personally telephoning Beaverbrook to ask for a meeting the day after his opening call to Goddard. Beaverbrook had no need to calculate whether the benefits of putting the King under an obligation would have been far greater than the benefits of a good news story; the King was his for the taking. He took full advantage of the King's invitation to 'name your own time' and set the appointment for three days later, Friday, 16 October.[4] In his book on the abdication he explained away the delay with a claim that he needed urgent dental treatment, but the historian A. J. P. Tylor, who edited the book and openly revered Beaverbrook, was for once sceptical and pointed out that Beaverbrook's appointments diary for the days between does not show his dentist but does mention Mrs. Simpson's husband Ernest late in the afternoon of Thursday the 15th.[5] It seems that Beaverbrook both wanted to make the King sweat a little and to check on the relationship between him and Mrs. Simpson before committing himself to suppressing what might have been a very major story indeed.

There is a small hint that the initiative for the King's attempt to solicit Beaverbrook's help came from Mrs. Simpson and that Edward himself might have been somewhat reluctant to see Beaverbrook, perhaps because of his previous distrust, perhaps because he dimly foresaw the political cost. On the Thursday after Beaverbrook's call to Goddard, Mrs. Simpson nagged Edward by post to perform 'Friday's job' and secure appropriately low-key press coverage.[6] Against this, there was ample reason to seek Beaverbrook's help. The King's plea to Beaverbrook was heartfelt and focused on his desire to protect Mrs. Simpson, 'ill, unhappy, and distressed at the thought of notoriety'.[7] Beaverbrook accepted this and in his usual style swung into a flurry of action, which would impress the King with his energy and commitment. The King cannot have put Beaverbrook fully into the picture as the first man that Beaverbrook contacted after they met was Esmond Harmsworth, whom the King had already brought on side. Beaverbrook and Harmsworth worked together to approach other national and local newspapers and won them over to a policy of restraint. Beaverbrook overcame the doubts of Sir Walter Layton of the left-leaning *News Chronicle*, which held the line of silence. Edward was ever afterwards immensely grateful for Beaverbrook's assistance, but in reality, Beaverbrook had got much for very little. His habitual exercise in dramatically exaggerated activity masked a far more modest performance. The silence of the *News Chronicle* was Beaverbrook's only solid achievement. He did not bother to get in touch with *The Morning Post*, *The Times* or *The Daily Telegraph*, the three dominant establishment papers. They were conservative papers which supported the government and were far more likely to follow an official lead than that of competitors whom they despised anyway. Discretion, inertia and establishment solidarity would hold them back from initiating a public scandal far more than anything Beaverbrook might do. Geoffrey Dawson, editor of *The Times*, knew that his paper 'will have to do something about the King and Mrs. Simpson' but that the prime minister must tell him 'what he wishes done.'[8] It is unlikely that any would have broken the silence spontaneously. The Labour *Daily*

Herald also kept silent without intervention; the Labour Party leader, Clem Attlee, had decided not to fish in the troubled waters of the King's affairs.

Beaverbrook had bought a claim on the King's gratitude very cheaply: a few phone calls to ask what was barely a favour of his competitors. The men he contacted had held the same line of silence over the King's affair with Mrs. Simpson and showed no inclination of breaking away on their own. All the press proprietors faced a fine calculation. Breaking the story of the King's involvement in the divorce might have brought a lift to circulation but was far from risk-free. Many of the public would disapprove of exploiting a seemingly sordid tale. There were also legal risks. Reporting divorce cases was legally restricted to strictly factual matters. Under the English divorce law of the day, Mrs. Simpson was presenting herself as the innocent party and that meant entirely innocent. There was a legal implication that she had been faithful to her husband. There was no such thing as a 'no fault divorce' and if you claimed it was your spouse's fault, the law supposed you to be entirely blameless. A newspaper story implying that Mrs. Simpson had some kind of relationship with the King could have been taken as a challenge to the legal basis of her case. In turn it might have brought a libel writ down on the paper. Beaverbrook and Harmsworth were thus pushing at open doors when they asked for the connection between the King and Mrs. Simpson to be suppressed in reports of her divorce case. By contrast the King had opened a Pandora's box by asking for Beaverbrook's help.

Intentionally or otherwise, the King had made a significant political choice in calling Beaverbrook to his assistance. There was a gulf between those papers which supported the government and those which did not. Beaverbrook was the most extreme example. Beaverbrook had also been a leading light in Lloyd George's coalition government, the 'thieves' kitchen', loathed by the traditional Conservatives championed by Baldwin. Beaverbrook had briefly benefitted from the Carlton House coup in 1922 by the traditionalists against Lloyd George when his fellow Canadian, friend and business partner, Andrew Bonar Law, was installed as prime minister instead of Lloyd George. Bonar Law had benefitted financially from the relationship, and Beaverbrook had benefitted in terms of backstairs political influence. Bonar Law was forced from office by a fatal cancer and his successor, Stanley Baldwin, showed no indication to grant Beaverbrook the same privileged position. This marked the beginning of Beaverbrook's bitter enmity towards Baldwin and gave an added edge to the dispute when they clashed over policy. Beaverbrook's genuine enthusiasm for the Empire led him to campaign vigorously against Baldwin on the issue of Empire free trade. When Baldwin was leading the Conservatives in opposition in 1929 and 1930, he had faced down a sustained attempt by Lords Rothermere and Beaverbrook to hijack the party's platform in favour of free trade within the British Empire. The battle culminated at the Westminster St. George's by-election in 1931 on which Baldwin staked his authority as leader of the party. The election pitted an official Conservative candidate against an 'Independent Conservative' backed by the press barons. On the day before the poll Baldwin famously denounced the *Daily Mail* for trying to exercise 'power without responsibility, the prerogative of the harlot throughout the ages'. Baldwin had never been a fan of the popular press but this episode instilled in him a bitter loathing of the press lords and their pretensions to convert mass circulation into political power. The official Conservative candidate won, leaving Baldwin in undisputed control of the Conservatives and inflicting a stunning defeat on the press lords for which they were bent on revenge. In early 1936, Beaverbrook was suspected of plotting with Winston Churchill, then struggling to return from the political wilderness, to remove Baldwin.[9] The King was concerned only to protect Mrs Simpson when he asked for the press's silence, but he had unthinkingly stepped into the camp of the government's opponents. He had strayed into a singularly venomous political feud. It was to have serious consequences.[10]

The fear that the King might try to mobilize press or political support to support his position against the government had weighed on Downing Street from an early stage. Baldwin authorized an MI5 operation against the King and his circle.[11] It was to take the government side a few weeks to dub Beaverbrook and Churchill 'The King's Party' but setting the security service, whose principal job was to protect Britain from the machinations of foreign powers working through spies and domestic subversive, onto the legitimate, unchallenged head of state shows just how deeply any campaign in his favour was seen as a threat to national stability.

5

Furnishing an American Queen

There is no doubt as to the original source of the most famous remark attributed to William Randolph Hearst. It appeared in *The Great Highway: The Wanderings of a Special Correspondent*, published in 1901 by James Creelman, one of Hearst's writers. Hearst had sent Frederic Remington, a famous and well-paid artist, to Cuba to cover its struggle for independence from Spain but he saw no sign of war and cabled to Hearst asking to be recalled. According to Creelman, Hearst cabled back, 'You furnish the pictures, and I'll furnish the war.' Down the years a minor but vigorous squabble has developed as to whether the tale is true.[1] A good part of the argument focuses on timing; whether the local revolution had broken out by the time Remington arrived. This, though, is beside the point. The war that was under discussion was the United States' intervention on behalf of the rebels, which Hearst did his utmost to bring about through a remorseless newspaper campaign against Spanish atrocities. By the 1930s the story was part of the established repertory of proof that Hearst was dangerously irresponsible. It served as the most flagrant example of the unaccountable power that major press organizations could deploy. Whether Creelman's story is true or not barely matters; Hearst was regarded as someone who could see the potential for something to happen in the real world that would provide good, commercially viable copy (and fit his political agenda) and to work for it to happen.

By 1936, Hearst was firmly established as a dominant, utterly self-willed press tycoon, soon to be immortalized as Citizen Kane in Orson Welles's 1941 movie. In parallel to his newspapers, he was building San Simeon, his vast castle in California, and filling it with treasures bought from round the world with no thought to cost. That year his greatest preoccupation was to ensure that the Republican Alf Landon won the US presidential election. Hearst had supported F. D. Roosevelt at the start of his presidency but had become a bitter opponent. He fully imagined that it lay in his power to replace him with Landon in November 1936. Hearst remained a practising newsman and his agenda in domestic politics did not blind him to the news possibilities inherent in the kingship of Edward VIII which must have been familiar to him following Frazier Hunt's biography of 1935. Much of Hunt's book had rapidly been overtaken by events but Hearst's perception of Edward closely followed the picture that Hunt had drawn. Hunt's experience of the new king also served as a guide to Hearst's other journalists in London.[2] At the start of the reign Hearst was treating Edward's accession more as a routine news story that certainly ought to be covered. When he wrote to one of his executives about the content in one of his leading titles, *New York American*, it came high in the list of items he discussed and he approved the amount of attention that his accession had been given, 'Edward VIII. gets all the space he is worth.'[3] There had been nothing exceptional in the coverage: routine news and a multi-part profile by a noted historian.

Hearst's press empire was almost entirely in the US. He owned the British edition of *Good Housekeeping* whose editor Alice Head was probably the highest-paid woman in Britain and one of his closest associates. But it was not a news magazine and Head's principal task appears to have been to liaise with the dealers who fed Hearst's insatiable appetite for fine art and collectibles. His strongest connection with Britain was St. Donat's Castle in Wales which he had bought on a whim and on which he lavished huge amounts of money, a European counterpart to San Simeon. St. Donat's became the usual final stop in Hearst's quasi-regal progresses through Europe, which occasionally had journalistic value, notably when he personally interviewed Hitler. Head was a regular member of Hearst's travelling court on these journeys. Hearst and his long-standing girlfriend, the film actress Marion Davies, became features in British society. At a house party at the Duke of Sutherland's home in Kent Davies met Edward, then Prince of Wales, and his brother George Duke of Kent.[4] The Duke of Sutherland was close to Edward and was appointed to be Lord Steward of the Household in one of his most senior court appointments after he became king. Davies later wrote that it was she who alerted Hearst to the King's intention to marry Mrs. Simpson, which she had gleaned at a party given by Philip Sassoon, the socialite politician.[5]

A few weeks into the new reign Hearst's attention was fired by the journalistic possibilities of Edward's marriage plans. He personally told one of his star reporters, Adela Rogers St. Johns, that she was to go to London and discover what she could about Mrs. Simpson. Hearst hinted that he saw diplomatic benefits in the relationship for America and that it was worth promoting on that score. He knew that Britain might soon be needing America's help. Hearst knew of the affair but not that the King was secretly set on marriage and set out his own breathtaking project to his employee, 'Let us see if we can make her Queen of England.'⁶ Rogers St. Johns's coverage was to be shaped to help the King make her his queen, but Hearst wanted to keep this firmly under wraps. Rogers St. Johns was to use a movie story as cover for her presence in Britain.

Rogers St. Johns sailed to Britain and set to work on what was a project of the deepest secrecy. She had been instructed not to report to Joseph Kingsbury-Smith, the head of Hearst's London bureau, supposedly to protect his standing in official circles. She was embedded in Beaverbrook's organization. Arthur Christiansen, Beaverbrook's top editor, had commissioned her to write a series comparing the British and US film industries but latched on to her true mission.

The only lead Rogers St. Johns brought to London was an introduction to Fred Bate, European head of the National Broadcasting Company, who was a regular guest at Fort Belvedere. She encountered widespread fascination with Mrs. Simpson and a wall of silence, but she was an experienced and persistent journalist. Her most important discovery was that Mrs. Simpson had been married before; at that stage only a handful of people in London knew of her first marriage to Win Spencer. Rogers St. Johns appreciated that this piece of questionable family history put a quite different complexion on the affair and immediately cabled Hearst. Had it been known about, the Simpsons' presentation at Court in 1931, the foundation of their standing as members of reputable society, would not have been permitted.

Rogers St. Johns returned to New York with a healthy stock of material on Mrs. Simpson but the conviction that Hearst's scheme was doomed. She knew that the notion of the King marrying a woman twice-divorced would provoke immense opposition in Britain. Moreover, an American woman almost certainly past child-bearing age fell far short of anything most British people hoped for in a queen. Hearst was not daunted and he replied by echoing the delusionally confident analysis projected by Hunt the year before, 'You underestimate the hold this man has on the heart of his people.'[7]

Hearst was still fixated on the project and had decided that he needed to speak to the King personally. 'You handle the story of Mrs. Simpson so she is a sympathetic figure, we may win their [the British people] hearts to this royal romance and present a case for it as an alliance ... so let us paint a portrait to perform our miracle.'[8] Marion Davies even suggested that Rogers St. Johns manufacture a story that Mrs. Simpson's first husband, who had been a naval officer, had been killed in battle, 'He wants you to create Helen of Troy and Cleopatra out of Wally Simpson.' Hearst was heavily invested in Rogers St. Johns's story and when she discovered that one of Mrs. Simpson's relatives, a grand lady in Washington high society, had childhood photographs of her, he pulled out all the stops to persuade her to let his newspapers use them, 'I feel it would be a good thing for the world if the King of England married this lady who is a member of your family.'

As Mrs. Simpson's divorce case loomed, two entirely different press strategies were being pursued. In Britain, the King with the active assistance of Beaverbrook and the instinct for silence and discretion of the establishment press, was striving for a practical news blackout, whilst in America, Hearst with the assistance, if not more, of Mrs. Simpson was softening the public up for the spectacular marriage that her divorce from Ernest Simpson would make possible. Two days before the divorce hearing in Ipswich, Hearst's *New York American* ran an authoritative prediction splashed across the front page under a huge headline that she would then marry the King:

KING EDWARD TO MARRY MRS. SIMPSON IN JUNE
Marriage Will Crown Their Romance
   Within a few days Mrs. Ernest Simpson of Baltimore, Maryland, U.S.A., will obtain her divorce decree in England, and some eight months thereafter she will be married to Edward VIII, King of England.
   King Edward's most intimate friends state with the utmost positiveness that he is very deeply and sincerely enamoured of Mrs. Simpson, that his love is a righteous affection and that almost immediately after the coronation he will take her as his consort.

It is stated definitely that King Edward is convinced that this is both the right thing to do and the wise thing to do.

He believes that it would be an actual mistake for a King of England to marry into any of the royal houses of the Continent of Europe, and so involve himself and his empire in the complications and disasters of these royal houses.

Opposes Royal Intermarriage

He believes further that in this day and generation it is absurd to try to maintain the tradition of royal intermarriages, with all the physical as well as political disabilities likely to result from this outgrown custom.

His brother, the Duke of York, has been extremely happy and fortunate in his marriage to a lady of the people, a commoner, so called.

King Edward believes that the marriage he contemplates would be equally happy, and that it would help him do what he wants to do – namely, reign in the interest of his people.

Finally, he believes that the most important thing for the peace and welfare of the world is an intimate understanding and relationship between England and America, and that his marriage with this very gifted lady may help to bring about that beneficial co-operation between English-speaking nations.

Wants Privilege of a Commoner

Primarily, however, the King's transcendent reason for marrying Mrs. Simpson is that he ardently loves her, and does not see why a king should be denied the privilege of marrying the lady he loves.

So, in all human probability, in June, 1937, one month after the ceremonies of the coronation, will follow the festivities of the marriage of King Edward VIII of England to the very charming and intelligent Mrs. Ernest Simpson of Baltimore, Maryland, U.S.A.

The article combined Hearst's vision of a marriage that would bring Britain close to the US with Edward's obsessive rejection of a dynastic marriage, which Frazier Hunt had trumpeted the previous year. Hunt's biography had also made much of Edward's affection for America. There had been practically no discussion of such a marriage for a long time so it is testimony to the strength of Edward's paranoid belief that the Court was trying to jockey him into marrying some stray European royal that as much space was devoted to rejecting this notion as to proclaiming his love for Mrs. Simpson.

The article was Hearst's own work. Widespread gossip amongst journalists held that it was 'dictated, word for word, by Mr. Randolph Hearst from his castle in Wales'.[9] This was supposedly the only time that he had ever done this. Alice Head, who was with him at St. Donat's, knew that he was taking a hands-on approach to coverage; the story of the imminent marriage was what 'he had already passed for publication'. One of Beaverbrook's London editors believed that Hearst had got the story directly from the King after visiting Fort Belvedere.[10] Marion Davies also told Rogers St. Johns that Hearst had made a secret visit to the Fort, but claimed that he had not told even her what had been discussed. In one draft of his memoirs the by-then Duke of Windsor gave Hearst a flattering acknowledgement for the article, 'Mr. William Randolph Hearst, the great American newspaper proprietor, then vacationing at his castle in Wales, went so far as to predict in his country-wide chain of newspapers that some eight months after [Wallis] had obtained her divorce she would be married to the King.'[11] If nothing else, this proves that the King knew of Hearst's presence in Britain, not something of which he might usually be expected to be aware. The Duchess of Windsor later denied the meeting had taken place, but in suspiciously qualified and circumspect terms.[12]

Hearst and his cohorts had miscalculated. Their plans were an open book to the British government through a low-profile but hugely valuable part of its intelligence operation. Downing Street knew that Mrs. Simpson was in direct and regular contact with the Hearst organisation, and took her to be the source of the *New York American* story.[13] Post Office clerks who were given cables to send simply passed these on to the Home Office if they appeared sensitive.[14] The supposedly private company responsible for Britain's international cable traffic, Cable & Wireless Ltd., was secretly controlled by the government, and operated its network as an arm of the state. Its chairman, Sir Campbell Stuart, fancied himself as an intelligence operative. This all gave Baldwin a full picture of the scheme to give the relationship between the King and Mrs. Simpson a positive diplomatic spin. Prime Minister Stanley Baldwin told the Australian high commissioner, Stanley Bruce, that 'Mr.* Simpson has an alliance with Hearst to write the thing up on the basis of a marriage of the King with an American subject would cement Anglo-American relations'.[15] Mrs. Simpson's links to an apparent press campaign in favour of her marrying the King helped harden the conviction in Downing Street that she herself was determined to achieve this goal. The British intelligence-gathering operation targeting the King had also reported that the Hearst organization was paying for the information it was being fed.[16] It was not an appealing picture – crude mercenary motives combined with an attempt to pressurize the government through a hostile foreign press organization.

The *New York American* article came and went in the welter of competing American and European press articles about the relationship without attracting the attention that it deserved. It provoked no significant reaction in British government circles or the higher reaches of the British press. It aroused practically no comment at Downing Street which might not even have got a copy until a month later.[17] Baldwin can have had little doubt that a marriage was in the offing and he was not the sort of man to be jockeyed into action by the foreign press.

What did throw the top level of British government into consternation in the days following the divorce case was the King's failure to comply with the unwritten rules of the era and adopt a measure of discretion as to his contact with a newly divorced woman. Instead, the King set out to flaunt his relationship with Mrs. Simpson so flagrantly that the hypothetical possibility of them marrying in six months' time paled into insignificance. The finalization of the divorce demanded that she maintain six months of 'innocence' following the Ipswich decree nisi but within days the King dined with her at her house in Cumberland Terrace and she had spent the weekend at Fort Belvedere.

The King was preparing for a showdown. On 11 November Hearst's London bureau reported that the King had set out to establish the true state of public opinion.[18] He was reported to have been confronted by the Archbishops of Canterbury and York, who had told him that the majority of his subjects would oppose his marriage to Mrs. Simpson. No

---

* More likely to have meant Mrs. Simpson.

record has survived of any survey undertaken by the King, but the report may have sowed a seed with Hearst himself who instructed his London wire service chief to prepare one.[19] The findings of the correspondents in the British dominions cannot have pleased Hearst. They ranged from tepid to qualified.[20] Hearst was personally overseeing the release of his Universal Service agency despatches and it seems that the survey was never distributed to agency clients.[21] Hearst's project to give Britain an American queen was proving more complex and challenging than bringing about a war between the US and Spain in 1898.

Hearst's front-line journalists were left manoeuvring on an obscure information battleground that their chief had helped to create. One of their reports epitomizes the challenges of the craft of royal reporting then and ever since.

Becoming more apparent amazing game [of] intrigue unprecedented [in] recent times being played around throne [of] England and that for next few months or until after coronation or when lady free king can act definitely one way or other we shall be flooded with insistent and persuasive rumors of propaganda [from] all quarters stop endeavoring keep as near facts as possible remembering always actors themselves frequently have [to] make tactical moves which may make getting accurate picture difficult at times.[22]

Hearst remained hopeful that there would be a Queen Wallis after the crisis broke and repeated once again what he had told Rogers St. Johns after learning of Mrs. Simpson's first divorce, 'Let us not despair. He has the support of his people.'[23] He was finally forced though to admit defeat and ruefully confessed to having misread the King, 'I'm sorry we failed … I have discovered that it is a grave injustice to overestimate a man. To expect more of him than he is able to give.'[24] Hearst bounced back from the disappointment and resumed his interest in the affair from a strictly newsman's point of view, 'I see no difficulty in sustaining the story. I agree the story is much less worth while now.' To his loyal employee Alice Head, he had still played a part in the crisis that had 'passed into history'.[25]

Hearst had good reason that autumn to retreat from his self-image as the man who could bend world affairs to his will through the power of his newspapers. When he returned to New York, he greeted the waiting reporters with a firm prediction that Alf Landon, the man he had elevated from insignificance as his anointed challenger to Roosevelt in the presidential election, would certainly win. Rogers St. Johns claims that she disagreed and told him, 'we're going to get our brains kicked out.'[26] Landon suffered a crushing defeat.

In the aftermath of the abdication Hearst still nursed hopes of extending the relationship. When he learned of the by-then Duke of Windsor's plan to visit America in the autumn of 1937 he offered him the use of one of his houses.[27] Perhaps unwisely the Duke declined Hearst's invitation. This might have saved him the furore which finally killed off his plan to go to America, which was to have been part of his programme to re-establish himself as a substantial figure on the world stage. Linking himself to Hearst for the exercise would have had the deep disadvantage of appearing to signal dissent from President Roosevelt, but it is unlikely to have aroused the near unanimous hostility provoked by choosing the Franco-American businessman Charles Bedaux as the sponsor and organizer of the journey. Bedaux's brutal time-and-motion study methods had made him a hate figure for American labour.

6

Editors as Statesmen

At the start of Edward's reign, Baldwin had made very tentative efforts to involve himself in the King's relationship with Mrs. Simpson but they had led nowhere. He then spent months resisting frantic pressure from courtiers and civil servants to intervene. There were other even more serious matters that occupied him. He was having to cope with the growing recognition that the Fascist powers posed a decisive threat to European peace: Mussolini's invasion of Ethiopia, Hitler's illegal reoccupation of Rhineland and the outbreak of the Spanish Civil War. On medical advice that he was at risk of mental breakdown, Baldwin left London for a period of complete rest over the summer. It was finally the news of Mrs. Simpson's divorce case that hastened his return to London with the King's matter at the top of his agenda.

Baldwin bowed to pressure from the hard-liners and a growing establishment chorus and spoke to the King about Mrs. Simpson on 20 October 1936. He asked the King whether he could get the divorce action stopped but the King declined, ostensibly because he did not believe he should interfere in the private affairs of a subject. The best that the government could hope for was that the divorce hearing did not provoke an open scandal but this would be no more than a breathing space. It was now clear that Mrs. Simpson – and perhaps the King himself – were working with William Randolph Hearst to flag their plans publicly and to put a positive spin on what was now openly their intention to marry.

The courthouse in Ipswich where Mrs. Simpson's divorce case was heard was besieged by foreign press. Despite the attempts by the local police to harass the foreign journalists, the case was fully reported in the international newspapers, including inevitably the Hearst papers with direct assertions that once Mrs. Simpson was free of her marriage, a wedding to her royal boyfriend would not be long in coming. By contrast the British newspapers reported the case in minimal form with no more attention devoted to it than to any other divorce case. No word of Mrs. Simpson's relationship to the King appeared.

The press silence on the relationship had not been challenged at any point by the government. In a predictable establishment response to potentially embarrassing behaviour by one of – if not its most – senior members, there had been no thought of giving it any publicity whatever, even of the most heavily spun nature possible. Behind this public black-out on news, the King's wayward behaviour had provoked a furious debate at the top level of government and civil service as to how to deal with such a threat to good order and discipline. Implicit throughout was that the problem would be addressed in a suitably confidential and discreet manner. The King's actions in the immediate aftermath of the court case affronted the code of the day so deeply that they came perilously close to bringing about a radical reversal in the government's stance and triggering the launch of a public campaign against the King's conduct.

Divorce law and practice in the 1930s was littered with hypocrisy and antiquity. Divorce was still unusual and widely frowned upon so, if irrational rules served as a deterrent to anyone contemplating it, so much the better. It mattered nothing if they were foolish or inhuman. Law and social custom fused happily on what should happen after the first court hearing. This could only grant the first stage in a divorce, a decree nisi, and there then had to be an interval of six months before the courts could grant the decree final, which completely ended the marriage. During this time the spouse who had brought the case was under the sternest of obligations to display their entire innocence. In particular, contact with another partner was considered unacceptable. This legal obligation had the happy social effect of masking the fact that divorces were very often undertaken to allow one spouse to marry someone else. In Britain's higher social reaches it was common for the 'innocent' party in a case to disappear abroad, returning after a suitable interval in which everyone could forget, or pretend to forget, the scandal of the divorce and remarry with as much decorum as possible. Many in government assumed that Mrs. Simpson would follow this pattern and damp down the scandal of her relationship with the King. But as mentioned above, Edward had no truck with any such weasel behaviour and only days after the hearing, dined with her at the expensive house in Regent's Park in which he had installed her. There was no thought of her leaving the country. The King was challenging convention head on.

The situation was bad enough for Baldwin to tell Neville Chamberlain, the Chancellor of the Exchequer and the number two man in the government, that '[h]e' thought it was necessary to give the King a real jolt to bring him to realise the situation'.[1] Baldwin was considering sending some kind of warning by 'the more responsible newspapers' as the 'real jolt'. Quite how serious Baldwin might have been is open to question. Chamberlain had established himself as the government's leading hawk on how to handle the King and had lobbied for severe measures that would have treated the sovereign as little more than an errant junior employee whose conduct was unsatisfactory. Baldwin may well merely have wanted to give his Chancellor the impression that he was taking the matter very seriously indeed. In the event, Baldwin chose another approach but a hand had run over the stopper to the genie's bottle of press coverage.

Baldwin's decision not to pull the stopper from the bottle had as much to do with tactics as principle. Baldwin was surveying a complex middle game in his chess match with the King and looking a good number of moves further ahead than either his opponent or the hard-liners who were urging him to act. The King was about to undertake a visit to the industrial areas of South Wales and to the Royal Navy at Portland. Both would showcase the King's talents as a public performer and were likely to be well received with accordingly positive press coverage.[2] If some newspapers chose to criticize the King's personal life, it would be recognized as an attempt to sabotage the boost to his popularity if it were launched in advance of the visits and as an attempt to dilute the boost to his influence if it were undertaken afterwards. It was not principle or discretion that held Baldwin back, it was a ruthless tactical calculation of media policy. The newspapers and public opinion were just pieces on the chessboard that he had to analyse. The King would soon have two very easy shots at bolstering his public standing by techniques that he knew and had mastered; a government-inspired negative campaign would be a high-risk exercise. For both sides of the game, actively putting an end to press silence was the nuclear option. Baldwin calculated that he would be the loser if he chose it then. In conversation with his civil service adviser, Sir Horace Wilson, Baldwin also came with another, rather more positive reason (or, more probably, pretext) for delaying action. The Remembrance Day service and the visits to the Fleet and South Wales would raise 'Kingly' thoughts in Edward's mind and make him amenable to a serious conversation when he returned to London.[3]

Baldwin's calculation kept the press silence alive, but it did not make it any less inevitable that it would end soon. By this point it was manifestly untenable. Few doubted it would end, but no one was going to take the responsibility for ending it. In the strict sense of the word the newspapers were already virtually playing a part in the crisis. Everyone who knew that a crisis was unfolding, knew that the newspapers would be involved, but no one knew when or how. Just as the establishment had in practice left the full job of dealing with the King to Baldwin, so it left him to choose when to end the press silence. But all this was a calculation amongst insiders. No one seems to have thought that the King's subjects might have been entitled to be told about something that was common gossip in the higher reaches of society. Insofar as public opinion mattered, everyone appears to have been content to leave the question of judging what the public might think about the King and Mrs. Simpson to the prime minister, who was, admittedly, a man who prided himself on his ability to read the public mood.

The newspapers which most recognizably made up the journalistic arm of the establishment saw the growing scandal as an issue of high policy and were ready to shape their coverage as and when the story broke, in a responsible fashion designed to support the government's handling of the issue. Their editors behaved as members of the great and good rather than mere journalists.

Newspaper editors had no journalistic work to perform, but two senior editors began to try to influence events directly by playing on their standing in the mechanisms of power. On Thursday, 12 November, Baldwin received a letter from Howell Gwynne, the editor of Britain's staidest newspaper, *The Morning Post*, the longest-serving national editor and a relentless meddler in politics.[4] Gwynne too envisioned the 'respectable' press operating as an arm of the government in dealing with the King. He had arrived late in the newspaper world from the imperial administration and he preferred shaping imperial policy to the grubby business of selling information to the general public. During the First World War he had sided with the generals against the prime minister Lloyd George to the extent of breaking the law to leak information that supported the generals' case. He was a die-hard imperialist, Tory and anti-Semite, prepared to contemplate military dictatorship. Between the wars Gwynne espoused conservative policies; he promoted as genuine the anti-Semitic fabrication *The Protocols of the Elders of Zion*.[5] *The Morning Post* was on its last legs commercially; its readership with their antique views of politics were dying out; in 1937 it was folded ignominiously into *The Daily Telegraph*.

However, Gwynne was the doyen of Fleet Street and could claim to be a spokesman for his colleagues to pass on their opinions to Downing Street. According to his letter to Baldwin, Gwynne's colleagues had warned him that it was becoming increasingly difficult for them to maintain the 'Great Silence' on the King and Mrs Simpson. Gwynne was claiming to speak for 'several of my confreres'.[6] Gwynne provided no evidence regarding which of his colleagues were concerned. Implicitly these were what he described as the editors of 'the more responsible newspapers' but if Gwynne had actually been in touch with them, these did not include *The Times*. Gwynne contrasted the responsible view with 'the sensational newspapers' which could 'deliver a deadly blow to the Monarchy'. It is suspicious that his letter should have coincided almost exactly with a big push by the cabal of hard-liners around the prime minister for brutal action.[7] In a rather different way Gwynne was sending the same message as the hard-liners: time was running out for the prime minister to keep deferring resolute action. For the time being, Gwynne claimed to be content to advise other editors to maintain silence, but ultimately, he said that the government had to give a lead. The threat of an uncontrolled breach in the press silence was both a danger in its own right and something that the hard-liners were using to goad the prime minister towards action.

To jog Baldwin into action and give the signal for the press to move, Gwynne had instructed William 'Bill' Deedes, then at the start of a celebrated career in journalism and politics as a junior correspondent on *The Morning Post*, to assemble a dossier of foreign press stories on Mrs. Simpson. When he later looked back on what he had done, Deedes recognized that his own motivation had been to be part of a simple journalistic scoop.[8]

Baldwin ignored the suggestion that *The Morning Post* should lead the ranks of conservative newspapers into breaking the news of the affair. After this brush-off by the prime minister, Gwynne tried his scheme out on the other claimant to the title of leader of the respectable establishment press, Geoffrey Dawson, editor of *The Times*. Unbeknownst to Gwynne, Dawson had already been trying to intervene with Baldwin, who had explained the tactical arguments against a press campaign to moderate the King's behaviour around the visits to South Wales and the Royal Navy. Gwynne tried to persuade Dawson that 'common action by the newspapers' was needed but Dawson had already gone over this ground with Baldwin. Between them the editor and the prime minister – with Baldwin more likely taking the lead – had seen the tactical moves well in advance. Baldwin had headed Dawson off from action then and Dawson had no difficulty in warning Gwynne of the drawbacks of organizing an 'official Press phalanx'. Dawson could take comfort from his certainty that Gwynne would not act on his own initiative without a lead from Downing Street. The rivals for leadership of the establishment press had been baulked of their desire for stern words against the King, but had the consolation that Downing Street was showing no particular favour to one or the other.

Geoffrey Dawson incarnated to a greater extent than any of his predecessors and successors *The Times*'s unique position as part of the British ruling class. Whilst it never took orders from a government department as though a mere propaganda tool, its editor was by definition a member of the establishment. Dawson himself had moved to journalism from imperial administration in its glory days when he was a member of Lord Milner's 'kindergarten' that controlled South Africa after victory in the Boer war. He held a fellowship of that uniquely British institution All Souls College, Oxford, which is formally part of the university but conducts neither teaching nor sustained research, serving in practice as a club for intellectual members of the establishment. Dawson was in close, regular and sympathetic contact with Baldwin, although he rather exaggerated his standing with the prime minister. He certainly overestimated how much advice Baldwin needed on press coverage. Dawson did not recognize that Baldwin had a very clear understanding of the press dimension to the crisis and took entirely at face value his *faux naif* claim to be 'quite unable to give advice [on whether to open criticism of the King's personal life]. The Press is an unknown world to him'.[9] Behind the façade of uninformed bumbling, Baldwin was instructing Dawson to hold his hand. Dawson saw his mission as public service in an almost diametrical opposite to the press barons' commercialism and pretensions to political power. He was a public servant and not a mere pressman.

Dawson knew that his paper 'will have to do something about the King and Mrs. Simpson' but that 'the Prime Minister must tell him what he wishes done'.[10] Dawson was, though, prepared to lobby behind closed doors after he had received a lengthy letter from a British man living in the US who felt that the affair with Mrs. Simpson had made the King an 'incalculable liability' to British prestige there. It was signed with limitless pomposity as 'Britannicus in partibus infidelium' (A Briton in infidel lands). It beggars belief that an anonymous letter-writer affected the way Dawson thought so it is far more likely that the letter provided a handy pretext for him to try to influence affairs. He first showed the letter to Major Alexander Hardinge, the King's private secretary. Hardinge was reliably conservative, a holdover from the court of George V but Edward VIII saw him as no more than a useful man to argue his own case to the politicians; Hardinge had no influence over Edward. Hardinge knew it would merely alienate the King if he tried to warn him and told Dawson that this was a job for the politicians.[11] Dawson took this as a pretext to escalate the affair to the highest level of politics and took the letter to Baldwin who thanked him but bided his time. He did not need prompting from someone who fancied himself as a moral arbiter. Dawson had even less joy when he tried to recruit the Archbishop of Canterbury to his cause.[12] Cosmo Gordon Lang had already been firmly rebuffed when he had tried to discuss the King's behaviour with him early in the reign and was not going to risk a second snub.

If Dawson hoped that *The Times* was going to be asked to take the lead in delivering the establishment's verdict on the King's matter, he was disappointed. Baldwin repeatedly warned Dawson off direct comment on the King's affair.[13] Baldwin wanted to avoid provoking the King any further once the 'real jolt' had been delivered as will be discussed in the next chapter. The prime minister feared 'that an admonition in the leading journal might send someone off the deep end'.[14] He also wanted to avoid playing favourites amongst the newspapers. Dawson still managed to sneak into an article on the new governor-general of, and thus the King's representative in, South Africa lightly disguised admonitions that the Crown should be kept from 'glaring public scandal' and held above 'public reproach or ridicule'. Dawson congratulated himself that the sub-text would be clear to the cognoscenti. He also spiced an otherwise routine survey of the programme for the House of Commons which included bills on supplying arms to Spain and new trunk roads with an exhortation to show it was, 'a Council of State, which is able to demonstrate its solid strength in any crisis that may arise, whether foreign domestic'. Even the cognoscenti might have struggled to spot the sub-text here. More with hindsight than anything, Dawson found that *The Times*'s positive coverage of a visit to Scotland by the Duke of York, very soon to become King George VI, was part of the same pattern of discreet intervention. Otherwise, Dawson was reduced to smug gloating that his lesser brethren had recycled the government line fed to the lobby correspondents that an emergency Cabinet meeting to discuss the King had been about Spain.

Both Gwynne and Dawson were wide of the mark in thinking that either of their titles would be the automatic choice for the government to use if it decided to intervene publicly. Dawson might have been correct in his later claim that Baldwin had 'seen a great deal more of me at this time than he did of any other journalist' but he appears to have been entirely unaware that it was one of his humbler competitors, the Berry brothers' *Daily Telegraph* that the prime minister actually used as his mouthpiece.

7

The Jolt

Baldwin had lifted his finger from the button that would have launched the nuclear option of a press strike against the King, but the near certainty that the press would break its silence featured prominently in 'the real jolt' that was finally delivered to the King, albeit in the most confidential fashion possible. The only option that went even further was the threat of an outright constitutional crisis and, almost by accident, this is what the King was confronted with.

It was the King's private secretary, Major Alec Hardinge who delivered the shock. Hardinge was in an invidious position; his main job was to liaise between the King and the government, but neither the King nor the prime minister were showing any inclination to conduct a dialogue. The King was pushing the boundaries of what he could get away with, whilst Baldwin was quietly waiting for the moment to act. Neither wanted serious advice from anyone else. Hardinge was in a doubly difficult position because he had a very weak relationship with his royal master. He had not been Edward's choice as private secretary; he would far have preferred Sir Godfrey Thomas, who had been his assistant private secretary as Prince of Wales, but Thomas knew Edward well and was only too well aware of how impossible the job would be. Hardinge had been assistant private secretary to George V and was placed in a difficult position following Edward's accession. By custom the private secretary and his assistant were left in the jobs with the change of monarch for the first six months of the new reign. Hardinge's chief, Lord Wigram, had severe doubts about Edward and took the opportunity to step down when the holdover period ended. George V's widow, Queen Mary, was anxious that her son would be surrounded as far as possible by the dependable courtiers of her husband's reign and Hardinge loyally took on the job. Edward saw this as a useful concession to his family. He was happy with a secretary who was respected and thus potentially a shield for him against any criticism of his own behaviour. He wanted an effective, passive representative and not an adviser. Hardinge's job was all the harder because he was not a popular man in his own right. He had neither the standing in government circles to force a policy nor the ability to persuade his royal master to improve his behaviour. His lack of self-confidence was a void that the hard-liners and other interested parties were more than willing to fill.

Hardinge knew better than anyone that the King's pretence that there was nothing serious to discuss was heading him for the rocks. His sense of professional duty impelled him to act, which made him a soft target for the civil service hard-liners who were frantic for brutal action to be taken. After agonized soul-searching, Hardinge wrote to the King setting out his concerns. It certainly delivered a sharp warning to the King but it probably went too far. If Hardinge had had a more comfortable relationship with the King he might have opted for a serious conversation. Putting his thoughts in writing gave the message an edge that spoken words might not have had. More important, the letter practically warned the King of an imminent constitutional crisis: the government might give him formal advice on his relationship with Mrs. Simpson and would resign if the advice were not accepted. Incorrectly, he warned that a twist in the legal divorce process would make the affair public; most likely the hard-liners had intentionally misinformed Hardinge. He rounded off with a direct exhortation to the King to send Mrs. Simpson out of the country; this might have been calculated to enrage his master.

Baldwin wanted to jolt the King and knew that Hardinge was writing to the King but it is an open question whether he saw the letter beforehand or even knew just how inflammatory it was.[1] Like many politicians Baldwin thrived on letting other people do his dirty work for him and Hardinge was the luckless victim. Hardinge's letter was the turning point in the crisis, although it remained deeply hidden, known to only a tiny handful of insiders. When Baldwin finally got round to briefing the Cabinet on the crisis a week and a half afterwards, he did not even hint at its existence.

The King read Hardinge's letter when he came back from the Royal Navy review at Portland on a late November afternoon. He was enraged. He assumed that Hardinge had simply written the letter as Baldwin's agent. He was unaware of the tensions within the government and viewed its doings as monolithic. He had persuaded himself that Baldwin's previous attempts to express his concern at the relationship with Mrs. Simpson were insignificant and could safely be ignored. When he was confronted with unarguable evidence that on the contrary the government took the matter very seriously indeed, he took it as an outright declaration of war and fought back. He even escalated the conflict when he summoned Baldwin to an audience on 16 November. Before the prime minister was allowed to say his piece fully, the King cut him short and blankly told him that he was unshakeably intent on marrying Mrs. Simpson and, unless he could marry her, he would leave the throne. Baldwin's reply, 'Sir, that is grievous news' can be read as his reception of an inescapable fact.[2]

In their separate accounts of the conversation both the Duke of Windsor, as he had become, and Baldwin treat the exchange as though a statement of fact were simply to be acknowledged and no more. It is one of the curiosities of the abdication crisis that no one seems to have questioned this. By any standards the King was taking a confrontational approach by opening the conversation with an ultimatum on a vital question. In his turn the prime minister's reply could be read as a flat rejection of the ultimatum. There is every reason to suppose that the King thought that he was in a position to issue an ultimatum and that he thought the prime minister would yield. He had told Frazier Hunt that no minister would dare to challenge his direct support from the public. He might have imagined that Baldwin would have to back down and tamely allow the marriage to go ahead. Mrs. Simpson was even more confident than the King and right up to the end of the crisis advised him that '...his popularity would carry everything'.[3]

Whether as a statement of fact or a bluff called, the opening exchange did not put an end to the affair. On his side Baldwin held open the hope that the King might reverse his decision. The King was rather more proactive. As he later wrote, he was not going to let Baldwin's statements go unchallenged. His first move was to ask Baldwin to keep the conversation quiet, which at the very least means that he was not expecting it to lead imminently to his abdication. He also asked Baldwin's permission to speak to two of his 'personal friends' in the Cabinet, Sir Sam Hoare and Duff Cooper, and sounded them out as to whether they would support him against the prime minister. He also set in motion a scheme which would take his stance before the court of public opinion.

8

King Edward's Contribution to Democratic Government

As he got ready to lock horns with his prime minister over the question of his relationship with Mrs. Simpson, the King was riding the crest of a wave of popularity. His programme of official engagements had resumed in full since his holiday at Balmoral and the old Prince of Wales magic was still working; any discontent provoked amongst his Scottish subjects by the Aberdeen Infirmary affair had not found their way southwards. He had been rapturously received at a massed meeting in the Albert Hall to mark Remembrance Day on 11 November which connected him to his constituency amongst veterans of the First World War. As Baldwin had predicted when he was calculating the odds in a public battle, the King's visit to the Royal Navy at Portland had been a resounding success.

The next date on the King's official calendar came days after the crucial audience with Baldwin. Baldwin had been right in thinking that the visits to his subjects would inspire 'Kingly' thoughts in Edward. The problem was that they were the wrong kind of 'Kingly' thoughts. They harked straight back to the manifesto for his kingship that he had set out to Frazier Hunt. The 'Socialist King' was going to challenge his capitalist prime minister's claim to legitimacy in the court of public opinion. By a curious and symbolic coincidence, it transformed into an arena of combat the site of one of his father's public triumphs in distant, happier days long gone. George V had fought a long battle of attrition to halt the encroachments on his power of elected politicians; his son was going over to the offensive

In June 1912, George V had been king for a little more than two years and was steadily making the rounds of his realm. That month his programme included a visit to Wales, in particular the Dowlais steel works in the heavily industrialized south of the principality. The royal visit set the seal on Dowlais's status as one of the key sites in British industry and economy. Dowlais had ridden the crest of the wave for most of the country's long industrial revolution since the eighteenth century, when a combination of coal and iron ore deposits nearby made it a natural site for large-scale iron production. Dowlais had turned to steel making early on and with 9,000 workers it was one of the counry's most important and impressive manufacturing sites. The visit was replete with symbolism. Britain stood at its imperial apogee and Dowlais embodied two of the great pillars of the empire. Steel was the vital raw material for the battleships through which the Royal Navy projected the power of the British Empire, the mightiest the world had ever seen. The choreography of the royal visit hammered home how the Dowlais works transformed natural resources into the substance of industrial and military power. The King and Queen Mary entered the works through an arch made of coal and left through one made of steel.

Less than a quarter of a century later George V's son and successor also visited Dowlais but the picture had changed radically. The iron ore deposits were almost exhausted and the coal was expensive to mine. Dowlais had already been uncompetitive but the Great Slump heralded by the Wall Street Crash of 1929 had destroyed its markets and sounded the works' death knell. Steel production was terminated and the last blast furnace was closed in 1936, throwing the last few hundreds of the thousands of men who had once worked there out of work. The relics of the equipment mouldered where they lay in a scene of profound desolation. The image of misery was underscored by the squalor of the houses where the hopelessly unemployed lived. Where the father had visited the pride of British industry, the son was visiting the symbol of industrial near-collapse. In the arid euphemism of government Dowlais was now part of a Special Area, one of the regions once dependent on old, heavy industry now seemingly doomed to permanent misery. At least half the men were out of work. Tentative government measures to improve conditions had achieved almost nothing. South Wales was an emblem of Britain's immense problems and there was deep significance in its having been chosen for the King's first, and as it proved only, major provincial tour.

The King's autumn tour of South Wales enjoyed a striking success. Everywhere he was received by rapturous crowds, delighted at the solidarity that their King was displaying with them in their plight. He was visibly moved and upset by what he saw. The accompanying press pack was very happy with such excellent copy and even happier when the King improved on it even further. He went far beyond a symbolic presence and made a very public statement that the people needed help. Precisely what he said, to whom, when and where has been lost beyond recovery, but no one argues that the much-quoted call 'Something must be done' captures the essence of what he said. Probably he said a number of slightly different things to different people. His words were reported throughout the press on Thursday, 19 November and went down in history almost immediately. Along with his abdication broadcast, the declaration features in almost all lists of his quotations. It has become a shorthand for the desperate sense of frustration inspired by the massive economic crisis of the 1930s and the inability or unwillingness of those in power to tackle the problems.

The implied criticism of government inaction was plain for all to understand but there was a doubly political edge to what the King was saying that went far beyond a generalized call for political action. He is reliably quoted as having told executives of the company that owned the Dowlais factory, 'These people were brought here by these works. Some kind of employment must be found for them.'[1] Any mildly well-informed reader would have known that the company in question was Guest, Keen, Baldwins and that it had been formed by a merger with the family company of Prime Minister Stanley Baldwin.

The King was acting out the playbook that Frazier Hunt had broadcast the year before. This was a step in saving the nation 'with her two million unemployed, her ten million over-population, her housing problems, her losses in trade, her vast discouragement and deep though silent unrest'.[2] He was not 'mix[ing] in politics or interfer[ing] with the orderly process of elective government' though. When he had briefed the German ambassador von Hoesch on the hostile reaction to his Albert Hall speech calling for the hand of friendship to be reached out to Germany in 1935, Edward had set out how he intended to operate. 'He believed, however, that the timidity and hesitation which, as is well known, were characteristic of politicians, were much slower in achieving results than a frank word spoken at the right moment, even though it might exceed the bounds of reserve normally maintained.'[3] In Edward's mind he was merely stating obvious fact, the illusion of amateur politicians down the ages. It was up to the politicians to apply his 'frank word' to the nitty gritty of policy.

Even if Edward had genuinely intended his remarks at Dowlais to be no more than 'a frank word spoken at the right moment', Esmond Harmsworth, his first and personally closest press ally, transformed his words into an unambiguously political statement in precisely the way that British constitutional rules are designed to avoid. Esmond Harmsworth's *Daily Mail* had given steady and friendly coverage to the King's activities and like the rest of the British newspapers it had only too willingly complied with the King's request to keep silent on his relationship with Mrs. Simpson. Days after Edward's return from Wales, it pitched in firmly on his side, albeit with no mention of the stand-off over his relationship with Mrs. Simpson. In its edition of Monday, 23 November it published a truly extraordinary editorial comment which gave Edward's words in Wales unprecedented significance. After a routine, albeit fulsome description of the King's sympathy for his subjects, the *Daily Mail* wiped away a few hundred years of constitutional development and wrote of the King as though he had executive power. It read uncannily like Frazier Hunt's manifesto:

Already he has talked with his ministers and prompted them into real activity ... **The King has called for action. He will want to review the Government's plans and to be kept posted of their progress.** [emphasis in original] Having once engaged in a task, the King maintains watchful pressure until he has seen it through.

King Edward's latest contribution to democratic government has been to give it a human aspect and a sharp, sudden access of drive.

A Contrast
He went to see for himself, personal investigation being the basis for every job of work the King touches. ... The contrast to the way in which national questions are customarily approached can escape nobody. How often does a Minister go boldly forth to see for himself and measure a problem by independent judgment, following this with immediate action?

Surely those who have recently confessed that they dared not tell the people the truth three years ago and who have since

accomplished so little towards defence will realise the gulf between their conduct and the King's methods in Wales. ... His character is the opposite of easy-going acceptance of inaction.[4]

The article broke new ground in two ways and it is impossible not to detect the hand of Esmond Harmsworth at work. Up till then dealing with unemployment had not been a particular topic in the *Daily Mail*. Nor had the constitutional role of the monarch featured. The leader seemed to be declaring the *Daily Mail's* allegiance to the King in an all-out constitutional conflict. It virtually claimed that the King and his ministers, notably the prime minister, were in direct conflict on the question of unemployment and that the King was firmly in the right. It contrasted the King's personal engagement with the problems of his subjects with what it castigated as the government's fumbling and remote bureaucratic methods. The leader went on to imply that the King's methods (and by implication, the King as a person) would offer the better approach to a far more vexatious topic on which Esmond's father Lord Rothermere had been campaigning for some years: the threat of air attack by Nazi Germany and the need to rearm to counter it. There is not the slightest evidence that Edward ever interested himself in rearmament in any respect so there must be a suspicion that Esmond threw this in to keep his father happy after hijacking his flagship newspaper.

The *Daily Mail's* hostile comments on the government rammed home to readers whose side it thought that they should be taking. There was an even less coded criticism of Baldwin than the King's dig at his family firm. The leader was glaringly topical. Baldwin had confessed to the House of Commons a week before that he had consciously downplayed the scale of rearmament required so as not to scare electors in a speech of 'appalling frankness'. He cultivated an image of passive and unhurried approach to action as part of his pitch to be seen as a solid, reflective and reliable man to lead the country, which his detractors spun into idleness and indecision. In reality, Baldwin was a master of timing and never signalled his intentions loudly before he had chosen his moment to strike. When he did strike, he did so hard and swiftly. The gulf between Baldwin's reputation and the hard record of his moves is an object lesson in the gulf between perception and reality.

The *Daily Mail* was straying into very dangerous territory by touching on another controversial political cause that it espoused alongside rearmament. It was promoting the image of a young, dynamic King unencumbered by the ballast of traditional politics, almost precisely the ideal of kingship held by Sir Oswald Mosley's British Union of Fascists (BUF). Lord Rothermere had been an enthusiastic supporter of the BUF, culminating in its celebrated *Daily Mail* headline 'Hurrah for the Blackshirts' in January 1934 which marked the highpoint of British Fascism as a potentially serious force in national politics. Lord Rothermere had withdrawn his paper's open endorsement of the BUF a few months later following the widely publicized violence against hecklers by BUF stewards at the massive Olympia rally, but this fell far short of open condemnation of Fascism and the *Daily Mail* remained broadly favourable towards Mosley and his movement.

Baldwin had no doubt what was truly at stake. He told his long-standing confidant Tom Jones, former assistant secretary to the Cabinet and occasional speech-writer, 'The *Daily Mail* is flying kites over the South Wales visit but really with the marriage business in mind.'[5] The languid phraseology masked a ruthless determination to defeat another attempt by men whom Baldwin saw as self-anointed interpreters of the public will to bully the elected government. The *Daily Mail*'s challenge to the government was direct and unambiguous. It revived the battle over Empire free trade waged by Rothermere and Beaverbrook that had been fought a few years before. By siding with the King against the government, the Harmsworths appeared to be mounting another attempt to take control of party politics. This time the stakes were even higher. The target was to influence government policy and not just the platform of an opposition party. It was a challenge that had to be tackled head on. The establishment struck back against the *Daily Mail* and predictably enough, did so through *The Times*, in that era the mouthpiece of the establishment generally and usually of the government of the day. It stood in proud contrast to the popular (or 'stunt') press, controlled by the newspaper barons with their freight of devious and irresponsible political ambitions. The day after the *Daily Mail* editorial it published a ferociously critical leader article of its own, practically written by *The Times*'s editor Geoffrey Dawson.

Dawson's editorial hammered home the dubiousness of the constitutional stance that the *Daily Mail* had taken. It was accused of the ultimate sin of trying to hijack the monarchy in the interests of a single political faction.

> But it is a wholly mischievous suggestion, and one altogether alien to the spirit of the Constitution, which would set his [the King's] well-known sympathy with the distressed against the measures taken by the Government, and which by implication would drive a wedge between the Monarch and his Ministers. The KING'S Ministers are His MAJESTY's advisers, and to contrast his personal and representative concern for the well-being of a section of the people with the administrative steps of his advisers is a constitutionally dangerous proceeding and would threaten, if continued, to entangle the THRONE in politics. To write of the KING'S visit, as one newspaper wrote yesterday ... is to strike at the very root of the Monarchy; for if the Monarch is to be dissociated, for the purposes of political argument, from some actions of his Ministers, then by inference he must bear a more direct responsibility for all the rest. The KING'S constitutional position is above and apart from party politics, and those who cherish the institution of the Monarchy will always strive to keep it so.

The high stakes press battle over the King's constitutional position was the turning point for the British media. Since the accession to the throne of Queen Victoria in 1837 the British monarchy had dwindled both as a political force and, by extension, an object of press comment. The Hanoverian kings had been major forces in politics and the target of vicious press comment that assailed both their politics and morals. They had taken deeply conservative stances on the great moral and democratic issues of the early nineteenth century: the reform of Parliament and the emancipation of Catholics. This pitted them against the politicians working for reform. Royal conservativism was strongly supported in Parliament, but on both issues, they were defeated. These were the last full-blown attempts by British monarchs to influence policy. Harmsworth was trying to wind back the clock.

9

The Filthy Newspaper and the Mind of the English People

In parallel to the open challenge to the authority of the prime minister against the King that the *Daily Mail* had launched, Esmond Harmsworth was working on another component of his plan, which he imagined could be presented to the government as a compromise. He thought that he could see a way out of the impasse of government hostility to the marriage and keep his friend on the throne, even if he did marry Mrs. Simpson. Whilst the King was in Wales, he invited Mrs. Simpson to lunch at Claridge's and unveiled his scheme. The nub of the plan was for the King to marry Mrs. Simpson morganatically without her becoming queen, albeit becoming a duchess on the strength of one of the King's less important titles. She would participate fully in the life of the court. The first obstacle to surmount was that the King was violently hostile to a morganatic marriage and Harmsworth knew that he had to begin with Mrs. Simpson, who was the only person capable of changing the King's mind. Over the weekend after he returned from Wales, the King was won over to the idea of a morganatic marriage by Mrs. Simpson, to whom it offered most of the advantages of being the King's wife without the requirement to participate in tedious official duties. Her influence was sufficiently strong to persuade the King to overcome his ambition to make her his queen in the full sense and to approve the scheme as a compromise solution to the impasse. As the King was to put it in his memoirs, 'at this stage I was ready to welcome any reasonable suggestion that offered hope of allowing me to marry on the Throne without precipitating a political struggle.'[1] According to Mrs. Simpson he was rather more direct, 'I'll try anything in the spot I'm in now.'[2] With the King won over to the morganatic scheme, the public part of the campaign could be unleashed and the *Daily Mail* editorial was published on Monday, 16 November. This explains the four-day gap between the King saying 'something must be done' and the *Daily Mail* editorial.

The next step was put the plan to the government. The morganic scheme would have to be approved by them. Downing Street gave Harmsworth the opportunity to do so. On the Friday that the King was coming back from Wales, Harmsworth had been summoned to speak to the prime minister. Harmsworth was ostensibly called in in his capacity as chairman of the industry trade association, the Newspaper Proprietors Association, to discuss how to manage the silence over the relationship that the British press had been maintaining voluntarily. It is, though, quite possible that Downing Street had an inkling of Harmsworth's direct involvement as an ally of the King. Over the weekend Harmsworth hid from Downing Street whilst Mrs. Simpson persuaded the King to accept the morganatic proposal. Harmsworth's office claimed, improbably, that no one knew where he was, which instantly triggered Baldwin's suspicions.[3] By the Monday everything was in place. The King had told Harmsworth personally that he was prepared to accept a morganatic marriage and the *Daily Mail* had fired the first shot in the campaign. Harmsworth could now unveil the scheme to the prime minister with the unspoken threat of an intensified press campaign on the King's side against the government if Baldwin demurred at the middle way out of the crisis.

Once again Baldwin was starting off on the front foot. The possibility of a morganatic marriage had been extensively discussed in the American newspapers already and the Hearst papers had even mentioned 'Duchess of Cornwall' as a possible title, which had only been discussed in a tight circle in the UK, so Downing Street knew that the leak had come from Mrs. Simpson's side.[4] The ensuing conversation was part of a constitutional battle for the highest stakes imaginable but Baldwin transformed it into the comic centrepiece of the chatty and breathless account of the crisis that he gave to his niece the following year. Light though it was in tone, Baldwin's loathing and contempt for the press barony is unconcealed. Harmsworth was 'a disgustingly conceited fellow and yet curiously timid at heart', an unsubtle dig at his subservience to his eccentric and megalomaniac father.[5] He was 'frightfully funny, though he did not realise it'. Harmsworth was presented as some idiot youth in a P. G. Wodehouse story desperate to persuade an elderly peer of the merits of some dubious money-making scheme. Before the prime minister could even broach the question of press silence, Harmsworth hurled himself into his arguments for the morganatic idea. Baldwin firmly squashed the idea that the *Daily Mail* somehow spoke for England, 'I told him that he and his filthy paper did not really know the mind of the English people: whereas I did.'[6] He followed this up with what he saw as the decisive argument against the morganatic scheme: that Parliament would never vote it through. Baldwin had seen off Harmsworth's father in alliance with Beaverbrook in 1931 from a far weaker position. Now he was prime minister of a government with a comfortable majority in Parliament and he had nothing to fear from Esmond. The King's chief newspaper ally in the battle over his marriage had been crushed like a cockroach.

At that point Baldwin was unaware that the King himself had espoused the morganatic scheme and wrongly thought that pouring cold water on the idea to Harmsworth and then not following it up would be sufficient to kill it off. He was wrong. After his initial reluctance the King had swung round to seeing the plan as an escape route. After a day seething impatiently for some kind of signal from Downing Street, he summoned Baldwin to see him and put to him the scheme much as Esmond Harmsworth had done two days before. If Baldwin had needed any confirmation that the King and Harmsworth were working together, this was clear proof that the government was facing its historic enemy in Fleet Street aligned with a sovereign with whom they were in disagreement.

Baldwin did not pull his punches with the King as to what he thought about the press. He warned the King very firmly off any idea of forming an alliance with the Harmsworths to support him against the elected government. He began by repeating the denunciation of the *Daily Mail*'s pretensions to speak for the people of Britain to which he had subjected Harmsworth two days before. Even in the restrained phraseology of the formal Cabinet minutes he called it 'the worst judge in England of what people were thinking'.[7] Baldwin hammered home his case with direct warnings as to the political cost to the King's image of getting into bed with the *Daily Mail*. The Labour Party would oppose anything that the *Daily Mail* advocated; then as now the *Daily Mail* was a committed enemy of the Labour Party. Worse, the King would be tarred by the brush of the *Daily Mail*'s recent, unhappy excursion into radical politics as Sir Oswald Mosley's supporter if he allied with it against the government. Baldwin quoted directly to the King the words of the Communist MP Willie Gallacher in Parliament (albeit unreported in Hansard), 'I see we are going to have a Fascist King, are we?'[8]

Baldwin did not stop at assailing the notion of a press campaign in favour of the King and went on to drop dark hints as to what would happen if he persisted. Baldwin acknowledged that the King was personally popular but emphasized that this kind of popularity was very much a wasting asset. If he continued in his scandalous behaviour, sentiment would swing against him and much of the 'fury' would be directed against Mrs. Simpson herself.[9] Faced with this onslaught, the King crumbled and meekly distanced himself from the *Daily Mail*, 'express[ing] regret that certain articles had appeared in the Press suggesting that here was a divergence [of views between him and his ministers]'. Thus the campaign to present Edward VIII as the champion of his people suffering in the face of an inefficient and uncaring government collapsed after only the opening shots had been fired.

The rest of the abdication crisis played out on the single issue of whether the King was to marry Mrs. Simpson. For the two and a half weeks that the King had left to reign, he featured only as a man so deeply in love that he was prepared to sacrifice one of the greatest inheritances on Earth to fulfil his love; Edward the social reformer was not mentioned again until he had left the throne. The only political organization that campaigned for Edward to remain on the throne was the British Union of Fascists. The King's side had made the tactical error of launching their campaign at half-cock in a mirror image of the adverse scenario that Baldwin had foreseen if the government side had opened hostilities. Harmsworth could fairly be accused of having tried to build up the King's popularity and influence ahead of the conflict over Mrs. Simpson. Beating him and the King up for this in private had been a lot more effective for the government than launching a public counterattack. The first and most dangerous attempt to use the media actively by either side during the abdication crisis was brought to a shuddering halt but the possibility of taking the argument to the public remained a distinct possibility throughout.

Squashing Harmsworth's press campaign was one thing, but dealing with the morganatic scheme was another. The King had asked for it to be considered so Baldwin would at least have to go through the motions. Baldwin was no more enthusiastic about the idea than the King had been before Mrs. Simpson got to work on him and spotted immediately that he could play a constitutional card in his first line of defence. A morganatic marriage would require formal consideration by the autonomous dominions of the British Empire: Canada, Australia, New Zealand, South Africa and, albeit tenuously, Ireland. The formal legal links between Britain and the dominions had declined to near invisibility, so the monarch was the most important single force uniting them. They would have to approve so radical a change in the royal family. And then the morganatic proposal would have to be put to the Cabinet. Telegrams were sent off to the dominion governments asking for their opinions. The replies were flatly negative or non-commital.

Baldwin had not neglected to line up his own allies if a public battle were to break out. The Berry family had long been his most reliable press backers and an emblem of solid Tory opinion.[10] William Berry had rescued *The Daily Telegraph* from near oblivion in 1928 and built it into a major force with a circulation of well over half a million, smaller than Beaverbrook's *Daily Express* or Rothermere's *Daily Mail* but still a potent force, albeit one step down in the pecking order from the ultra-establishment *The Times*. The Berrys resembled Beaverbrook and the Harmsworths in their hands-on style of management and the huge commercial success of their newspapers, but they had none of their rivals' political pretensions or desire for more than conventional success. They were establishment and social insiders in contrast to the resolute outsider stance of their more famous competitors. Throughout the crisis J. C. C. Davison, Baldwin's confidant and fixer, took care to keep *The Daily Telegraph* fully informed of all developments. When Baldwin mused at launching a press campaign to put the government's case, it was *The Daily Telegraph* amongst national newspapers that he had in mind. He knew that the dam could not hold forever, although he wanted to wait for the dominions to give their answers 'before taking any action, which might begin with a press campaign provided the Berry Press & the provincial papers were prepared to take part in it. We should then see what the real feeling of the country was'.[11] It was *The Daily Telegraph* that first applied the damning term 'King's Party' to Edward's supporters which reminded readers of Charles I's backers who had helped trigger the English Civil War.

10

Round Trip to New York

T he establishment's chief press backers might not have been marching fully in step, but this was nothing compared to the shambolic strategy that the King was conducting. Just as Esmond Harmsworth was setting his campaign to promote the King as a champion of social justice into motion, the King's other great press friend, Beaverbrook, who had cooperated in keeping news of Mrs. Simpson's divorce case to a minimum, was disappearing from the scene. Beaverbrook had set sail across the Atlantic aboard the German liner *Bremen*, ostensibly at least for a long stay. His asthma was troubling him and he hoped that a winter in the dry air of Arizona would help. He had made a tentative attempt to contact the King before he left but that had led nowhere. Just as he had let the King sweat in the run-up to the divorce hearing, Beaverbrook was in no hurry to flag his interest to the King too vigorously and cheapen the price at which he would sell his support. He had calculated correctly and he soon found that the King was desperate for his help. He had hardly set sail when he found himself bombarded by pleas from the King to return to Britain. He accepted the challenge and came back to the UK as quickly as possible, but he had to stay aboard for the whole voyage. He spent less than a day in New York and recrossed the Atlantic on the *Bremen*, the fastest option available. Scheduled flights between Britain and America only began in 1939. Even though Beaverbrook went to Fort Belvedere direct from Southampton when the *Bremen* landed, there was thus a gap of at least a week between the defeat of the first of the King's press champions and the entry of the second into the lists.[1]

When the King told Beaverbrook what had happened in his absence, he knew that the King had committed a series of disastrous tactical and political errors that would need to be made good. Only then would his newspaper empire serve any purpose. To cap it all, the prospects of a concerted campaign in favour of the King by Beaverbrook working together with the Harmsworths had gone backwards and not forwards. With his habitual desire to compartmentalize to the maximum, the King had concealed from Esmond Harmsworth that he had summoned Beaverbrook to come to his assistance and now asked Beaverbrook to help him to continue to hide this inconvenient fact. Gratuitously the King had created the basis of mistrust between his two best allies in the press. Beaverbrook understood immediately that the King had placed his fate in the hands of the government by asking for the morganatic scheme to be considered. He tried desperately to persuade Edward to mitigate the damage but with no success. As ever Edward was immune to advice although Beaverbrook's agitation at the King's indiscreet talk over an open telephone line was strong enough to instil his fear of wire-taps and a direct telephone line was installed between the Palace and Beaverbrook's office, one of only five such private lines.[2]

Harmsworth had been motivated by a desire to help the King and Mrs. Simpson; embarrassing Baldwin was a collateral benefit for him. Beaverbrook's priorities were the other way around. He saw a golden opportunity to dislodge Baldwin from Downing Street. If the King was obstinate and forced the government to resign, the way would be clear for a new prime minister to be installed with Beaverbrook's assistance. He could nurse fond memories of the First World War when he had helped manoeuvre David Lloyd George into Downing Street to replace Herbert Asquith. Beaverbrook fancied himself as the hidden force pulling political strings from the shadows and wildly exaggerated his true influence. This rather set the pattern for Beaverbrook's modus operandi; he imagined that a combination of backstairs intrigue and his newspapers provided a powerful mechanism for him to control British politics. The distant threat of government resignation was a handy extreme outcome for Baldwin to hold over the King but it was never a likely option. You had to look far back into the late eighteenth century to find the last time that disagreement between sovereign and government had actually forced the government to resign. Even at the height of the constitutional crisis over Lloyd George's 'people's budget' in 1911 there had only been a slight danger that the government would resign.

Beaverbrook's vision of the political chessboard was set by his fantasies rather than any serious analysis. His only prospect of achieving anything lay in the one major piece that he could influence and, even here, his reading of the situation was out of touch with reality. The Conservative politician Sir Samuel Hoare did not share Baldwin's detestation of the press lords and had developed a close, but far from overwhelming partnership with Beaverbrook, which eventually translated into the offer of a secret £2,000 annual subsidy – a colossal sum for the days – and arguably an outright corrupt arrangement. Hoare was in the front rank of government politicians. He had held Cabinet-level office since 1922 and in 1936 he was the First Lord of the Admiralty, in political charge of the mighty Royal Navy. He was, however, neither liked nor trusted, nor did he speak for any significant constituency in Parliament or the public. He was widely known as 'Slippery Sam' after a popular card game of the era. He had also cultivated a relationship with Edward; his country house was not far from the royal estate at Sandringham. When Edward finally grasped that he might need political support for his project to marry Mrs. Simpson, Hoare was one of two Cabinet ministers to whom he turned. The other one was Duff Cooper, the war minister, who was more of a personal friend to the King.

Hoare understood the realities of the situation far better than either the King or Beaverbrook. He had nothing to gain from fishing in the troubled waters of the King's relationship with Mrs. Simpson. An elementary assessment of the political odds meant that loyalty to Baldwin's conservative approach to the affair was the only viable strategy for him. He gave the King the cold shoulder and gave Beaverbrook no support. He did, though, stay in close touch with Beaverbrook through the crisis, but operated more as a double agent on the fringe of what came to be called the King's Party, feeding information back to Downing Street on what the opposition was up to. Duff Cooper was more sympathetic, but apart from vainly advising the King to delay, provided just as little practical assistance.

The only hope for Beaverbrook to make anything out of the crisis was for the King to commit to an all-out battle with the government. As a newspaper proprietor Beaverbrook was only a side player; it would take one of the major players in the conflict to open full-scale hostilities for him to become a significant force. Beaverbrook was chafing at the bit to throw his newspaper empire into a struggle, in which Baldwin might be defeated and humiliated. Like a general assessing the balance of forces ahead of a major clash, Beaverbrook totted up the readership of his newspapers together with those of the Harmsworths, his putative allies, and set the total against the circulation of the papers supporting the government. To Beaverbrook's eyes the figures were favourable: 12½ million for the King's stance and 8½ million against. Long after Edward had abdicated, he fed these numbers to him to use in his memoirs, couched as though they conferred some kind of democratic legitimacy on his crusade against Baldwin. In Beaverbrook's mind, buying one of his newspapers was the same as endorsing his political programme. Beaverbrook does not appear to have given the smallest thought to the possibly disastrous effects of a fight between the King and the government: a bitterly divided nation, perhaps ruled by an anti-constitutional monarch with little idea of how to use his power, or alternatively nursing the wounds of an abdication that had practically and visibly been forced on the King. At least afterwards the by-then Duke of Windsor claimed that he had rejected the thought of splitting the nation.[3]

Finding someone to replace Baldwin took second place in Beaverbrook's mind to simply toppling his detested foe. The best that he could come up with was Sir Archibald Sinclair, the leader of the opposition wing of the Liberal Party after it had split over the policies of the national government in 1932 but the idea never seems to have progressed beyond Beaverbrook's musings; there is no sign that the idea was discussed between them. Perhaps as well because it was laughable; the opposition Liberals had a mere twenty-one MPs and they were divided amongst themselves. As he had to admit to himself, Beaverbrook knew that the only possible candidate that he could run was Winston Churchill, which was tantamount to a confession that his scheme was almost impossible. Churchill was so marginal and divisive a figure at this stage in his career that only the most colossal upheaval would have placed him in power.

11

The Dam Bursts

T he press silence on what was now unarguably a crisis was looking ever more fragile. A left-wing Labour MP, Ellen Wilkinson, had even asked a question in the House of Commons as to why pages had been torn out of two reputable American magazines imported into Britain.[1] Insiders instantly understood that these pages would have contained articles about the King and Mrs. Simpson. Fortunately for the government the question was asked of the industry minister who denied that his department was involved, but did not question the facts behind the question. Wilkinson told journalists that she would put the question to the Home Secretary as the minister likely to have ordered such censorship but she did not follow through. No government record has survived that mentions removing articles from imported magazines and it might simply have been undertaken spontaneously by the distributors.

Mrs. Simpson was broadening her line-up of press allies. Her distant cousin, Newbold Noyes, edited *The Washington Star* and she accepted his suggestion of his crossing the Atlantic for an interview. The couple saw him at Fort Belvedere in an atmosphere of well-lubricated conviviality in the hope of generating a flattering profile of her.[2] Noyes was accompanied to the Fort by another US-based pressman, Otis Wiese, editor of *McCall's* magazine. Wiese was promised a follow-up interview. The King's camp was also preparing moves for a breach in the press silence. On the suggestion of Walter Monckton, a friend of the King who had unofficially taken over the job of liaising with the government, the editor of the left-wing and intellectual weekly the *New Statesman* was put on standby to come out with a piece setting out the King's position in the constitutional wrangle with the government.[3] This would have been far more dignified and low profile than an obviously political campaign in mass-circulation newspapers, but by the time that the plan was in place, events had moved on and it was abandoned.

With the barely noticeable exception of the Grenadier Guards' complaint, the King had escaped anything like serious public criticism in Britain on any score during his reign up till then. His luck was about to run out and the criticism he did face lit a short fuse which detonated a pile of explosive material heaped against the façade of normality masking the truth of his personality and doings. Perversely, it was neither his relationship with Mrs. Simpson nor his capricious behaviour that attracted complaint. He became a collateral victim of a squabble between different factions within the Church of England. A modernizing wing led by the Bishop of Birmingham had seized on the format of the service for the coronation, scheduled for May 1937, as a battleground, and sought to eliminate holy communion from the proceedings so as to accommodate non-conformists. The traditionalist wing of the Church fought back and one of its leaders, Alfred Blunt, the otherwise unknown Bishop of Bradford, responded with an aggressive statement of their case in a speech delivered at his diocesan conference. He hammered home the religious and sacramental meaning of the coronation service. Almost as an afterthought he slipped in a single sentence expressing the wish that the King would give 'more positive signs of his awareness' of this dimension to the coronation. The King's father, George V, had been an assiduous church-goer, a stout Anglican and a good friend to the Archbishop of Canterbury so the contrast with Edward VIII's casual and spasmodic attendance at church was painful and made an obvious target for comment. Blunt's remark was unprecedented and severe by the standards of the day; it is little surprise that it inspired suspicions of being the opening move in an orchestrated assault on the King whose true target was his intention to marry Mrs. Simpson. Blunt denied this ever afterwards and claimed not even to have heard of Mrs. Simpson at this point. No evidence of collusion has emerged.

Another argument against Blunt being part of a conspiracy lies in the reaction of Geoffrey Dawson, editor of *The Times*. On the evening that the speech was made he was alerted to the fact that one of his provincial colleagues had pre-empted the national papers and decided to use Blunt's speech as an excuse to break the press silence about the King's matter. *The Yorkshire Post*, the powerful paper that covered Blunt's region, was going to publish an editorial that disclosed the crisis. Its long-standing editor, Arthur Mann, had spoken to Dawson when he was in London the previous week so cannot have been unaware of Dawson's strategy of waiting for a lead from the prime minister. Other provincial newspapers were following *The Yorkshire Post*'s lead. That night Dawson consulted the other establishment national newspapers, Howell Gwynne, editor of *The Morning Post*, and Berry, the proprietor of *The Daily Telegraph*, as to what to do. It was inevitable that the silence would break; all that had to be decided was whether to join in the first chorus. Dawson opted for reticence and *The Times* published a verbatim report of Blunt's speech with no commentary whatever. Quite apart from the Mrs. Simpson dimension, Blunt's criticism was striking, so Dawson was indulging in some astonishingly flat-footed journalism as part of his insistence on subordinating his newspaper to what he saw as the interests of the government. Discretion and inertia smothered the imperative to provide readers with news. Provided that his colleagues in the establishment national press did likewise, Dawson was comfortable in appearing to be responding to stories in the less important and, by implication, less responsible provincial newspapers. In their later accounts of the crisis neither Edward nor his press ally Beaverbrook held back from criticism against anyone they felt had plotted with the government. Beaverbrook depicted Mann's meeting with Dawson as conspiratorial and portrayed Mann as a pawn of Dawson but admitted that *The Yorkshire Post* leader was written on Mann's initiative. The best that the Duke of Windsor could come up with was to accuse Blunt of being a Communist agent.[4]

The stories inspired by Blunt's speech did not merely terminate the great silence, they wrecked one of the key delusions that had shaped the King's calculations. He had wildly overestimated his positive image in the press and, far more dangerous, had assumed that this would automatically extend to blind endorsement of his wishes, in particular his plan to marry Mrs. Simpson. The press coverage on the morning of 2 December put him brutally straight on the point. The fantasy that he would be able to face down his ministers because of his personal popularity that Frazier Hunt had retailed on his behalf, crumbled into dust. *The Yorkshire Post* endorsed the accuracy of stories in reputable American newspapers (without saying what these were about) and warned of deep disappointment if the King allowed a constitutional dispute with his ministers to develop. But the most fatal was the editorial in *The Birmingham Post*, the largest paper in the Midlands. The King was due to make a royal visit to the Midlands a few days later, which would have given him the opportunity to tap the same wells of goodwill that had he had tapped in South Wales and, perhaps, to renew his call over the head of the government for urgent action. The Midlands were not in as abject a state as South Wales but they had not been spared from the ravages of the depression. *The Birmingham Post*'s editorial did not even mention the planned visit and gave a wholehearted endorsement to what it depicted as Blunt's 'reproof' of 'one particular phase of his Majesty's private life [which] is not without its basis of solid truth', although it did not mention Mrs. Simpson.[5] The editorial stated simply that Blunt's admonition was unprecedented in modern times and faulted it only on the grounds that it had not been delivered by someone more senior in the Church hierarchy, implicitly the Archbishop of Canterbury himself. The piece concluded with the ringing assertion of the fact that the King had long tried to wriggle away from, that 'the private and the public life of the King Emperor are inseparable'.

The Birmingham Post had torn the guts out of the King's plans and when he summoned Baldwin to an audience that evening, it was clear that it had badly damaged his morale. He kept returning to the article, constantly picking up his copy of the paper and moaning to the prime minister, 'They don't want me.'[6] The King was well ahead of the game in thinking that *The Birmingham Post* was somehow voting for his abdication but it had crossed a threshold. The paper almost certainly did not know and certainly did not report that the King had trapped himself with his insistence that the government accept his marriage plans or face his abdication. Unlike *The Yorkshire Post*, it did not even mention the danger of a constitutional crisis. The delusion fostered by the rapturous public reception that he was accustomed to receiving was being shattered. He was no longer above criticism – 'admiration and allegiance are not blind hero-worship' – and a direct statement that the 'Stuart maxim that "The King can do no wrong" was no longer accepted'.[7] Unthinkingly, he had gambled on the overwhelming strength of his public popularity, but when the acid test of a truly controversial issue had presented itself, his error was brutally apparent. Like so many celebrities before and after he was learning the bitter lesson of the fickleness of the press.

The King had swung around from a mood of bland and unreflecting confidence. He now feared that there was even worse to come. Egged on by Beaverbrook, the King imagined that *The Times* and Dawson was his most ferocious opponent amongst the establishment press. He and Mrs. Simpson were wracked by fears that *The Times* would follow up the provincial press with a venomous personal attack on Mrs. Simpson's reputation. He begged Baldwin to protect him. He was deaf to Baldwin's statement that he could no more control *The Times* than any other newspaper and badgered his prime minister into telephoning Dawson. The King's initial demand for a veto on the article had been scaled down to getting Baldwin merely to read the article before it was published, presumably to warn him if it contained anything especially outrageous. Dawson fell in with this and sent a proof copy round to Downing Street, but by this time everyone was fast asleep and the proof went unread. It is improbable that the King or Mrs. Simpson would have found anything to complain about at the time. *The Times*'s editorial of 3 December simply referred to a 'marriage incompatible with the throne' and announced the paper's intention of following the government's lead. This did not prevent Beaverbrook from believing that Dawson had written an editorial personally attacking Mrs. Simpson which he claimed was being circulated around Fleet Street in samizdat form.

12

A Friend on Fleet Street

In the long years of the futile exile that the Duke and Duchess of Windsor were to spend together, one of her favourite points on which she scolded him was the failure of the media campaign he conducted during the crisis. One of the weaknesses for which she berated her husband was that he had been working on a do-it-yourself basis, relying on his own flawed judgement to make his decisions. She complained that the King could have kept his throne if only he had used a 'first class public-relations man from New York'.[1]

As ever the Duchess was rewriting history to conceal an awkward truth. The one man who might have given the King media advice had become his friend through the Simpsons. He was Bernard Rickatson-Hatt, the chief editor of Britain's dominant international news agency, Reuters. He knew the couple through his friendship with Ernest Simpson, with whom he had served as an officer in the Coldstream Guards during the First World War. Simpson and Rickatson-Hatt enjoyed a cosy, posh Englishmen's relationship with erudite discussion of the Classics over late-night drinks. Ernest Simpson and Rickatson-Hatt were close enough friends for the King to take the bizarre step of announcing that he was determined to marry Simpson's wife to them jointly rather than to Simpson alone.[2]

At an early stage in the affair between Mrs. Simpson and Edward, she had persuaded Rickatson-Hatt to use his acquaintance with the head of Hearst's international syndication operation, Universal Service, to suppress reporting of the affair.[3] Mrs. Simpson was delighted when Hearst ran a story that referred to the Simpsons as a couple.[4] Rickatson-Hatt was not the perfect candidate to serve as an adviser on broader questions of media. Wire service journalism focuses above all on hard content with very little interpretation. In those days Reuters' content was almost entirely factual. Moreover, Rickatson-Hatt was far more of a manager than a journalist. He was the right-hand man of the agency's autocratic boss, Sir Roderick Jones. Rickatson-Hatt was able to make Reuters enforce the same silence on the King's affair as the British domestic newspapers, but this was a purely negative move on his part. When the story broke, agency coverage did not play a significant part in shaping opinion compared to the newspapers, but Rickatson-Hatt was all the King had left. The King's two press baron champions had fallen by the wayside: Harmsworth's attempt to bully the government into swallowing the morganatic scheme proved a miserable failure and Beaverbrook was unable to persuade the King to overcome Mrs. Simpson's hostility to the idea of a full-blown press confrontation with the government. Rickatson-Hatt could also feed the King with Fleet Street gossip and in the final days of the crisis his Fleet Street 'friend' was practically his only direct avenue into the media and they were in touch until the end.[5] Rickatson-Hatt told the King of the poor reception that the morganatic proposal was receiving in the dominion capitals and his final contribution was to alert the King to the collapse of his plan to smuggle Mrs. Simpson secretly to refuge in Cannes, which degenerated into a media circus as the world's press pack pursued her conspicuous Buick limousine through the winter roads of France on a nightmare two-day journey.

Nonetheless Mrs. Simpson retained considerable confidence in Rickatson-Hatt's talents and contacts. When she was confronted by what she saw as unfavourable coverage following the abdication, she hoped that Rickatson-Hatt might be able to improve the situation in the run-up to their wedding. She told the Duke to get Rickatson-Hatt to find a 'good press liaison officer'.[6] There is no sign that he delivered, but Rickatson-Hatt was one of Mrs. Simpson's few visitors at the Château de Candé in the Touraine to which she retreated when her first place of exile on the Côte d'Azur became uncomfortable and where the couple's wedding would take place. The sole tangible result of the visit was that the couple's beloved Cairn terrier, Slipper, died of a suspected snakebite which he suffered when Mrs. Simpson accompanied Rickatson-Hatt on a round of the chateau's private golf course.

Rickatson-Hatt was a blind avenue in the couple's search for someone to help them establish positive media coverage. There is also good reason to suspect that he was actively working against their interests. After serving alongside Ernest Simpson in the Coldstream Guards during the First World War, Rickatson-Hatt had remained in the army and had gone to Turkey during the confused phase of Allied attempts to occupy parts of the former Ottoman Empire. Initially despatched there on the depressing duty of graves registration, he had risen to command the British detachment of the Allied Police Commission under the title of Provost Marshal.[7] His story then reads like something from one of Eric Ambler's novels of seedy intrigue in the Balkans. He helped confiscate a large sum of money from an Armenian clerk, who had been denounced by his business rivals, which various British authorities spent much effort in trying to recover from him over the succeeding years, together with supposed overpayments in his salary.[8] He found it convenient to plead that his absence in the Balkans and Caucasus on 'special work' had disrupted his attention to administrative matters, and thereafter added intelligence work to his curriculum vitae.[9] It is an open question as to whether there was any substance to his claim, but his card would have been clearly marked in the bureaucracies of Britain's security agencies.

There is clear sign that Britain's domestic security agency, MI5, had a source close to the Simpsons, the royal household or both from an early stage in the crisis. When Baldwin authorized an outright MI5 operation against the King when the divorce action became public in mid-October, MI5 came on stream with information so rapidly that the source must have been in place beforehand. Moreover, circumstantial evidence links the operation's early intelligence to Rickatson-Hatt. The MI5 reports consistently and mistakenly depicted Churchill as the true author of the morganatic scheme, almost certainly because the King believed this to be the case. Rickatson-Hatt certainly thought that the morganatic scheme was Churchill's work and briefed a friendly German journalist to this effect.[10] Unknown to Rickatson Hatt, this journalist was also friendly with Downing Street and the story got back there in an object lesson in the perils of covert intelligence: a false story was fed to the agency by a source who then unwittingly fed it indirectly to the agency's customer. An incorrect story thus became its own confirmation. The jaundiced view of Mrs. Simpson in the final MI5 report could easily have come via Rickatson-Hatt from his friend Ernest Simpson, who had tried to sabotage their divorce earlier in the week.

Rickatson-Hatt's later career suggests that he had made himself powerful friends and has given rise to the suspicion that he was the beneficiary of 'people in high places looking after a friend'.[11] His patron at Reuters, Sir Roderick Jones, was finally defenestrated in 1940, leaving Rickatson-Hatt's career on the rocks, but another powerful individual bailed him out. Montagu Norman, the Governor of the Bank of England, was a long-standing ally of Sir Horace Wilson, the chief civil service adviser and right-hand man to Baldwin and then to Neville Chamberlain, and in 1941 he offered Rickatson-Hatt the job as the Bank's first ever public-relations officer. The job had to be cleared with Major Desmond Morton, Churchill's intelligence adviser, who in turn had to obtain approval from the Foreign Office, MI5 and Walter Monckton, who had moved on from acting as Edward's adviser during the abdication crisis and its aftermath, to the grander job of running Britain's propaganda operation.[12] Rickatson-Hatt was shoehorned into the job but appeared to view it as something rather greater: he insisted that he was not merely the Bank's press officer and passed himself off as the Governor's adviser on international affairs.[13] After leaving the Bank, Rickatson-Hatt slipped into an equally comfortable berth at another relic of Britain's imperial past, the Bank of London and South America.

Rickatson-Hatt's relationship with the King was sufficiently prominent for it to attract the attention of some watchful and well-funded individuals or organizations. When he died in 1966, the auction catalogue of his effects included 'Simpson divorce case papers', which featured correspondence between the two.[14] The letters were available for inspection in advance of the sale and contained some references to managing newspaper publicity during the crisis. They were withdrawn from sale and have never resurfaced, which suggests that someone with an interest in keeping their contents private and a lot of money made the executors a high enough offer.

13

A Powerful Propaganda Agency

Most of the press was far less restrained than *The Times* when the story broke. Mrs. Simpson was catapulted from an obscure socialite, known only to a few as the King's mistress, to being one of the best-known women in the country. Her photograph appeared on almost every newspaper front-page on 3 December, except for those which followed the antique practice of reserving the front page for classified advertisements. The couple were horrified, especially Mrs. Simpson who was appalled to see her photograph 'grossly magnified … [in] a sensational newspaper'.[1] The photograph concerned covered little more than a quarter page and Hugh Cudlipp of the *Daily Mirror*, in which it appeared, complained fairly that it was a posed portrait photograph commissioned by Mrs. Simpson herself.[2] Even if the photograph was not 'delightful' as Cudlipp described it, it was hardly offensive.

There was practically no direct criticism of Mrs. Simpson in the stories that appeared, but she fully understood that she would carry the blame for any difficulties. Under the mentality of the day, it was the woman rather than the man who was held to be responsible for the ill-effects of any sexual misconduct. In Mrs. Simpson's mind it would be a short step from popular complaints that she had spoiled the life of Britain's Prince Charming to mobs attacking her. She was terrified and told the King that she wanted to flee the country that night. The King inevitably complied and rapidly organized the journey. A small party consisting of Mrs. Simpson, Lord Brownlow, one of the King's trusted courtiers, a chauffeur and a police bodyguard would take the ferry from Newhaven to Dieppe and drive to the house of Mrs. Simpson's friends, the Rogers, on the Côte d'Azur in a conspicuous Buick limousine. The King was unaware that Brownlow was deeply involved in a conspiracy with Beaverbrook to keep the King on the throne by persuading Mrs. Simpson to give up the idea of marriage.

The end of the press silence offered Beaverbrook the shining prospect of a full-blown campaign by his newspapers in favour of the King and against the prime minister, Stanley Baldwin, which would force the government to accept the marriage and, far more important in Beaverbrook's eyes, force the removal of Baldwin. He was doomed to bitter disappointment. The vital task for the King was to shield Mrs. Simpson from the publicity that terrified her. Beaverbrook knew full well that Mrs. Simpson dominated the King entirely and that her instincts would control his decisions. When the dispute with the government had come into the open, the King's priority was to shield Mrs. Simpson and not to fight his corner.

Beaverbrook knew the strength of the press assets available and favourable to the King, but that it would take a clear commitment from the King to make full use of them. 'We had a powerful propaganda agency at our service, if only we were allowed to use it.'[3] But Beaverbrook's hands were tied:

I was personally forbidden by the King to explain that no constitutional situation had arisen. He was the source of my information and I had to obey him.

All through these days the King constantly interfered with the presentation of the case by the newspapers he could influence. For days the papers which I control were completely ineffective on that account. And here let me dispel any misunderstanding. That influence was entirely directed (1) to dampening down controversy; (2) to avoiding conflict with the government and Mr. Baldwin, and (3) to limiting as far as possible the references to Mrs. Simpson. All three seemed to be major propositions with him, in moments when abdication should have been the principal consideration.[4]

Throughout all the days of public controversy he shackled the press that was favourable to himself. He would allow us no liberty in expressing our views or in arguing strongly for his cause. His chief desire was to secure a minimum of publicity for Mrs. Simpson.[5]

Beaverbrook looked enviously at what he incorrectly imagined was the freedom that Esmond Harmsworth enjoyed to shape a campaign, unfettered by the King's feeble concerns.[6] The Harmsworths did not rule their newspapers as absolutely as he did. The *Sunday Dispatch* was a fading star in the journalistic firmament, but its editor, Collin Brooks, was a trusted personal adviser to Lord Rothermere, which gave him the standing to refuse point-blank a direct request from Rothermere to write an article proclaiming, 'I support the King.'[7] The elder Harmsworth had no greater affection for Baldwin than Beaverbrook, but he was not driven by the same all-consuming hatred and desire to wreak revenge and demonstrate how a press lord could decide the nation's political fate.

The Beaverbrook and Harmsworth newspapers did come out in favour of the King but well short of a full-throated campaign against the government. The most vocal title was the *Daily Mirror* which belonged to Rothermere's younger brother Cecil and operated quite independently. In the hypersensitive eyes of Downing Street though, this was an attempt 'to produce a form of mass hysteria in favour of the King's right to a free and unfettered choice ... which sprung ... from rather sinister political motives and personal ambitions of a very small group'.[8] A senior Tory back-bencher judged that both the *Daily Express* and the *Daily Mail* were 'sitting on the fence'.[9] Senior staff of the Beaverbrook organization felt that their boss was behaving indecisively and should have come out wholeheartedly in favour of the King, albeit because they scented an opportunity for large extra sales and not because they supported the King.[10]

The newspapers of the King's Party were given only a brief time window in which to operate. By Saturday, 5 December, the King had practically decided to abdicate. Beaverbrook told Churchill on the Saturday morning, 'Our cock won't fight' but Churchill was carried away by the drama of the moment and continued to beg for the King to be given more time in a disastrous speech to the House of Commons on the Monday afternoon that was so badly received that Churchill thought it had ended his career. By this point the end-run was clear and Churchill got practically no support in any newspaper, including the Beaverbrook or Harmsworth titles. One even shifted its stance. The day after Churchill's speech the *Daily Mirror* performed a smart about-face from its initial slavish praise of the King to praise for the prime minister.

The last journalistic hurrah of the King's Party came on the Tuesday morning in response to a statement that Mrs. Simpson made from Cannes in which she claimed to be willing to renounce the King. This was the solution that Beaverbrook – no friend of Mrs. Simpson – had been promoting for some days and it briefly looked as though it had come to fruition. The *Daily Express* trumpeted Mrs. Simpson's announcement as the end of the crisis even though this would have meant that the dispute between King and prime minister had been laid to rest and with it Beaverbrook's fantasies of removing Baldwin. The other newspapers spotted just how hollow Mrs. Simpson's promise was and gave it perfunctory notice.

Perversely enough, Beaverbrook did succeed in bringing one newspaper proprietor firmly out on the King's side. Sir Walter Layton presented a radical contrast to the buccaneering self-indulgence of the press lords. By training a statistician, he had been committed to public service until he entered the world of the press, where his greatest achievement was a three-way merger of the *Daily News,* the *Westminster Gazette* and the *Daily Chronicle* into the *News Chronicle* which was recognized as the forum for Britain's then still immensely powerful non-conformist religious community. Beaverbrook had lobbied Layton to secure press silence over Mrs. Simpson's divorce and now did so again to win his support over the marriage. He was almost embarrassingly successful and presented this as a major defeat for Baldwin.[11] On one point at least, Beaverbrook had been less than open with Layton. The *News Chronicle* was the only paper that had come out immediately in favour of the morganatic proposal on the Thursday – in the government's eyes 'the one amazing exception'.[12] Beaverbrook was fully aware when he spoke to Layton that the government had firmly buried the morganatic proposal, but left Layton with the impression that it was still a real possibility. The non-conformist community, however, showed no indication to follow the lead of its house journal and there is no sign that Layton's decision translated into noticeable public support for the marriage. Beaverbrook had a poor grasp of how much newspapers could lead opinion and how much they were obliged to follow opinion for commercial reasons. By the Tuesday the *News Chronicle* too was having to row back. Even Beaverbrook could not claim credit for the most surprising of all the press calls in favour of the King, delivered by *The Catholic Times.*

Beaverbrook also entertained hopes of bringing the *Daily Herald,* in practice the organ of the Labour movement, out in favour of the King. Its managing director, Julius Elias, was personally receptive to Beaverbrook's case but his mainly left-wing journalists were rather more high-minded and politically inclined. The King was not the champion of the working classes that Harmsworth had cracked him up to be. The leadership of the Labour Party had already swung behind Baldwin so there were no dividends to be garnered from the call that 'something must be done' when the true nature of the crisis was revealed.

These were the exceptions; otherwise, the country's newspapers solidly supported the government's line. The morganatic solution barely registered and the overwhelming press reaction was to accept Baldwin's judgement. This was a spontaneous reaction to the decision of Downing Street; the newspapers did not need to be led. There was almost no mention of the King's dilemma, still less of his 'right to choose' and no one suggested that Mrs. Simpson was fit to be queen. *The Birmingham Post* followed up the criticism on the first day that had so shaken the King with a pointed reference to the fact that the King would be Mrs. Simpson's third husband. This was trumped by a supremely catty phrase in *The Manchester Guardian* (parent of today's *The Guardian*) referring to the King being 'anxious to become the third husband of a lady of American birth who became a British subject by her second marriage'.

In the aftermath of the crisis Beaverbrook criticized Baldwin ferociously for trying to influence the media to support the government's case. He seemed to think that using the press to manipulate public opinion was something that only press proprietors were entitled to do. Unintentionally, he was letting slip the mask that covered the frustrated ambitions and jealousies that drove him. The principal target of his assault was the relationship between Baldwin and Geoffrey Dawson, the editor of *The Times*, whom he depicted as working hand in glove to impose their own solution, 'The man behind the scenes was Geoffrey Dawson, editor of *The Times*. He was Baldwin's intimate adviser and he did much to make the Abdication a certainty.'[13] Unwittingly, Beaverbrook was setting out how he imaged a prime minister could operate through the agency of a press figure. In his fond fantasy that was how he and Bonar Law would have ruled Britain had Law's death not robbed him of his destiny.

Baldwin was perfectly happy to make use of Dawson but Beaverbrook wildly overestimated his influence. Dawson certainly entertained hopes of deploying his newspaper as a national institution on the side of the establishment, but Baldwin had as good a nose for bad journalism as anyone. *The Times*'s wordy pronouncements on the constitution and Mrs. Simpson's unfitness for the throne might read sonorously in the eye of history, but Baldwin knew that he needed something more in tune with the journalistic demands of Britain's middle class to do his work. It was his long-standing consigliere J. C. C. Davison who put the work in the hands of William Berry, Baldwin's favoured press proprietor.

one of the most interesting features of the crisis was the fact that it was the making of *The Daily Telegraph*. For the first few days of the crisis Robin Barrington-Ward [Dawson's deputy] was in charge of *The Times*, and had been magnificent; but when Dawson came hastening back from Canada* the newspaper lost its character and even its information became forty-eight hours out of date. I thought that it was essential that one respected national newspaper should be properly informed so that it could give the nation a lead; I accordingly saw to it that *The Daily Telegraph* was kept completely informed of all developments. The confidence I placed in the proprietor was not misplaced; nothing secret was disclosed, and of course I made no attempt to influence the newspaper's attitude. But it was very striking how accurate was the information carried by the *Telegraph* and how out-of-date was that carried by *The Times*.[14]

Setting the coverage of the crisis by the two newspapers side by side shows pompous wordiness in the grander title and crisp, clear factual reporting in the upstart's. *The Daily Telegraph* was also briefed on and fully understood one crucial aspect of the crisis. Once the morganatic scheme had been eliminated, the King faced a simple and brutal choice: abdication or renunciation of Mrs. Simpson. On the morning of Friday, 4 December *The Daily Telegraph* ran a story under the strapline 'No Question of Compromise' (which appeared twice on the page just in case anyone had missed it) which set the alternatives out starkly. It was written in such authoritative terms that it could only have come from a direct briefing by the government. It came as a severe shock to the King when Baldwin stated this binary choice to the House of Commons that afternoon, but he had been paying attention to the wrong newspaper. In his obsession

---

* It is unclear what Davison is referring to here. Dawson was in Britain throughout.

inspired by Beaverbrook that *The Times* was the government's mouthpiece, he had not realized that he should have been reading *The Daily Telegraph*. The leader in *The Times* of the same day merely rehearsed the arguments against Mrs. Simpson being acceptable as a queen followed by a long disquisition on why a continental European practice such as a morganatic marriage would not work for Britain.

After the crisis Downing Street did produce a secret briefing paper on the press handling of the crisis designed to exonerate the government of trying to manipulate public opinion through the affair in contrast to the dubious actions of the Beaverbrook and Harmsworth groups.[15] It did admit to one conversation between Baldwin and William Berry, but it did not refer to *The Daily Telegraph* at all.

14

A Fireside Chat

Rather late in the day the King awoke to the possibility of using media other than newspapers to promote his cause. His basic judgement was sound but almost everything about the way he tried to put this into practice was weak. Above all, the plan that he presented faced an almost insurmountable constitutional obstacle, but he still wasted valuable time and leverage with the politicians in trying to promote it. The media outlet on which it depended was under firm government control. Not only did the episode fail to improve the King's position, it convinced the hard-liners in Downing Street that it was a sinister part of a plot against the government. The end result was one of the most memorable moments in the crisis, but this served more as a tombstone for the King's early hopes.

It took a number of days for the King to face up to telling Mrs. Simpson fully of his predicament: that in practice he was confronted with the choice of giving her up or abdicating. She comforted him with the glimmer of an idea that she had picked up from the journalist Newbold Noyes, her cousin by marriage whom she had called to her assistance.[1] She saw a chance of using American political methods to escape the trap: using radio to address the public directly, bypassing the politicians.[2] It was still a relatively young medium, but President Roosevelt had recognized its potential whilst still governor of New York. He had used radio to appeal directly to the public in his battle to overcome strong Republican opposition to his policies, but by calling his broadcasts 'fireside chats' he had adroitly softened their function as a tool in party politics. She was much taken by what seemed to her to be a way of breaking the impasse on the King's terms. What she did not take into account was that Roosevelt was one of the most ferociously crafty politicians of the day who had succeeded in palming off a significant coup as something easy and natural. It would require political skills of a high order to replicate both the organization and the delivery of the chats on the more complex topic of the boundary between the King's private and public lives. The King had made a number of radio talks, including one in which he set out his ambitions for his reign, but the reaction had been respectful rather than enthusiastic. The cornerstone of his popularity were public appearances in the flesh and caught on newsreel.

To begin with the couple kept the idea to themselves but as the vice closed on the King, they tried to turn it into a reality. Coming late in the day it appeared little more than a distraction. Much as had happened with the morganatic scheme, the idea of a radio broadcast was sprung on the government without proper preparation or forethought. There was no well-argued, persuasive project that might have had a chance of success; instead the prime minister was just presented peremptorily with a vaguely set-out idea. The King had firstly tentatively floated the principle behind the idea to Baldwin. Baldwin had already successfully nailed down support for his approach to the crisis in Parliament and with the opposition parties, which was a perfectly reasonable, democratic way of proceeding but it did rather beg the question of what the public might have thought on the question. In the King's eyes, Baldwin was merely expressing an opinion on a question that had not been put to the electorate when he stated that the public would be opposed to a marriage with Mrs. Simpson.[3] A broadcast had the added attraction to the King that it would give him the chance to pre-empt any criticism of Mrs Simpson in a hostile press. At this stage, Baldwin seems to have been caught off-guard by the proposal and did not challenge the King's right to broadcast, but only pointed out that as not everyone in the country had heard of her, a broadcast would draw attention to her with possibly disastrous consequences. 'He would have to mention her name. Everyone would want to know who she was and all about her, and the newspapers would be full of gossip.'[4]

Baldwin's lukewarm reaction when the idea was put to him was no more effective than his initial reaction to the morganatic scheme had been in killing it off and the King became passionately excited about the broadcast. His desire to make the broadcast was so extreme that one of his household thought he was 'quite "insane" on this issue'.[5] He set about trying to make the broadcast a reality. The first step was to tell the prime minister formally what he intended to do, and Baldwin was summoned to an audience at 6 p.m. on Thursday, 3 December at Buckingham Palace. Despite the constitutional issues involved, the King seems to have thought that Baldwin's assent would be a formality. As had happened with the morganatic scheme, the King had made up his mind and did not want or seek any advice as to the wisdom of his plan. He behaved with the same unthinking impetuosity and launched the plan with no significant outside advice. His adviser Walter Monckton and his solicitor George Allen were allowed to help him polish the draft, but there is no sign that he wanted an opinion on whether the idea was a good one or not, still less on how to implement it. He held one high card in practical politics: the situation in which the sovereign and the government were in disagreement over his private life was unprecedented. The usual constitutional rules apply to matters of governing the country, but the King never thought to point out that if any question deserved to be treated as exceptional, his plans for marriage did.

The King's launch of a half-baked proposal had the added drawback of allowing his enemies at Downing Street to prepare their defences. Baldwin had immediately alerted Sir Horace Wilson, his hard-line civil service adviser, of the scheme and Wilson moved immediately to get the key potential player on side. At the time, the BBC had a monopoly on broadcasting in the UK and Sir John Reith, its autocratic founding director-general, was a man of the establishment, fully aware of the value of the support that the top level of the civil service could give to him. Wilson set out to warn him but could not find his home telephone number. This did no more than delay the conversation. Somehow Reith had independently picked up the possibility that the King might want to broadcast and had sought direction from his first patron in Whitehall, the head of the civil service, Sir Warren Fisher, the following morning, Thursday, 3 December. Reith was summoned to see Fisher and Wilson, who told him to say that 'we must consult the P.M. before agreeing' should the King ask to make a broadcast.[6] The BBC would be working for Downing Street.

Reith was thus forearmed when the King tried to bounce the BBC into beginning preparations for a broadcast by sending his assistant private secretary, Sir Godfrey Thomas, to speak to Reith and make him put the arrangements in hand. When Thomas arrived at Reith's office late on the Thursday afternoon, he was in such a bad state of nerves and stress that Reith had a whisky and soda sent up for him. Reith did not have much of a rear-guard action to fight. Thomas told Reith that the King was going to ask the prime minister for permission for the broadcast, so they seem to have deferred any discussion of practicalities until it was given.

Sir Horace Wilson's reading of the situation worked in an extreme interpretation of the proposed broadcast. He 'knew from other sources that the King was being urged to press his request: it was one phase of the attempt to set up a "King's Party"'.[7] Having teetered on the edge of inaccuracy since the inception of the operation, MI5's reports had finally come up with a picture that was almost the opposite of reality. Beaverbrook would far rather that the King had authorized him to launch a conventional press campaign and sniffily dismissed the broadcast as 'an effort of his own'.[8] Beaverbrook and Churchill had been shown the draft of the broadcast but spotted immediately the constitutional objections to the King making it. Wilson was painting the King's allies as the enthusiastic promoters of a constitutionally dubious project, rather than the hapless followers of another hare-brained scheme that had been half-explained to them too late for them to give any meaningful advice on it. The MI5 view fitted comfortably with the near-paranoid image that Wilson had formed of an unscrupulous and resolute conspiracy to topple the government by whatever means it could find. MI5 had either fallen into the classic intelligence trap of allowing their informant to work out which way their thinking went and inventing material, which would be well received because it confirmed this preconception, or it had accepted as true material that was simply wrong. Given the King's blind and overwhelming enthusiasm throughout the Thursday for the idea of a broadcast, it is quite possible that he had convinced himself that his allies would share this enthusiasm and had told this to MI5's informant. Perhaps it was a combination of both. Yet again, the government – or at least its hard-liners – found itself making decisions on the basis of narrowly procured and untested covert intelligence rather than analysing the verifiable facts that were available to them.

The King did not help his cause of trying to win his prime minister round to the idea of a broadcast by organizing the audience in a way that was so inconsiderate as to verge on insulting, and it began in an atmosphere of grim farce. The time was firstly put back to 9 p.m. as the King wanted to say goodbye to Mrs Simpson as she left Fort Belvedere on the first leg of her flight from Britain; he had to get back to Buckingham Palace afterwards. This message was given to Downing Street by Bateman, a former Royal Navy telegraphist, whom the King had taken on to man a private switchboard at Buckingham Palace. This had been part of the drive for security inspired by Beaverbrook's obsessive fear of phone taps.[9] Bateman was already the object of suspicion in Baldwin's entourage and it was seen as offensive for someone so junior to be used as the conduit between monarch and prime minister.[10] The King's household at Fort Belvedere was so small and the circumstances so exceptional that this was a pardonable breach of etiquette, but the reaction shows how little personal sympathy there was for the King at Downing Street by then. Baldwin and his parliamentary private secretary, Tommy Dugdale, were left with most of the evening to kill and first went for a drive in Hyde Park, which was enlivened by a collision with another car, and then to dinner at Buck's Club, where the waiters tried to stop the prime minister from smoking his pipe in the dining room.[11] When Baldwin was allowed to come to Buckingham Palace, he was sent to the back entrance and, in a final humiliation, made to climb in through a window. As seemed to happen so often with the King's attempts to preserve secrecy, all these arrangements failed and a press photographer snapped a photo-flash picture of Baldwin huddled in the back of his small car. It is a tribute to Baldwin's equanimity that he took all this in his stride and conducted the audience with calm and courtesy, although he did treat the following morning's Cabinet meeting to an account of some of the unconventional preliminaries.[12]

The King began the audience by thrusting a copy of the draft of his proposed broadcast into the prime minister's hands, but if he had entertained any hope that he would simply be allowed to make the broadcast, Baldwin dashed them. He told the King firmly that the question was one for the Cabinet to decide, but after reminding the King that he had already informed him that the members of the Cabinet, the leaders of the opposition and the dominion prime ministers were opposed to marriage, he said bluntly that the broadcast would be 'to go over the heads of his ministers and talk direct to the people ... a thoroughly unconstitutional procedure'.[13] The King was abashed enough to acknowledge the constitutional point, but Baldwin was not finished with his objections. The broadcast could even hurt the King's cause: 'the King would be telling millions of people throughout the world, including a vast number of women that he wanted to marry a married woman.' It should have been clear to the King that the whole idea of a broadcast was hopelessly flawed, but as Baldwin described the King's reaction: 'This was another instance of a certain lack of comprehension which he had observed in the King.' There was no serious possibility that the broadcast would happen, but the King was so insistent that Baldwin agreed to discuss the idea in Cabinet the following morning, where it would inevitably be buried with full constitutional honours.

The King certainly failed to understand that there was practically no possibility that he would be allowed to make the broadcast and he ploughed on undeterred, apparently assuming that the Cabinet would approve. After the audience with Baldwin just before midnight, he told Godfrey Thomas to telephone Sir John Reith to tell him to arrange broadcasting facilities at Windsor Castle because 'the King would probably broadcast tomorrow [Friday] night – the PM agreeing'.[14] Thomas had only the King's account of the conversation with Baldwin to go on, so may have been misled as to whether the broadcast had been approved, but after his conversation with the civil servants that morning, Reith was not going to do anything without clear evidence that the prime minister approved. All he did was to inform Fisher and Wilson of Thomas's midnight call the following morning, Friday.

That Friday morning Baldwin formally presented the proposal to the Cabinet. Just as the King's request for the morganatic scheme to be considered had obliged Baldwin to look into it, so his wish to broadcast had to be given proper attention. Proper, but not supportive attention; Baldwin opened with an account of the bizarre treatment that the King had subjected him to the previous evening and began by saying that he had only brought the broadcast to the Cabinet for discussion because '[t]he King had used every argument to urge the broadcast and asked him [Baldwin] to consider it. He had promised to do so'.[15] The discussion was a formality; there was no doubt in anyone's mind that the proposal was unconstitutional. Even Duff Cooper, the nearest thing that the King had to a supporter in the Cabinet, knew this:

There was no doubt ... in the mind of any member of Cabinet that this broadcast could not be allowed. So long as the King is King, every utterance he makes must be on the advice of Ministers who must take full responsibility for every word. If, therefore, we could not advise him to make this speech, we could not allow him to.[16]

The mood and dynamics of any discussion can be fragile things, especially in as fraught a situation as the Cabinet faced that day, and they are as vulnerable to accident as to deliberate intervention. It would have been a simple matter to drive the final nail in the broadcast's coffin by reading out the King's draft, but Sir John Simon, the eminent lawyer and Home Secretary, had forgotten to bring it with him. However, he had remembered to bring his own analysis of the legal position, with which he proceeded to divert his colleagues when one minister was unwise enough to ask him what it was. If there had ever been any risk of the ministers not grasping that the King's request was impossible, it was firmly laid to rest. Eventually Simon's draft was brought in for him and the discussion resumed. Simon used the draft as a launch pad for a two-pronged assault on the King. He tutted at the King's ignorance of constitutional law, so lamentable in someone who had been taught law at Oxford University by no less a luminary than Sir William Anson, the author of that standard work on the topic, *The Law and Custom of the Constitution* – an ignorance, Simon insinuated in a piece of intra-lawyerly bitchiness, which was shared by the King's adviser and Oxford contemporary, Walter Monckton, who was a high-powered barrister in his normal occupation. Simon then moved on from Inns of Court cattiness to a point that demonstrated the tactical legal skill that made him one of the most formidable courtroom advocates of his day: the proposed text showed that the King was backtracking on his willingness to abdicate. The King's claim, 'I could not go on bearing the heavy burdens that constantly rest on me as King unless I could be strengthened in the task by a happy married life; and so I am firmly resolved to marry the woman I love when she is free to marry me' showed that he still aimed to marry Mrs Simpson and remain on the throne.[17] Despite the verdict of the dominion governments and what Baldwin had told him about prospects in Britain, he was also still pursuing a morganatic marriage: 'Neither Mrs. Simpson nor I have ever sought to insist that she should be Queen.' Not only did this sound like an attempt to appeal over the government's head to be allowed to make a morganatic marriage, but the scheme was now inextricably linked to the King's Party, and as such anathema to the hard-liners.[18] The Cabinet decision was unanimous and was communicated to the King, their only piece of formal advice during the crisis. The broadcast idea was unconstitutional and it would not occur.

At no point either as King or Duke of Windsor did Edward appear to understand that a broadcast putting his case directly to the people, could have split the nation. This is impossible to reconcile with his later claim that he rejected Beaverbrook's wish to launch an all-out newspaper campaign in his favour because it would have been divisive. The crucial difference between the two ways the King's case could have been presented to the nation is that Mrs. Simpson wanted the radio broadcast but she rejected a newspaper campaign; the King obeyed her.

In his draft for the broadcast the King had announced his intention 'to go away for a while so that you may reflect calmly and quietly, but without undue delay on what I have said'.[19] Even after the Cabinet had blocked the broadcast the King wanted to carry out this part of his scheme. He was feeling the stress and needed the break himself, even if the British people would not be needing the time for reflection. He set out to implement unilaterally this project and in the process further damaged his already poor standing in the eyes of the powers that be. It deepened suspicions that he was involved in some great conspiracy against the government. He ordered that his private de Havilland Rapide aircraft be made ready to take him to Zurich on the Sunday morning, but the government got wind of the plan and the courtier who was in charge of arranging it was told bluntly that it was not going to happen. The only definite result was to give the Downing Street hard-liners led by Wilson a pretext to tap the King's telephones so as to give warning of any similar initiatives which they automatically assumed were part of the sinister machinations of the King's Party.

The constitutional position changed after the King had abdicated and become the Duke of Windsor the following week. He was a private person, no longer bound by the advice of his former ministers. He then insisted on making a broadcast to explain to the British people why he had decided to cease being their King. It was the next best thing to explaining why he wanted to marry Mrs. Simpson against the advice of his government. Thus came about the celebrated radio speech on the evening of his abdication. Its most famous statement that 'I have found it impossible to carry the heavy burden of responsibility and to discharge my duties as King, as I wish to do, without the help and support of the woman I love' repeated almost exactly the words that he had hoped to use to make the British people override their government's wishes: 'I could not go on bearing the heavy burdens that constantly rest on me as King, unless I could be strengthened in the task by a happy married life; and so I am firmly resolved to marry the woman I love, when she is free to marry me.'[20]

The Duke of Windsor's broadcast is now widely known and is a stock feature of almost any documentary of the crisis, but it was not so at the time. The BBC attempted to expunge it from history immediately and long denied that there was any recording. In fact, some of its engineers had disobeyed orders and made one.[21] Britain's record companies revived the self-censorship that the newspapers had practised up to 2 December and declined to issue a gramophone record of the speech.

* * *

As abdication became the certain outcome of the crisis and immediately afterwards, the establishment side had no intention of letting the now Duke of Windsor have the last word on the crisis. Both overt and covert means were used. The focus of the campaign was Edward's social circle in general and Mrs. Simpson in particular. Edward himself came in for criticism both directly and indirectly. The loudest voices against them belonged to institutions that had played only peripheral parts in the crisis itself but gained in prominence because of what they said at the end and afterwards.

The Times might not have been the dominant force on the government side that its editor Geoffrey Dawson had imagined it was or Lord Beaverbrook persuaded himself had been the case, but it delivered some trenchant verdicts through its leader (opinion) columns. On the day of the abdication *The Times* had played to its readers' image of themselves as an elite schooled in the Classics at public schools. It claimed that it could not resist using as a judgement on Edward a 'well-worn' verdict that the Roman historian Tacitus had passed on one of the shorter-lived emperors which it quoted in the original Latin: '*Omnium consensu capax Imperii nisi imperasset*'. Today it is hard to judge how often educated British people were dropping this line into conversation. Only at the end of the sentence did the leader deign to provide the translation into English, 'that all men would have judged him worthy of the Throne if he had never ascended it.' Three days earlier *The Times* had been equally forthright about Mrs. Simpson, stating that had a morganatic marriage taken place it would have made her 'carry in solitary prominence the brand of unfitness for the Queen's Throne'. The phraseology was severe, but the substance was slight. Spurred on by Beaverbrook, the couple had feared that *The Times* would publish a far more comprehensive leader detailing Mrs. Simpson's unfitness.

Edward had used a radio broadcast to justify his decision to abdicate and it was another radio broadcast that passed the most damning verdict on his reign. The attacker was Cosmo Gordon Lang, the Archbishop of Canterbury, who had played no more than a fringe role during the crisis, but now catapulted himself to near the head of the now Duke of Windsor's list of guilty men. In a radio broadcast two days after the abdication, Lang savaged Edward for abandoning his duty because of his craving for private happiness and damned his circle of friends for good measure in blatantly xenophobic terms.[22] 'Even more strange and sad it is that he should have sought his happiness in a manner inconsistent with the Christian principles of marriage, and within a social circle whose standards and ways of life are alien to all the best instincts and traditions of his people.'[23] There is no sign that the BBC imposed any kind of control over what the Archbishop was going to say as it had on the Duke's farewell broadcast and Director-General Sir John Reith thoroughly approved of what he said.[24]

Lang's words reflected the sentiments of Baldwin as well and it is not hard to see his influence on the broadcast. During the crisis, Baldwin had talked of Mrs. Simpson as his principal opponent and he held a very low opinion of her, 'I have grown to hate that woman. She has done more in nine months to damage the monarchy than Victoria and George the Fifth did to repair it in half a century.'[25] On the Sunday, 6 December, Baldwin had manufactured an opportunity to speak to Lang, giving him a chance to share his views of Mrs. Simpson. Lang had been summoned to Downing Street to advise on the religious aspects of a short-lived scheme to accelerate Mrs. Simpson's divorce proceedings by Act of Parliament. Baldwin had been overruled by his ministers and the scheme had been aborted, but the summons to Lang was not cancelled. Apparently, a charade was maintained that the scheme was still live and Baldwin had the opportunity to talk privately to Lang. No formal record was kept of the conversation but in Baldwin's account, 'he had told the Archbishop that what-ever he were to say said would get him shot at:

remain silent, and be condemned for not having spoken; speak and offend many.'[26] Lang, though, cannot have been left in any doubt as to the prime minister's opinion of Mrs. Simpson. This supposedly disinterested advice has the flavour of Baldwin manoeuvring someone else into doing his dirty work for him, whilst ostensibly washing his hands of the outcome much as had occurred with Alec Hardinge's letter.

Immediately afterwards Baldwin congratulated the Archbishop warmly:

> You said just what was wanted and, if I may say so, just what you ought to have said.
>
> I know how difficult a task you had, but you triumphed over all the difficulties and you were indeed the voice of Christian England.[27]

Lang's broadcast was widely and ferociously criticized for its unchristian appearance of kicking a man when he was down. It inspired a celebrated rhyme:

> *My Lord Archbishop, what a scold you are!*
> *And when your man is down, how bold you are!*
> *Of Christian charity how scant you are!*
> *And, auld Lang swine, how full of cant you are!**

The Duke of Windsor shared the sentiment fully and ever afterwards referred to his former Archbishop as 'auld Lang swine'.[28] Afterwards Baldwin tried to distance himself from what had become an unpopular intervention with some thoroughly two-faced comments about it. He told the Duke of Windsor's adviser Walter Monckton, 'He thought the Archbishop would have done well to have shown more charitableness over it.' To his son and later biographer, Windham, he claimed that he had left Lang a genuine choice.

Baldwin was not the only person working on Lang. The Archbishop had also received a visit from Alec Hardinge, the King's private secretary whose letter had triggered the final crisis, immediately after the abdication.[29] Hardinge had developed a very poor opinion of his

---

* The Archbishop of Canterbury's ecclesiastical signature is Cantuar.

royal master and was critical of the company that the King had kept. The broadcast expressed a hostile verdict on the former king that was widespread amongst such conservative courtiers.

Mrs. Simpson was also the target of a venomous smear campaign in the aftermath of the abdication. The story gleaned by the Metropolitan Police Special Branch in 1935 that she had been triple-timing both her husband and Edward with the car salesman Guy Trundle was quietly circulated, notably to the new American ambassador Joseph Kennedy.[30] The conduit here was an impeccably establishment figure, the prominent merchant banker Sir Edward Peacock of Baring Brothers who also worked closely with the Bank of England. An even murkier tale was broadcast by unnamed 'supporters' of Baldwin and a courtier, Major Jack Coke, which alleged that Mrs. Simpson had had a Chinese lover whilst she was in Shanghai during the 1920s, which would have been deeply shocking at that period.[31] These allegations served to justify the royal family's ostracism of the Duchess of Windsor. Coke is reported as having described the Duchess of Windsor's 'personal record [as] so shocking that no English gentleman could properly advise Queen Mary to receive her or in any way relent'. Part of this campaign was to refer to the 'China dossier' of intelligence on Mrs. Simpson.

Another widespread rumour was that Edward had abdicated because he did not want to be king. It was strong and persistent enough for the Duke of Windsor to see the need to deny it in 1940. At the start of Edward's reign Baldwin had expressed his doubts to Clem Attlee, leader of the opposition Labour Party, as to whether the new king 'would stay the course' and after the abdication he mused to Sir Horace Wilson, his civil service adviser, that Edward's '"hunted" look' then was because he realized that 'he had missed his opportunity to get out and would now find it much more difficult to do so'.[32] Wilson believed that it was common knowledge that the then Prince of Wales had been telling his friends that he had no wish to become king and that it would be better if his brother, the Duke of York, did. Any suggestion that Edward had not wanted the throne validated Baldwin's actions during the abdication crisis, but it did not reflect well on the ex-King. Two and a half years after the abdication Baldwin believed that what people really felt was that he had quit his job, and let them all down in doing so.[33] It is harder to trace how the story became current.

There were also widespread (but entirely false) rumours that the King drank heavily through the crisis. As Baldwin told Lord Hinchingbrooke in February 1937 that one of the two important facts to remember about the crisis was that the King did not drink at all: it is highly improbable that Downing Street fostered the rumour. Baldwin's other key fact was that the King had been entirely honest with him except for denying involvement in Mrs. Simpson's divorce, which Baldwin was willing to excuse.

15

A Thoroughly Efficient Horse-Whipping

Just as she had not been braced for the scale of publicity that struck her when the press silence crumbled, Mrs. Simpson was not braced for other aspects of becoming a public figure. Under the stress of her flight to France and the abdication itself, she failed to develop the sense of proportion that a celebrity requires to navigate the tortuous and treacherous paths of fame. She was incensed that Madame Tussauds should display a waxwork of her, which she considered 'too indecent and awful to be there any way'.[1] To this day the museum displays waxworks of the royal family as a matter of routine so this was hyper-sensitivity pushed to extremes. She had to be told that unless there was something in the figure or the way it was displayed that defamed her in some specific way, say by grouping her with the murderers in the Chamber of Horrors, she had no grounds for action. Her waxwork appeared decorously clad in an evening gown in Tussauds's Main Hall with figures from French history, which admittedly included Marie Antoinette on one side and famous British generals on the other. She would just have to live with this part of her fame.

The Duke of Windsor had barely stepped off the throne when the couple was confronted with the ingratitude and untrustworthiness of press men. Mrs. Simpson's cousin by marriage, Newbold Noyes, reneged on their agreement that he would simply write a profile of her. He spun the tale of his dinner at Fort Belvedere into an account of Edward and Mrs. Simpson's life together. It was anodyne and disclosed nothing material, although it quoted Edward joking that as a member of the family, Noyes might be there to impose a shotgun marriage on the couple.[2] This might have brought uncomfortable memories of the speculation provoked by the incorrect story that her lawyer Theodore Goddard had brought a gynaecologist with him when he flew to Cannes to see her. Noyes's articles threw her into a fury and she issued a press statement denying that Noyes was her cousin and that she had given an interview; conversation at the dinner was 'solely of a general nature' and had not taken 'the confidential turn' Noyes had indicated.[3] She had 'authorized him only to publish a portrait in words of herself with the object of rectifying many fantastic reports concerning her personally'. Quite how dinner party chit-chat was to have provided the substance for a profile was left unexplained. She also objected to the articles having referred to the King, although it was rather late in the day to worry about their names being linked. The statement rounded off with the fact that she had retained a Parisian lawyer to defend her interests in a foretaste of the couple's long-term media strategy.

Her loathing of publicity was fused with horror at the way she was almost universally labelled simply as Mrs. Simpson, which still endures. This led to the bizarre decision to change her name legally back to the surname of her birth, which became effective a fortnight before her wedding. As the Duke insisted, he was marrying Mrs. Wallis Warfield. Thus, Ernest Simpson and her first two marriages were to be air-brushed from history. It was not a promising project; in two weeks Mrs. Warfield was not going to make anyone forget Mrs. Simpson and her months of notoriety.

The Duke of Windsor's newly discovered litigious instincts found a better outlet amongst the inevitable crop of instant commentary on the abdication, which contained similarly unwelcome comments on the couple. A well-established author Geoffrey Dennis had been finishing an instant biography of Edward as the new king when the abdication forced him to tack on a couple of extra chapters covering the end of the reign. They were not kind. His book *Coronation Commentary* claimed, 'For Queen of England an itinerant shop-soiled twice-divorcée was *not good enough*.' [italics in original][4] It set out the King's behaviour in the Aberdeen Infirmary episode and quoted the graffiti in Aberdeen 'Down with the American whore!'. The King was accused of dilatory performance of his duties including 'neo-Kaiserly' annotations of state papers and prolonging the crisis to obtain more money. The US edition was even more savage, 'He left his land with kingly dignity and repaired to the welcome of company of rich American Jewesses ... with full trunks and full pockets'.

The Duke instantly took legal action and forced the withdrawal of the book, albeit not before avid readers had stampeded to the bookshops to secure their copies before it became forbidden fruit. A glance at AbeBooks confirms that very many succeeded as copies are still plentiful and cheap.

Undaunted, the Duke ploughed on with a full-scale libel case against author and publishers. Most of the book's claims were given in the form of reporting rumours, which the defence could have argued was just reportage, but it did leave two fatally open flanks to legal attack. Dennis suggested that Edward had kept up his courage with drink during the crisis – damaging but difficult to prove (and actually false). Far worse, he insinuated clearly that Mrs. Simpson had been Edward's mistress. A specific allegation of sexual misconduct, then as now, is unarguably defamatory and often hard to prove. The British legal authorities had found this out for themselves when they set out to investigate this point in the hiatus after the decree nisi of October. They were investigating whether there might be grounds under the weird and antique rules of the day for blocking the final decree absolute which would otherwise have been due in May 1937. The couple had been extremely discreet in their conduct and left no evidence. The world had taken them to be lovers, but in the remorseless world of British libel courts much more by way of hard evidence would be needed.

The publishers had apologized after the first writ and made no attempt to justify Dennis's allegations. Beyond the weak claim that the book was merely reporting rumour as 'a valuable review of an important period ... recording the reactions of ordinary people', the defendants barely raised a defence and settled on undisclosed terms. The judge would clearly have preferred to have been able to deliver a stinging judgement against author and publisher in open court:

> These particular libels, a jury might think appear almost to invite a thoroughly efficient horse-whipping. It may well be that a criminal prosecution will follow.
> Reluctantly and with hesitation I allow this record to be withdrawn.[5]

The Duke had secured a resounding legal victory which held back criticism of him for the rest of his life. It also opens the intriguing question of what the couple's sexual relationship had been before they were married. As Prince of Wales, Edward had been prepared to swear a Mason's oath to his father that his relationship with Mrs. Simpson was innocent and his legal action against Dennis automatically exposed him to the possibility of having to state on oath that he and Mrs. Simpson had not been lovers.

Mrs. Simpson's friend and sponsor in her advance up the social ladder, Emerald, Lady Cunard told the journalist Robert Bruce Lockhart that she was 'sure that the Duke of Windsor has not lived with Mrs. Simpson, and that he worships her as a virginal saint'.[6] The assertion that the couple had not been lovers before their marriage mattered deeply to the Duchess and continued well after the Duke's death. It was the centrepiece in the campaign waged by Maître Suzanne Blum, the sinister French lawyer who took control of the Duchess's life as she faded into vegetative senility, to dominate the narrative of the abdication, using her control over the Duchess's correspondence as her trump card. She obsessively repeated the claim that the couple had not been lovers and insisted it was true at every occasion.[7] At the British embassy in Paris it was understood anyone who suggested otherwise 'would find themselves at the wrong end of a legal process conducted with no quarter'.[8] She blocked the publication of a book on the abdication by the well-known popular historian Alain Decaux, to whom she had granted access to the papers, but which included a single, slight piece of evidence suggesting that the couple had been lovers.[9] In the event the letters between the couple were published verbatim.

It has been widely speculated that Mrs. Simpson used exotic sexual techniques – possibly acquired in Shanghai brothels – to dominate Edward, another outgrowth of the rumoured 'China dossier'. This is entertainingly prurient but can be set against another, simpler explanation, which would also explain the insistence that the couple never committed adultery. Mrs. Simpson might just have used the word 'no', a time-honoured and generally effective way for one half of a couple to dominate the relationship. She might also have restricted their physical relationship to something that allowed him to deny that it was sexual, as President Clinton did with Monica Lewinsky.

The savage legal treatment of Geoffrey Dennis set a useful precedent. The Duke and his legal henchmen were vigilant and aggressive towards any similar attempt to expose the couple to criticism. Next in their sights was *Ordeal in England* by a very distinguished and reputable journalist, Sir Philip Gibbs, embarrassingly enough also published by Heinemann early in 1937. The book addressed broad social and intellectual conditions in England but did also mention the abdication. The publishers were told that references to Mrs. Simpson's mother's time keeping a boarding house and other comments that might reflect badly on her social status were defamatory.[10] As were, naturally, suggestions that the relationship between the King and Mrs. Simpson was 'guilty'. Heinemann was not going to take the risk again, withdrew the book and republished it in a form that not only eliminated the objectionable material, but included direct statements that some foreign press comment at the time was unfounded.

The Duke's side had rather less luck with *Westminster Watchtower* by the Canadian-born Westminster MP, journalist and socialite, Beverley Baxter, who had known the Simpsons personally. He was also of one the clique of friendly journalists around Neville Chamberlain who had been the most powerful champion of a hard line against the King during the crisis. Baxter's Atticus column in *The Sunday Times* vigorously supported Neville Chamberlain's policy of appeasement and Baxter had been called upon to extricate Chamberlain from a tight spot when he had unwisely told the Duke of Windsor that he would be allowed to return to Britain. Here the target was rather more elusive as the book was not yet published in Britain and only review copies had been circulated, although it had appeared in Baxter's native Canada. The Duke endorsed his solicitor's proposal to 'frighten' the publisher with the fact that he had got hold of a copy.[11] The Duke thought that *Westminster Watchtower* was worse than Dennis's book. Baxter claimed – fairly – that on Mrs. Simpson's side love played little part in her considerations and stated baldly that Edward had not abdicated to marry but because he was unfit for the throne.[12] The King's circle were 'intellectual second-rates ... who put social ambition before moral values' and that Mrs. Simpson and her circle were a 'useful medium for propaganda'.[13] The publisher agreed to make the author withdraw the offending material, but it does not appear that the book was published in Britain.

The Duke was also taken aback by the antics of the Reverend Douglas Jardine, the Church of England priest who had defied his bishop's orders and performed the wedding ceremony for the couple at the Château de Candé. Afterwards he emigrated to the US where he tried to trade on his celebrity, eventually opening a wedding venue in California under the name 'Windsor Cathedral, Wedding Chapel', prefiguring the character of Dennis Barlow in Evelyn Waugh's novel *The Loved One*, who blackmails the respectable English community in Hollywood with the threat of setting himself up in business as a non-sectarian clergyman. Here the Duke's advisers wearily recommended doing nothing.

16

The Brand of Unfitness

The Duke and Mrs. Simpson were making the same discovery as so many celebrities: that it is one thing to use Britain's friendly court system to suppress unwelcome comment, but quite a different thing to get favourable media coverage that matched the image that they wanted to project. As an ex-royal, the Duke was also playing on a distinctly uneven playing field against a current and practising royal.

Unwittingly the Duke had been responsible for this. Mrs. Simpson's divorce action had been timed so that they would be free to marry before his coronation which had been set for May 1937. His brother, now King George VI, had inherited the coronation arrangements unchanged including the date, but the Duke stuck to his determination to marry Mrs. Simpson as soon as possible after her divorce was finalized. Marriage and coronation would thus coincide in a brief period and comparison between the two would be unavoidable. The six-month gap between accession and coronation was unusually short, but there was not the normal requirement to mourn the previous sovereign. It was also in the interests of both monarchy and government to secure George VI on his throne with the pomp and magnificence of the coronation service to pre-empt any discussion of the process of how he came to be there. Unspoken but obvious in the calculations of the establishment was the fear that the wedding might overshadow the coronation, either because it provoked greater public enthusiasm or, more probably, that the Duke of Windsor might try to disrupt or pre-empt the success of the coronation.

The establishment had the advantage that two key issues had been left outstanding when the Duke had abdicated and it was far better placed to influence the outcomes than the couple. The Duke's headstrong determination to bring the crisis to a swift end had given the government and the court a large leverage over him. They had a few months' breathing space in which the Duke could not afford to provoke the men who would decide the couple's future. A financial settlement had to be fixed in agreement with government and Parliament; this would take months to finalize. In the few weeks after this had been signed off, the establishment ran no risks. Even more unsettling for the couple, Mrs. Simpson's divorce was still not complete and was still vulnerable to intervention by the King's Proctor, which created the risk that the couple might be left in limbo, unable to marry. The King's Proctor was a legal official charged with enforcing Britain's arcane divorce laws. Time was on the side of the establishment.

The court faced only one ticklish news management decision. The Duke and Duchess of Windsor were going to be treated as pariahs by his family, but the news had to be drip fed to them slowly to soften its impact and to reduce their scope for protest. Only in the immediate run-up to the wedding was the word spread that it would be viewed extremely poorly by the new court if anyone prominent in society attended it. Similarly, members of the Duke's family on whom he had counted, including his brother the Duke of Kent and his cousin Lord Louis Mountbatten, who long before had promised to stand as Edward's best man as Edward had done for him, would not be amongst the guests. The British legal process threw in a week or so of unanticipated delay before the decree absolute was formally issued. The Duke bowed to the inevitable and set his wedding day for three weeks after his brother's coronation.

The gap between coronation and wedding created an opening for the most brutal piece of news management against the Duke. The court and government were able to delay the formal decision, and thus its announcement, on an issue that was to become the focus of the longest-lasting and most bitter animosity between the ex-king and his family. The question of the Duchess of Windsor's full title is emblematic of the estrangement between the ex-king and his family and their refusal of any serious contact with his wife. During the frantic days before the abdication, the Duke of York, now George VI, had promised his brother that he could keep the Royal Highness title without, apparently, thinking through the full implications. At this point the Duchess of York was prostrated by influenza and her husband almost certainly did not discuss the question with her. Fatally, Edward had assumed that this promise would apply to his wife-to-be.[1] As the wedding approached there was a rethink and in March 1937, George VI had told the government that he wanted to avoid the Duchess of Windsor becoming a Royal Highness.[2]

There are good grounds for suspecting that Queen Elizabeth was the main force behind this. George VI lobbied hard for the title to be withheld and the ingenious lawyer and Home Secretary Sir John Simon obliged with a convoluted retrospective legal structure to give the decision a faint legitimacy. Simon had to reconcile two apparently common-sense arguments that came to utterly different conclusions: a wife acquired her husband's status automatically so simply by marrying a Royal Highness Wallis would become one as well, but royal titles fall entirely within the sovereign's prerogative so he or she can do entirely what they choose. From the start it was clear that the choice would be political as much as legal; the timing of the announcement would be crucial.

Simon's fiction that the Duke had been recreated a Royal Highness on a purely unique and solely personal basis is an utterly unconvincing contrivance manifestly designed to rescue George VI from the unconsidered consequence of his spontaneous generosity to his brother. The validity of the ruling is still argued over today, but this rather misses the essential question: whatever the Duke of Windsor's wife might have been called or titled, she would still have been ostracized as the person whom the family held responsible for the abdication. Moreover, no British sovereign had ever voluntarily abdicated before, so it is idle to claim that any particular legal precedent can be correctly applied.

There was no doubt that the decision would be the source of controversy and the question of whether it would be expedient to deprive the soon-to-be Duchess of Royal Highness status was debated in the corridors of power just as vigorously as the legalities. The latter extended to quasi-philosophical ruminations as to whether Royal Highness was a 'title' or merely an 'attribute'. The mood of a meeting of courtiers and lawyers called by Simon to study the options was that withholding Royal Highness status 'would be considered by large sections of the public as vindictive and would do more harm than good'.[3] Eventually Simon decided it would be expedient, but he was alert to the timing of the announcement and stipulated 'it would be possible after the coronation'.[4] Walter Monckton who liaised between the Duke and the government, saw immediately the dangers in barring the Duchess-to-be from the status of Royal Highness and unsuccessfully warned against it. He wrote to Simon accurately predicting that it would bring a 'real risk of a complete family rift and it might not be easy to damp it down or keep it hidden'.[5] He knew George VI would be blamed by a vocal majority who felt that Mrs. Simpson had been hard done by. Monckton underlined that the public would automatically know about the title decision. He reminded Simon that the morganatic scheme had been opposed in part because it would have given different statuses to husband and wife, but the title ruling did exactly the same thing. Baldwin did not like it when the Letters Patent that embodied the ruling were presented to his final Cabinet meeting as prime minister and he foisted the responsibility for contacting the dominions governments about it onto his successor, Neville Chamberlain.[6] Baldwin was widely and unfairly blamed in the US press for the decision. *The Times* had predicted that a morganatic marriage would have marked Edward's wife with the 'brand of unfitness'; refusing her the designation Royal Highness had the same effect. None of this cut any ice with government or the court. The government made no attempt to pass over it in silence and both the BBC and the newspapers were informed immediately.[7] When he was told about the move days before his marriage, the Duke of Windsor remarked bitterly that it was a fine wedding present.

The best that the couple could come up with by way of a publicity counter-offensive was for Mrs. Simpson to urge her husband to get their friend the Reuter's editor Bernard Rickatson-Hatt's advice on finding someone to ensure favourable coverage. If Rickatson-Hatt was indeed MI5's man in Edward's circle, he was the last person who should have been given this job, quite apart from his weak credentials. In the event, there is no sign of any work being done to promote the couple's take on the event. The world's media flocked to the Château de Candé for the ceremony but this was simply professional journalistic treatment of a newsworthy event. The photocall in the château's gardens and the posed photographs of the newlyweds and their sad handful of guests in the courtyard provided a painful contrast with the age-old pageantry and splendour of his brother's huge coronation ceremony in Westminster Abbey.

The media impact of the Windsor wedding was further diminished by a piece of spontaneous self-censorship which replicated and fed off the same instincts that had driven the British press's silence on the relationship between the King and Mrs. Simpson and the burgeoning political crisis that this triggered.[8] The newsreel coverage of the abdication itself had been slight, in large measure because it featured no set-piece events that could have been filmed by the technology of the day, but this did not stop the respected trade journal *World Film News* labelling the newsreel companies as 'infinitely more cowardly' than the newspapers, themselves accused of 'ostriching'.[9] Paramount newsreel had put together a major piece featuring archive shots of Mrs. Simpson, due to be broadcast on 7 December 1936, but it was pulled for reasons that have never been explained. The blackout was to get even deeper. A couple of days after the coronation the heads of the five main newsreel companies in Britain met at the offices of Movietone News in Soho. They swiftly decided that the Windsors' wedding was not going to be covered in British newsreels. There is no sign that they were guided by government or court and it was probably a commercial decision: the run of public sentiment against Mrs. Simpson was strong enough for them to fear anything that smacked of favourable publicity for her would provoke anger in a significant number of their customers, the cinema-going public, and no compensatory positive reaction from her small number of supporters. This would have been in line with the industry's practice of keeping its output as uncontroversial as possible, notably on the Spanish Civil War which broke out in 1936.

The newsreel blackout endured after the wedding. The footage captured of two significant news stories involving the couple later that year was never shown in a newsreel despite their obvious newsworthiness. A few months after the wedding the Duke launched a campaign to re-establish his image as a significant world figure and to showcase how he wanted his Duchess to appear as someone worthy of the same respect. Disastrously, he chose to visit Nazi Germany where he and the Duchess received a high-profile public welcome. The footage of the visit is a stock feature of almost any documentary on his life but it was not shown to contemporary viewers in the cinemas of Britain. As with the decision not to show the wedding, this was probably a commercial choice and not a political choice, still less an inspired refusal to support the Duke's attempt to relaunch himself on the world stage. Even when the Duke and Duchess made a far less potentially controversial visit to the World Exhibition in Paris (with a side visit to the dressmakers in the Eighth Arrondissement) in the autumn of 1937, the British public were deprived of film images, which show him being treated as a dignitary by the authorities. They also serve to show that the Duke's knowledge of French was probably weak. The couple's Buick limousine still carried the embarrassing and conspicuous British licence plate CUL 457 it bore when Mrs. Simpson used it for her nightmare flight to the South of France in the days before the abdication.[10]

The self-censorship by the British newsreel companies lasted until the outbreak of the Second World War when national propaganda considerations brought a change. The Duke's arrival in Britain in September 1939 provided the material.[11] The return of the couple after an absence of nearly three years was certainly newsworthy in its own right. However, the upbeat tone of the item's prediction that the Duke of Windsor would soon take up an appointment in the service of the country for the war betrayed the propagandistic agenda. It was left to viewers to draw their own conclusions from the fact that the couple were staying with Major 'Fruity' Metcalfe, whom some but no means all would have known as his former courtier and friend, rather than at a royal residence with the Duke's family.

The lack of newsreel footage in Britain from the wedding at the Château of Candé was all the more pointed because the coronation of George VI was given full coverage in cinemas. The forty technicians involved had to wear formal dress and their output was censored by the Archbishop of Canterbury and the Duke of Norfolk, Earl Marshal and traditional organizer of the ceremony. They were terrified that the film might expose the new king's stammer but all they had to expunge was a shot of the new King's mother, Queen Mary, brushing away a tear. Television cameras had not been allowed in the Abbey but the procession was the subject of the BBC's very first outside television broadcast, seen by several thousands of viewers, with many gathered round the tiny number of television sets then operating.[12] The broadcast required the installation of a dedicated eight-mile copper cable between Hyde Park Corner and Alexandra Palace, site of the BBC's transmitter, and a four-ton truck for the mobile studio from which the journalist Freddie Grisewood delivered his commentary. It was the first great moment in Britain's television age.

The Duke did make one highly visible public appearance in the media, which rebounded against him. In May 1939, the Duke made a broadcast to the United States for the American National Broadcasting Company (NBC) from the First World War battlefield of Verdun pleading for peace. This had been initiated by his friend Fred Bate, the network's European chief. The Duke was speaking as a still major public figure who hoped to use his standing to prevent war, but his motives were instantly suspect. He seemed to be trying to pre-empt his brother George VI who was on a liner to the US for the first visit to the country by a reigning sovereign. With conflict in Europe looming, it was a good (and successful) way of building ties to a potential ally, so the Duke's broadcast could have been seen as giving support to the powerful isolationist movement that was firmly opposed to any US involvement. There is no reason to question the genuineness of his motives but his appeal to 'all nations' now sounds excessively even-handed considering that Hitler had torn up the Munich agreement and seized the remainder of Czechoslovakia less than two months before. NBC offered the broadcast to the British but it was declined. *The Times's* report pointedly mentioned that it was not relayed either by the BBC or its Canadian counterpart, without giving any explanation. Even the Beaverbrook newspapers criticized the broadcast. Had the broadcast been intended to upstage the King, it was a miserable failure. The royal couple were rapturously received and the King no longer needed to feel he was permanently in the shadow of his older brother.

When George VI's visit to the US had first been announced in late 1938, William Randolph Hearst had seized on the opportunity to revive the fantasy that the by-then Duchess of Windsor was the key to a rapprochement between Britain and the US. A visit to the Windsors in France by his brother, the Duke of Kent, had inspired reports of a broader (and imaginary) reconciliation between the Duke of Windsor and his family. Hearst latched onto these and set his journalists on the hunt for copy to support his analysis. Having spurned an American queen in 1936, Britain supposedly now needed the US and in order to win their goodwill, would allow her to return to Britain and give her royal status. Hearst wanted William Hillman, one of his most senior men in Europe, on the job to provide a story along the lines of, 'And the King will come over and say[,"] see what we did for American [the Duchess], and please forgive us our debts."[']¹³ Fortunately for the British, their royal diplomacy toward the USA did not need to make any such pitch.

On a more mundane level, Hillman had also had to travel to Rome to speak to Joe Kennedy, the US ambassador to London who was there to attend his son's first communion at the Vatican.¹⁴ His mission was to report a complaint from the Duchess of Windsor that Kennedy's wife was snubbing her and 'playing the English game'. Rose Kennedy had declined to dine with the Duchess as she would have been expected to curtsey to her, for which she had been excoriated in an article that Hillman brought with him. Kennedy took great delight in telling Hearst's man that he knew 'of no job that I [Kennedy] could occupy that might force my wife to dine with a tart' and retelling the story to Queen Elizabeth a few weeks later when he was a guest at Windsor Castle. Kennedy was no friend to President Roosevelt but that did not mean he was automatically going to do favours to the protegée of Roosevelt's avowed enemy, Hearst. The British establishment smear campaign against the Duchess was paying dividends.

17

The Behaviour of Those in Power

The Duke of Windsor was not just enraged at what he saw as false and hurtful stories about him and his new wife, he began to develop a deep and lasting bitterness at how he had been treated in the crisis. The most bitter blow was to be rejected by his family, but his anger focused on the government. He rapidly developed a narrative of the crisis that ignored his own mis-steps: his attempts to bluff out his relationship with Mrs. Simpson; threatening the government with a press campaign promoting himself as the friend of the poor; finally, his precipitate determination to marry Mrs. Simpson even at the cost of leaving the throne, despite being advised by almost anyone he had asked that patience could bring him a happier solution. It was all everybody else's fault but his own. He cast himself as the victim of a concerted effort by the establishment to thwart him and remove him from the throne.

The consensus across politics, Church, most of the media and the court that Baldwin's handling of the crisis had been correct was not universal. Public demonstrations in favour of Edward's stance were minuscule, limited to the Fascists and eccentrics, but many dissented from the government more quietly. It is practically impossible to estimate the scale of this support; no opinion polls were conducted and the Mass Observation survey group only started in 1937. There is only anecdotal evidence to go on and it is far from unanimous, although in the view of novelist Robert Graves and writer Alan Hodge writing a couple of years afterwards, 'Most ordinary people were for the King; most important people were against him.'[1] After the abdication practically every newspaper fell in line. The one high-profile media figure to dissent was David Low, star cartoonist for the Beaverbrook newspapers, whose cartoon 'Secretly in the Dead of Night' showed 'public opinion' being gagged whilst top-hatted figures carried away the throne and the crown, with the mottoes 'silence' and 'mystery'. Many people thought the ex-king had been ill-treated and one of them volunteered to help and might have been a powerful ally, albeit not one obviously to the taste of the establishment.

Compton Mackenzie was one of the foremost literary figures of the day with a string of successful novels to his name, some of which steered close to the winds of contemporary sexual morality. His semi-autobiographical novel *Sinister Street*, published in 1913, was praised by the critics and sold in huge numbers, even though some of the circulating libraries banned it. He was also one of nature's instinctive controversialists and positively relished disputes. A Scot, he was an early proponent of Scottish independence partly from childhood tales of Jacobite romanticism, partly from distaste at their Hanoverian successors. His broad-minded approach to relationships had not stopped him being received into the Catholic Church. The First World War had interrupted his writing career; the horrors of combat at Gallipoli had been succeeded by work for the Secret Service in Athens where manoeuvring against Britain's French allies was a far greater preoccupation than the war against Germans, Austrians or the Turks. This ultimately led to his first major brush with authority when he published a memoir of his time as an intelligence officer in 1931 which led to him being convicted under the Official Secrets Act and fined modestly. He believed that this episode had personally offended George V.[2]

At the time of the abdication, Mackenzie was in close contact with one of his former subordinates at Athens, Wilfred MacCartney, who had become a Communist and Soviet agent for which he had just served eight years in prison. MI5 took a close interest in the relationship. MacCartney's influence led Mackenzie to pepper his language with left-wing tropes and it was MacCartney who urged him to offer to put his pen at the service of the Duke of Windsor in a campaign to right the supposed wrongs of the abdication with an account of the crisis that redressed the balance.[3] He was pushing at an open door. Mackenzie had met and had a friendly conversation with Edward before his accession. He was appalled when the BBC changed its normal running order of items on the day of the abdication in a way that suggested it shared Neville Chamberlain's concern as Chancellor of the Exchequer that the crisis was bad for business:

a black rage which had come over me at hearing *immediately* after the news of the abdication the prices on the Stock Exchange read by the six o'clock announcer out of their usual order. Was that the true anodyne for a nation's sorrow, a rise in the shares of some wretched motor-car company? Had Elgar's *Land of Hope and Glory* been played as an overture to this eructation of bad taste? Financial anxiety is intelligible, but decency, even if was but a piece of humbugging decency, should have kept Stock Exchange prices at such a tragic moment in their proper place in the lees of the news.[4]

Mackenzie had telegraphed his congratulations to the Duke on his wedding, trading faintly on the fact that they had both been at Magdalen College, Oxford, albeit years apart, and he had complained publicly at the record companies' failure to issue recordings of the abdication speech.

The Duke responded warmly and swiftly to Mackenzie's offer and proposals in early July 1937. He saw an opportunity to expose and punish 'the recent behaviour of those in power towards me'.[5] The book's task would be 'to counteract the false impressions which had been created by malicious gossip about the Duke and the Duchess, and to relate in a dispassionate and historical manner the whole truth'.[6] It would rewrite the story of the abdication from the point of view of its victims and chief actors.

Mackenzie accepted the Duke's suggestion that they meet in Paris and discuss the project. Mackenzie would become almost the Duke's ghostwriter. Here Mackenzie made what proved to be a tactical error and suggested that the project be broadened out from an account of the crisis in isolation into a full biography, supposedly in line with his publisher's wishes. He sent a synopsis of what he proposed, which in practice would serve as a questionnaire to establish the Duke's version of the story.

At this point the Duke mentioned the project to his friend and adviser Walter Monckton who immediately saw the dangers. He had no objection to Mackenzie writing what he wanted but was horrified at the idea that the Duke might give any kind of authority or supply any information for a book that would revive the controversies of the abdication. Monckton had been Edward's trusted adviser in the final weeks of the abdication crisis when he had in practice replaced the King's private secretary, Alec Hardinge, as the link to the government. After the abdication, Monckton had continued in this role, but he was anything but the Duke's slavish assistant or propagandist. He had transferred his allegiance to the new king George VI who was grateful enough for his work during the

crisis to confer on him the first knighthood of the new reign. Monckton
kept his position as Attorney General to the Duchy of Cornwall, which
administered the kings' private assets. He thus had a foot in both camps
and foresaw the dangers of the Duke launching a media war:

> My own feeling is that at all costs, in the Duke's interests, the
> controversy must not be resuscitated – particularly in this way.
> Undoubtedly the book will be a "best seller". Undoubtedly people
> will rush to take sides. Undoubtedly the prospect of the Duke's
> return would be further postponed if not put out of the question for
> ever. Indeed this question ought not to be aired in public now from
> the point of view either of the Duke or the public interest, though,
> no doubt, there will never be a better moment from the point of view
> of [sic] the pockets of publisher and author.[7]

Monckton had one foot firmly inside the establishment camp and shared
the government view that the firmer a line that could be drawn under
the whole embarrassing episode, the better. He certainly did not believe
that the Duke had been hard done by. At first the Duke did not disclose
to Monckton the full extent of his discussion with Mackenzie but in the
autumn of 1937, around the time the Duke catastrophically tried to rebuild
his (and his wife's) public profile by visiting Hitler in Nazi Germany, the
full magnitude of the potential calamity had become evident. Monckton
set out to bring the Duke back to the straight and narrow path but he
knew the challenge he faced:

> The Duke is very reluctant to take advice … Mackenzie's method
> really makes the Duke his own spokesman and widens the field of
> controversy in a most disputatious form so that it must bring out new
> enemies of the Duke and Duchess. It is hopeless to present any case
> by the mouth of someone who feels that he is struggling against the
> world. … I think the Duke ought to ask Mackenzie, whatever the
> sacrifice, not only not to claim authority but also not to write the
> book at all.[8]

The easy part of Monckton's task was to persuade the Duke to withdraw
– reluctantly – the authorization he had given Mackenzie for the crisis

book. Here he could attack the flank that Mackenzie had opened when he switched to the idea of a full biography from an account of the crisis. This had happened after the Duke had written the letters which approved the stand-alone crisis book, so it could be fairly said that he had done no such thing for the biography. The Duke duly wrote to Mackenzie purportedly expressing surprise at the upward creep in the author's mission to 'a publication of so intimate a character' and saying he would not be able to help him with information.[9] His description of the biography project was composed almost word for word by Monckton. He left any further discussion to Monckton and his solicitor George Allen. Mackenzie's early hopes of a joint project had manifestly foundered.

The more ticklish work was to persuade the author himself to abandon the project entirely. Word had started to leak around Fleet Street that the Duke was authorizing a biography and Mackenzie was in the frame as the writer. Anything Mackenzie wrote would seem to carry the Duke's blessing whatever the truth of the matter. Here things did not go Monckton's way. Mackenzie had told the Duke that he would write nothing without his say-so and the Duke here was letting Monckton down. The Duke was playing a double game: withdrawing public approval of Mackenzie but tacitly endorsing his work. When Mackenzie asked Monckton point blank whether the Duke did not want him to write the book at all, Monckton had to confess that he doubted whether the Duke would instruct him not to. Mackenzie was free to write his own book without the active help of the Duke, but he could take advantage of a nebulous association with the Duke's wishes. Monckton was equally unsuccessful when he tried to prevent the book from appearing as a newspaper serial which would have emphasized its sensationalist character.

The advance publicity for Mackenzie's writing was every bit as bad as Monckton could have feared. The direct connection between Mackenzie and the Duke was splattered across the newspapers when the *Sunday Dispatch*, with which Mackenzie's agent and publisher were negotiating serial rights for the biography, ran a highly misleading piece designed to stimulate interest ahead of publication. It implied that the Duke's approval would be forthcoming and made the extraordinary suggestion that the Duke would actually receive royalties, a fiction that can be traced back to Mackenzie's publisher. The publicists even invented an implication that highly confidential material was going to appear by claiming that it had been necessary to consult an eminent lawyer on whether the Official Secrets Act might have been breached. This adroitly played on Mackenzie's public track record as a divulger of state secrets. The Duke's solicitors could only respond with a public denial that he would not approve the biography or supply information; what they could not do, was to deny that there had been close contact between writer and Duke or that he and Mackenzie had agreed to write a joint book on the crisis. Mackenzie's publishers in turn put out their own statement pointing this out, thus milking the record to build up the maximum image of a book that had been practically authorized by the Duke.

The orgy of public dispute got even worse. After its unnatural silence over the King's scandalous affairs, Fleet Street gave full rein to lurid sensationalism, admittedly over the Duke's literary projects and not directly his private life. A delicious squabble broke out in which a number of publications assailed Mackenzie for overstating his credentials. The limited scope of the Duke's solicitors' statements created a trap for unwary commentators, who mistakenly gave it an extreme reading. Mackenzie spotted one headline, 'The Duke of Windsor Repudiates Compton Mackenzie'. The British libel courts are perilous places but Mackenzie's side was running little risk in using them as a publicity machine. Mackenzie's solicitors fired off writs for libel to no less than five publications in a lawyers' paradise that gave a glow of authenticity to the book. The establishment was faced with the horrible prospect that the letters between the Duke and Mackenzie might find their way into open court, but all the defendants surrendered and settled before Mackenzie's cases came to any hearings.[10]

Hard on the heels of all this publicity courtesy of Mackenzie's enemies in the press and British libel law, came another blast, this time from a notionally friendly camp. At the outset Mackenzie had given the *Sunday Pictorial* first refusal on the serial rights and had negotiated a very healthy fee of £5,000, albeit one that he would have to split with his agent and publisher. There was enough left over for Mackenzie himself to pay for a cottage in Hampstead, which gave him a London base. In the interval there had been a change in the *Sunday Pictorial's* editor's chair, which was now occupied by the 25-year-old Hugh Cudlipp at the very beginning of his long and aggressive career in Fleet Street. Cudlipp could not escape paying the fee but in a weird exercise in undoing his predecessor's legacy, publicly denounced Mackenzie's work. Under the front-page headline 'The Duke: Appalling Book' he condemned the biography for its supposedly salacious treatment – of which ample specimens were quoted – of the history of the British royal house. For good measure, a photo of a dummy cheque to Mackenzie for £5,000 was plastered over the page to demonstrate the scale of the financial sacrifice that the *Sunday Pictorial* was making in the name of decency and illustrating the greed of the man who would have used it as a tool to offend that decency. Given the normally sensationalist content of the *Sunday Pictorial*, Cudlipp's stance was preposterous; stories on the same pages as his diatribe carried headlines such as 'Kissed Wife – Vanished' or 'Wife's Cry Clue to Man's Death'. The hypocrisy was widely remarked on in other newspapers, none of which supported Cudlipp's position. Monckton clearly understood that the dishonest denunciation of the book by this 'disgusting paper' merely served to publicize Mackenzie's 'mischievous' project and drag the whole project deeper into the mud.[11]

The *Sunday Pictorial*'s sister Sunday paper, the *Sunday Dispatch*, was only too happy to pay Mackenzie £1,000 for the serialization rights. According to the *Sunday Dispatch*'s own account, its circulation soared by several hundred thousands from its previously rather depressed level. Never one to miss an opportunity for controversy, Mackenzie went on to publish a pamphlet attacking the *Sunday Pictorial*'s actions and statements. The *Sunday Pictorial* had only paid Mackenzie his roughly half share of the fee so he could point out that the cheque shown in the story was a dummy.

Mackenzie worked frantically to write *The Windsor Tapestry* which set the abdication in the context of the amours of the British royal family and it appeared in less than a year. Of course, it had no access to inside information on the crisis from the Duke or anyone else directly involved; it told nothing more than informed Fleet Street stories, Mackenzie's historical prejudices and the fruits of diligent work by an Oxford graduate acting as his researcher in the libraries. What emerged was a rambling account of the private lives of the Hanoverians, supposedly demonstrating that morganatic marriage was an established practice, together with venomous criticism of contemporary writers of whose comments on Edward or the crisis Mackenzie disapproved. A particular bugbear was Hector Bolitho, who had been on the fringes of Edward's court when he was Prince of Wales but had defected to a hostile stance. Its sole contribution to the historiography of Edward's reign was one dubious anecdote from his time at Oxford University of his habit of switching from charming over-familiarity to regal froideur at the drop of a hat that was observed by US journalists in London in the 1930s.

The grubby, commercial dimension to Mackenzie's work was emphasized by an advertisement that appeared on the same page as one instalment of the serial in the *Sunday Dispatch*, 'If COMPTON MACKENZIE offered you a cigarette, it would be a de Reszke – of course' featuring a large photograph of the author. *The Time's* review condemned the book for attributing the worst motives to politicians and sneered at a trivial error of fact about the English Civil War; W. H. Smith & Son, then the mightiest power in the book trade, blocked its stores from promoting the book actively. But this was no bar to its success and it went through several editions. It is not a good book though. MI5 kept a scrapbook documenting the travails of Mackenzie, the errant secret service man.[12] This was not the end of the interest of the security services. Mackenzie's emotional devotion to the Duke's cause was entirely genuine and he went on to found a weird little secret society called the Octavians to promote the cause of the ex-king which occupied the attentions of the police's Special Branch for some months.

Monckton made one last desperate attempt to block Mackenzie's book. He wrote to Sir Horace Wilson, now all powerful as the eminence grise to Prime Minister Neville Chamberlain and his most fervent supporter in the policy of appeasing the Fascist dictators, which had come to dominate government thinking.[13] Monckton's greatest fear was that Mackenzie would succeed in passing off his work as an authorized account from the Windsor side, 'fathering' the book on the Duke. Unspoken was Monckton's hope and plea that the government had in its arsenal some hidden weapon – presumably from his secret service days – to pressurize Mackenzie and would be prepared to use it. The two men discussed the problem a few days later but it seems that Monckton had to be disappointed as publication went ahead.

Just as Monckton had feared would happen, the Duke's attempt at self-justification had turned to disaster with a series of resounding, lurid and frequently entirely manufactured press squabbles which did nothing to improve his reputation. He had not even managed to publicize his own tendentious narrative of the crisis. He had the worst of both worlds, tarred with a willingness to revive the bitterness of the crisis but without having got his own version of it to the public. He had neither spoken clearly nor had he maintained a dignified silence. He had bowed to Monckton's judgement, but his heart remained in taking the fight to the men whom he saw as his – and his wife's – traducers. Fleet Street could rejoice in a deluge of good copy and Mackenzie could relish the financial proceeds of his efforts but any hope that the Duke might take up some recognized position after a period of calm had gone by the board. The support that Edward had promised to his younger brother when he took over the throne had taken a distant second place to his own interests as he saw them. The affairs of the royal family had become fair game for literary and journalistic vendettas and they have remained so ever since.

18

Careful and Delicate Handling

As Walter Monckton was deep in the throes of untangling the mess that the Duke had created by his precipitate agreement with Compton Mackenzie, he saw the opportunity for a far more satisfactory way to bring about a book that would keep everyone as happy as possible under the circumstances. It was one that allowed him to leave open the question of whether the book would be authorized, inspired (recognizably guided by its subject) or apparently independent. The key advantage lay in Monckton's confidence in the historian involved.

Philip Guedalla's first qualification was that he knew both Monckton and, unlike Mackenzie, the Duke of Windsor well. He and Monckton had been part of the same glittering circle at Oxford just before the First World War. Guedalla had been two years ahead of Monckton and had eased his path at the prestigious Oxford Union debating club of which Monckton too became president. Guedalla gave a widely noted performance as Mark Anthony in an Oxford University Dramatic Society production of Shakespeare's *Julius Caesar*. He graduated with a first-class degree but he was not universally admired. One contemporary sniffed cattily with a touch of the disdain for Jews which was then socially acceptable, 'his mind was a little *too* brilliant, and his hair a little *too* brilliantined'.[1] His promise at Oxford was never quite fulfilled in part because of his war record or lack of one. Whilst contemporaries such as Monckton were fighting and winning gallantry decorations in the trenches, Guedalla avoided military service on health grounds and enjoyed a comfortable billet in the Civil Service. He came up with the arrogant and fatal comment, 'I am the Civilisation they are fighting for.' He stood for Parliament five times but was never elected; in part because of his faithfulness to the waning Liberal Party, in part because of his war.

Against these disappointments he became a successful popular historian with a string of high-selling books about the nineteenth century, notably *The Duke*, a biography of the Duke of Wellington, to his credit. Today their ornate and allusive style reads as affected and precious; they are barely read. Guedalla also established himself as a leading figure in various bodies promoting links between Britain and South America, so he had absorbed some of the deferential instincts of public service. Through this he had met and struck up a warm relationship with the then Prince of Wales in the course of the royal visit to Argentina in 1931 which showcased the Prince's talents in promoting British business. Guedalla was a guest at the only official dinner Edward gave as King on 30 October 1936 in honour of the Argentinian ambassador. But for the abdication, Guedalla would have been well placed to enjoy a glittering career in public service, but like many who had hitched their star to the new King, this prospect vanished overnight. He wrote articles in support of the King during the crisis and in the aftermath was part of a small group headed by one of the ex-king's former courtiers, Sir Godfrey Thomas, which set out to find ways to respond to hostile press coverage.[2]

Guedalla's writing career had continued to thrive and serendipitously his most recent book created an opening for a discreet literary partnership with the Duke. He had enjoyed enormous success with his book *The Hundred Years* which had been published in 1936. It charted the one hundred years of history from the year before Queen Victoria rose to the throne in the author's allusive and mildly ironic style. It had concluded with the funeral of George V and the approving depiction of his successor as a man of extensive experience, widely known by his subjects. The picture of British politics was of torpid stability and its calm was contrasted to Germany's frantic rearmament and dictatorship. Baldwin was not mentioned by name but appeared in a snapshot comically dressed in Privy Councillor's uniform and 'smiling gaily' (and inappropriately) for his sovereign's funeral.

What Guedalla now planned was to follow on with a book about 1936, *The Hundredth Year*, which would look at the momentous events of the year. This had merits from Monckton's standpoint. The progression from one book to the next was natural enough to conceal the extent it accomplished the Duke's agenda. The abdication would naturally feature very largely, but the risk that the book would appear to be a polemic about the crisis would be diluted by the other momentous global episodes that were discussed: Hitler's reoccupation of the Rhineland, the outbreak of the Spanish Civil War and the US presidential election. Guedalla

Edward Prince of Wales, the first celebrity royal, pleases the crowd.

EP Ranch, the Canadian refuge.

Frazier Hunt, neighbour in Canada and publicist.

The Prince of Wales takes to the
microphone in Canada in 1927.

Fort Belvedere, the
Surrey refuge.

An unsuitable image of monarchy.

William Randolph Hearst in appropriately baronial setting.

Adela Rogers St. Johns. Hearst wanted her to build up Mrs. Simpson to be the 'American Queen'.

The King's summer holiday provides copy for the non-British press.

St. Donat's Castle, Hearst's base in Europe.

The fateful visit to Balmoral in September 1936. From left: the King, Mountbatten, Esmond Harmsworth, Mrs. Rogers and Wallis Simpson.

Hearst's New York American foretells the marriage.

Dowlais, 'Something must be done.'

Stanley Baldwin with Walter Monckton in the background.

Geoffrey Dawson, editor of *The Times*.

Mrs Simpson 'grossly magnified'.

Bernard Rickatson-Hatt, the King's friend in Fleet Street and perhaps more.

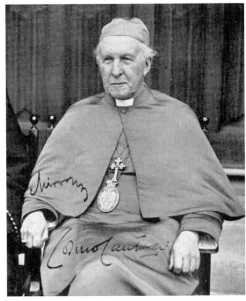

Cosmo Gordon Lang, Archbishop of Canterbury, mouthpiece for establishment criticism of the ex-king.

Appeasing the press with a photocall at the Rogers' villa. From left: Lord Brownlow, Mrs Rogers, Mrs Simpson and Mr Rogers.

King George VI and Queen Elizabeth. The new regime.

Walter Monckton, the indispensable linkman.

Compton Mackenzie, the first would-be champion of the ex-king.

Philip Guedalla, the establishment choice of champion.

The Windsors do their bit.

Charlie Murphy, the ghost-writer caught in crosscurrents.

Lord Beaverbrook trying to remake history.

Sir John Simon, news management with a mailed fist in a velvet glove.

Geoffrey Bocca, Beaverbrook's chosen literary assassin.

Alec Hardinge, the scapegoat fights back.

James Pope-Hennessy, the official historian with shaky allegiance.

squeezed in a discussion of Mussolini's invasion of Abyssinia in 1935 by some chronological sleight of hand. Baldwin too would feature naturally as would other aspects of his policies. Criticism of his role in the abdication would form part of a rounded verdict of Baldwin's performance as prime minister. Crucially, Guedalla had assured Monckton that his book would not claim 'any sort of authorisation' from the Duke.[3] Therefore the book would not be marked down as a biased work steered by the Duke and there would be no repetition of the embarrassing fiasco of first promising Compton Mackenzie authorization and assistance, and then having to withdraw the offer publicly.

Monckton enthusiastically endorsed Guedalla's qualifications to serve as the Duke's literary ally to Sir Horace Wilson, who had remained at Downing Street as the prime minister's eminence grise when Neville Chamberlain succeeded Stanley Baldwin in May 1937:

> it would be wiser for him [the Duke] to trust to Philip Guedalla's proposed book ... I know Guedalla well and am sure the book will have a bias towards the Duke, but it will not claim authority nor will it stray from history of his usual kind.[4]

Other factors worked in Guedalla's favour. He had been born a Sephardi Jew, albeit in a secularized family, but over time he more closely embraced his Jewish identity, becoming president of the British Zionist Federation and a leader of other Jewish groups. This strengthened his credentials to defend the Duke against widespread accusations of favouring the Nazi regime, a charge of which Guedalla himself was very aware. Guedalla's workload and schedule was another attraction. Guedalla was committed to a lecture tour in the United States and would only be able to start work in the summer of 1938 so the best part of three years would have gone by before his version of the abdication would appear. His book would not be rushed into print so the risk of reigniting a recent controversy would be less.

Monckton arranged for Guedalla to meet the Duke in November 1937 and the two resumed their cordial relations. The Duke enthusiastically endorsed Guedalla's idea for *The Hundredth Year* which would be written from the Duke's perspective of how badly he had been treated in the crisis. There does not seem to have been any formal agreement but once he had returned from America, Guedalla began to visit the Duke regularly in France to garner information for the book. Guedalla's visits had the added benefit of providing the Duke with something more than an outlet for his litany of complaints. The catastrophe of the Duke's journey to Nazi Germany and the aborted plan to go to the US had left him ever more isolated. Guedalla's company was all the more valuable as it gave him stimulating and intelligent conversation as well. As Prince of Wales and King, Edward had preferred unchallenging social company, but his duties exposed him constantly to more substantial individuals operating in a complex and engaging world. This had all disappeared after the abdication and the micro-court of an ex-monarch was no substitute. Guedalla was joined by his wife and the couples became good friends.

Guedalla was in close touch with Monckton whilst he was writing which in practice gave Monckton a veto over the text. Monckton took special trouble to tone down what Guedalla wanted to write about the circumstances of the now Duke of Windsor's departure into exile in Austria immediately after the abdication. The first draft noted that the British government had done nothing to help organize the journey and asked pointedly whether this was the first instalment in the 'lifelong friendship' of which Baldwin had spoken in his speech to the House of Commons when he gave his side of the crisis. The Duke of Windsor was offended at what he saw as a hypocritical fiction by the prime minister and returned to it frequently in the aftermath. Baldwin appeared genuinely to believe that he had remained friends with Edward. The Duke had a case on Baldwin's protestations of friendship, but his complaint about the travel arrangements reveals that he had failed to grasp that his circumstances had changed. He was provided with a private train with squads of French riot police to fend off intrusive journalists, but fawning British officials were conspicuous by their absence. To all intents and purposes, he was now merely a private citizen. Monckton wanted to avoid any 'traces of partisanship' and asked Guedalla to revise the passage. All that survived of the Duke's bitterness in the published version was the fact that he had had to arrange somewhere to stay under his own steam with the insinuation that this was something that ministers might have attended to.

As a politician Baldwin was fair game for public criticism. Guedalla adroitly skewered a number of points on which Baldwin was open to attack before he even needed to turn to the crisis. He accused him of having been overpromoted as a reward for stabbing Lloyd George in the back in the Carlton House coup.[5] Baldwin had been indulgent towards a Cabinet minister, Jim Thomas, who had been forced to resign over an insider trading scandal, in a way that he had not been charitable towards the King.[6] But most important, Guedalla could join the growing chorus of voices that blamed Baldwin for having allowed Hitler's Germany to rearm and dominate Europe with little attempt by Britain to intervene. This was a far more damning case than anything that could be said about the abdication and one where Baldwin's record could quite fairly be held up to severe examination. Guedalla came down firmly against him and questioned whether he had a foreign policy at all, exploiting Baldwin's reputation for being far more comfortable with domestic politics than international diplomacy.[7] Above all, the debate over Britain's military weakness in the face of Hitler had progressed directly from minimal analysis to polemic. Guedalla's portrayal of Baldwin's 'unruffled equanimity' towards Germany's massive rearmament and his assertion that British rearmament was 'not unduly hurried' chimed happily with the mood of the times after the Munich crisis, however unfair it was. In the brutal equations made at the top of the pyramid of power, Baldwin was an expendable ex-prime minister who would have to take his medicine of criticism in a foretaste of history.

Rearmament and chance coincidence gave Guedalla an opportunity to compare King Edward with his prime minister to the former's advantage. Both had made speeches on the evening of 12 November 1936. Baldwin's was a catastrophe for his reputation and features in practically every charge sheet for the conduct of his premiership ever since. Confessing 'appalling frankness', he admitted that public hostility towards the idea of rearmament had helped shape his campaign in the 1935 general election when he had promised that there would be 'no great armaments'. More often than not, honesty in politics is its own punishment and Baldwin appeared to have admitted to putting party political considerations before the security of the nation. By contrast, the King's speech to the crew of the aircraft carrier HMS *Courageous* on his visit to the Royal Navy at Portland just before Hardinge's letter transformed the crisis into an outright confrontation, was one of the last hurrahs of Edward's golden days as the monarch of all his people. It was wildly well received by the lower deck and offered a highpoint of his inspection of the Fleet, where he provided a brilliant vignette of monarchical resolution placed besides a politician's prudence. Despite a torrential downpour the King wore only his dress uniform of Admiral of the Fleet and was drenched to the skin, whilst Sir Sam Hoare, accompanying him in his job as First Lord of the Admiralty, was swathed in protective oilskins. The *Courageous* speech served both as a warm-up for the King's tour of South Wales and what proved to be a dangerous reaffirmation to the King of his faith that his personal popularity would translate into public support in the burgeoning dispute with the government.[8]

The Hundredth Year showcased the Duke's most bitter complaint against the government: that the prime minister had blocked him from mobilizing the public support that he believed was his most important asset. He constantly challenged Baldwin's pretension to be able to judge public opinion. The Duke's direct influence on the book is clearly visible in the passages about the King's broadcast plan. Guedalla noted that Baldwin had failed to mention the King's request to broadcast to the public in his speech to Parliament. Guedalla presented a broadcast as something that would have provided a genuine test of public opinion, whilst all that the Westminster politicians learned from visiting their constituencies was a narrow feedback from party hacks. Without any direct evidence Guedalla accused Baldwin of milking up public opinion against the King. Guedalla implied that Baldwin deliberately concealed from the public that they could lose their King by failing to make it clear in his 4 December statement to Parliament that the only alternative for the King if he wanted to marry Mrs. Simpson was to abdicate once the morganatic proposal was off the table.

The public opinion issue was the strongest point in an otherwise thin – and often dishonest if it came from the Duke – criticism of Baldwin's handling of the crisis. The tale he told Guedalla about the fateful audience with Baldwin on 16 November was so misleading as to be fiction. There was no mention of Hardinge's letter that triggered the conversation. Instead, the Duke claimed that he had been driven by a recognition that it was his duty to inform the government of his intention to marry. Baldwin might have set a Christmas deadline for the King to decide, but it was the King who rejected all advice to be patient. Unwittingly, Guedalla echoed the only substantial question mark that Sir Horace Wilson had left over

Baldwin's performance in his account of the crisis: that he might have acted sooner. Guedalla's version assumed incorrectly that Baldwin would have known about the divorce case well before the middle of October and anyway begged the question as to why the King did not actively address the certainty that his marriage plans would cause controversy in advance.

Guedalla's thumb was firmly on the Duke's side of the scales. His account of Baldwin's speech to the House of Commons was peppered with sceptical observations but the Duke's post-abdication radio broadcast was quoted verbatim with a few notes on how it was delivered. *The Hundredth Year* included insider knowledge which was only likely to have come from the Duke or, at its most innocuous, well-informed surmise. Guedalla let the mask slip when he noted that the Duke's praise of Baldwin was pencilled in as 'kindly afterthought' on the text for his farewell broadcast. The reader was invited to set this alongside Baldwin's refusal to include in his speech to Parliament a pencilled note from the ex-king praising Mrs. Simpson for her efforts to dissuade the King from forsaking the throne for her, even though he did include a similar note claiming to be on the best of terms with his successor.

Guedalla trotted out the litany of complaints to which the Duke treated him and which were to echo down the years as the Duke put his case forward in an assortment of forums. Some were substantial but many were trivial. They provide a catalogue of the irritations – some real but others imagined – that had grated on him. When the Archbishop of Canterbury accused him of a 'craving for private happiness', he was accused of failing to understand that Edward was stating a literal truth in claiming that he would have been unable to perform his royal duties had he not married Mrs. Simpson. Edward had had to resist pressure to make a semi-arranged dynastic marriage, whilst his marriage to Mrs. Simpson was a true love match. Guedalla extended his protection to Mrs. Simpson over her connections to the Nazi ambassador which had fed much hostile comment. She had met von Ribbentrop only twice 'at other people's tables'. But the Duke let his own sympathies slip in the claim that his holiday on the *Nahlin* would have been a useful opportunity to make a rapprochement with Mussolini, but for the obstinacy of the Foreign Office. He needed an undemanding social circle in which to unwind from his heavy duties. Others were just as responsible for sacking servants at Sandringham; insiders would have spotted the dig at his brother, then still

Duke of York, who had prepared a report on the costs of Sandringham. The umbrella story received the first of its many outings. One minister had supposedly complained that he had sacrificed royal dignity by walking whilst he should have used a limousine; another minister had revealed the government's hypocrisy by soliciting an introduction to Mrs. Simpson early in the reign. And many more.

The Duke and Duchess were delighted with the product of Guedalla's labours when he brought the final text to them in the South of France in July 1939. They had high hopes that it would swing public opinion back in their favour when it was published on the first Monday of September, but fate and Adolf Hitler intervened. That was the day that the German invasion of Poland started the Second World War. The publishers leapt on the act of God clause in the contract and refused to put the book out and only after much wrangling did *The Hundredth Year* appear on 3 June 1940, just as Hitler invaded France. The British public had other things on their mind and by the time they might have been able to devote some attention to their ex-king the world had moved on. The Duke had been side-lined into a minor colonial governorship, an irrelevance in an existential struggle to survive. *The Hundredth Year* sold well but did nothing to swing opinion in favour of the Duke of Windsor; it features little in bibliographies of books on the crisis.

Guedalla reprised his criticism of Baldwin's performance during the abdication crisis in *Mr. Churchill: A Portrait* which appeared in 1941. It praised Churchill for supporting the King in the crisis but acknowledged that this had sabotaged his far more important campaign in favour of rearmament. Guedalla himself died in 1944 at the comparatively early age of 55 so his pen and voice which might have served again in the Duke's defence were lost. Guedalla's health had been badly weakened by a gruelling period as a squadron leader doing publicity work for the RAF and gathering material for a book on the air war in the Middle East which still stands the test of time as an analysis of air warfare, albeit incongruously rendered in his Edwardian style of writing.

19

Interlude

The outbreak of war rescued the Duke of Windsor from the most extreme depths of the pariah status to which he had been consigned after the abdication. He was allowed to resume public service and to contribute to Britain's war effort. He remained, though, on probation. Originally, he had been offered the choice of a job either in Britain as Deputy Civil Commissioner for Wales or one with the British Army in France, but finally had been told that it would have to be the second option. He was still to be kept out of the country. Commissioned as a major-general, far below his honorary rank of field marshal, he was given a nebulous task of liaising with the French Army. His hunger for favourable publicity was undimmed and he demanded that it should be publicized that he was receiving no pay for his military work.[1] The War Office ignored him; no other member of the royal family was being paid either.

His ally during the abdication crisis, Winston Churchill, was brought back into government. Churchill had bounced back from his humiliation at the end of the abdication crisis but he had not been beaten into conforming with government policy. Once again, he had been nearly a lone voice proclaiming the dangers of Adolf Hitler's Nazi regime in Germany, castigating the folly of Neville Chamberlain's appeasement policy and calling for rearmament. It would have been impossible not to bring him back into government but the politicians who had paid the penalty for supporting his stance were only very partially rehabilitated.

Lord Beaverbrook, who had also opposed the government during the abdication, was left firmly on the outside. Unlike Churchill he had pursued a resolutely anti-war stance during the appeasement years. Whilst he was never invited to join the press phalanx that championed Chamberlain's policy, centred on *The Times* under the editorship of Beaverbrook's long-standing foe Geoffrey Dawson, he had campaigned for an isolationist stance as a way of keeping Britain out of war. When war finally came his support for the war effort was no more than lukewarm and he foresaw major problems for the country.

In early 1940, Beaverbrook tried to take his defeatist programme a large step forward. He met the Duke of Windsor, who was in London on leave from France, and set out a scheme adroitly calculated to satisfy the Duke's hankering after a position that would restore him to some form of high-profile national leadership. He and the Duke of Windsor agreed that a swift negotiated settlement with Germany would be the best outcome for Britain.[2] Beaverbrook urged the Duke to give up his army job in France and come back to Britain at the head of an active movement to achieve this securing the support of financial circles and launching a public campaign, which Beaverbrook predicted would be a huge success. Mercifully, Walter Monckton was present at the meeting and able to warn the Duke that this would expose him to UK taxation, usually a decisive consideration for him. Monckton may also have actively pointed out that the plan was little short of treason against his brother, George VI. Beaverbrook might have been doing more than testing the water for a major exercise in mischief and did not pursue the scheme, but the Duke's defeatist instincts remained strong. He was less than discreet and some of his anti-war and anti-Chamberlain remarks found their way to the German ambassador in the Netherlands who reported them to Berlin.[3]

The Duchess did war work with the French Red Cross which gave her an elegant uniform with which to pose alongside her husband in his general's uniform, but the British media showed no inclination to give her coverage in this guise. The Duke tried to enlist Bernard Rickatson-Hatt to correct this.[4] He doubled down on his indiscretions when the German invasion of France in May 1940 forced him and the Duchess to flee to Spain and then to Portugal. There he spent much time with locals who supported the German cause and shared his defeatist thoughts with them. This was still hidden from the British government, now under Winston Churchill, and the Duke tried to exploit the government's anxiety to bring him back into a purely British sphere of influence and out of reach of the Germans by trying to extort some public recognition of the Duchess's status in exchange for his cooperation.

The Duke was finally prevailed upon to cross the Atlantic to take up the job of Governor of the Bahamas, where he was to serve out the war years.

It was an insignificant backwater where his contribution to the war effort could be allowed to pass almost unnoticed. William Randolph Hearst did not though entirely forget his protegés and his star journalist Adela Rogers St. Johns was dispatched to the Bahamas to write a flattering profile of the Duke and Duchess in the autumn of 1940.

*   *   *

In May 1940, the German invasion of France also brought an end to the phony war and with it Chamberlain's time as prime minister. Churchill was put into 10 Downing Street with a remit to prosecute the war seriously which soon meant leading the nation in a fight for survival. He could not depend on the full support of the established Conservatives who had so recently backed Chamberlain's appeasement to the hilt and knew that the Labour Party, which he brought into a full national government, still had reservations about him. He needed allies who could offer him some protection from the established parties. Foremost amongst them was Beaverbrook, to whom he gave a seat in Cabinet and the newly created job of Minister of Aircraft Production, in which he jolted the bureaucracy out of its complacent peacetime ways but appalled the commanders of the RAF by putting their cherished programme for an all-heavy-bomber force on hold in favour of smaller and obsolescent types.

As well as doing his work in government, Beaverbrook wanted to reshape the way people saw the past and to distract attention from his questionable stance during appeasement and the phony war. Three of his journalists set to work on an instant book which accused the previous government of full responsibility for entering the war in a state of desperate unpreparedness. *Guilty Men*, published under the pseudonym Cato, was an instant and immense success. Beaverbrook had no avowed involvement in the book but he did later joke that he was living off its royalties. It tapped into widespread public shame at the enthusiasm with which appeasement had been welcomed. Predictably Stanley Baldwin featured high in the list of *Guilty Men* and it marked the beginning of an assault on his reputation from which it has never fully recovered. Beaverbrook was widely but incorrectly suspected of engineering the affair of the gates at Baldwin's country home Astley Hall, which were requisitioned by the government as scrap. Baldwin applied for exemption on the grounds of artistic value, for which he suffered a savage parliamentary and press criticism, led by the columnist William ('Cassandra') of the *Daily Mirror*.

* * *

The abdication itself inevitably faded from view during the war and its aftermath. The leading figures in the government camp ranged against the then King were also vanishing from the scene. Chamberlain had died from stomach cancer soon after resigning as prime minister in 1940. Two of Beaverbrook's chief villains in the affair soon followed: Dawson of *The Times* was next in 1944 and the former Archbishop of Canterbury, Cosmo Gordon Lang, in 1945. When Baldwin died in 1947 this left the field clear for Beaverbrook's version of the story. William Randolph Hearst died in 1951 at the age of 88 but the Duke was to find a new ally in America.

20

Despatches from St Helena

illiam Randolph Hearst was going to have one final bite at the abdication cherry when the Windsors arrived in the Bahamas in 1940, exiled from Britain and placed out of reach of the Nazis. His dreams of furnishing Britain with an American queen had crumbled to dust but he knew full well that it was still a marketable story, as he told Adela Rogers St. Johns whom he tasked with the work.

> What people are curious about makes news. Before ... there were not five hundred women in the United States who had ever heard of her. Now I doubt if there are five hundred who will not be deeply interested in what you find out about their life today and in what, for the first time, they have to tell you about their own love and about the abdication.[1]

Rogers St. Johns had deep reservations about the assignment; she felt she had had enough of the couple without ever having interviewed either. She knew that she had developed a strong prejudice against the Duchess and had already turned down Hearst's request for her to cover the wedding at Candé. Hearst sent Louella Parsons, the Hollywood gossip columnist, instead of her. In Rogers St. Johns's view Parsons had 'been writing about the movies so long she couldn't tell the difference' but the Bahamas interview was a huge journalistic opportunity presented to her on a plate. All the other newspapers, magazines and book publishers had been turned away but thanks to the support that Hearst had given during the crisis and the gratitude this had earned him, he was being given an exclusive. He never had his interview with Queen Wallis at Buckingham Palace but the first extended interview with the exiled governor and his wife was not a bad scoop. His organization would have practically unlimited opportunity to interview the couple on the record and take photographs.

Rogers St. Johns understood full well that this came at a price. She knew that the Windsors did not want a warts-and-all portrait and, more important, her boss shared their view for simple commercial reasons:

Mr. Hearst was sure what his readers wanted. If I went to Nassau he'd hope I'd be sitting in a seat where it looked to me as though Happy Ending won the Love Story of the Century Handicap.

Rogers St. Johns salved her professional self-esteem by making it plain that she wanted to write the truth, but she took the job despite Hearst's politician's response which non-committally deferred the real decision, 'You need not write anything but the truth. Let us cross the bridge of what is the truth in this case when we come to it.' Her friend, the writer Damon Runyon, overcame her final scruples by pointing out that the interviews would give her the chance to get fascinating copy.

When she got to Nassau, Rogers St. Johns saw the Duke's immense attraction and charm without being swept away, but disliked the Duchess as much as she had expected to. She also swiftly learned that the couple had managed to upset local people. Her copy was splashed over the Hearst papers and syndicated throughout the United States in fourteen daily instalments. It is an entirely professional piece of work, anything but a slavish puff article, but it did give the couple a platform from which to deliver their complaints. Her criticism of the Duke and Duchess is almost invariably heavily coded.

She had caught the Duke at a perfect moment for an indiscreet interview. He was close to outright clinical paranoia about the British authorities:

we have ample evidence of their activities on this side of the Atlantic and that the persecution of the Windsors goes on relentlessly. We know from reliable sources that they more or less control news regarding ourselves in America, that they go so far as to encourage any lousy publicity, and that disgraceful and libellous lies are rife even in Washington. I have good reason to believe that the latter emanate from the F. O. at any rate, the British Embassy has taken no steps to deny them.

I am only beginning to realise the virulence of the campaign that Official England launched against me the day I ascended the throne, and how, with macchiavellian cunning, used the fertile soil of the American press in the fabrication of sufficient evidence against me to justify the its ultimate aim of having me out. However, who knows that this appointment in the Bahamas ... may ... prove to be the first opportunity we have as yet had to frustrate their game.[2]

The Duke accused 'government "fifth columnists"' of trying to sabotage the reception of Philip Guedalla's *The Hundredth Year* which he had used as platform to present his version of the abdication.

The most strident complaint was the plain fact of the Duke's minor job in the Bahamas, coupled with continual references to the discomfort of its climate and discouraging surroundings.[3] The Bahamas were frequently denigrated as St. Helena, the isolated and unwelcoming South Atlantic island to which Napoleon had been exiled. The Duke had the degrading position of 'shiller [tout] for a winter resort'. The Duchess repeatedly protested that her husband would be capable of far more important work. The Duke gave a strong hint of what he had in mind with a fanciful account of his time as Prince of Wales. He and his father supposedly worked in a close partnership in which Edward was tasked with delicate and unavowable missions. The Duke seemed to be angling to recreate this arrangement with a slot as official older brother whilst George VI handled the mundane business of kingship. There was a strong insinuation that he could have done a better job of preventing the war than his brother if he had been given the chance. The Duke permitted himself a sharp dig at his brother, the King 'whose self-confidence he had always tried to build up'. , insinuating that Georg VI's acute feelings of inferiority which fed off his stammer were well-founded.

High on the list of complaints at the family's behaviour was the refusal to give the Duchess the title of Royal Highness. The Duke's snobbism shone through in the resentment that his two commoner sisters-in-law – Queen Elizabeth and the Duchess of Gloucester – were entitled, but not his American wife. Even many years later the Duke relished the fact that he was one of only a handful of people in Europe to have exclusively royal blood in their veins. Here Rogers St. Johns also detected a powerful psychological motive for the Duke's anger: a feeling of masculine inadequacy that he had failed to provide his wife with something.

In the Duke's version of the crisis Baldwin was 'of the old order' and working to defend the interests of 'every reactionary in England of church and state' who were 'trembling' at 'a young King who had said We must do something for the poor – for the labouring man, for those in need'. Rogers St. Johns mused that history would unearth other reasons for the abdication than merely Edward's desire to marry Mrs. Simpson, endorsing the Duke's belief that he had been made to suffer for his instincts in favour of social justice. In the Duke's rewriting of history, his desire to broadcast over the head of the government to swing opinion in favour of the marriage became a generous offer of a pause for thought that the government refused. The 'people who had so long loved him as Prince of Wales' might also have been given the opportunity to decide on 'other things': the last echo of the vaulting fantasies of clawing constitutional power from the elected politicians that he had shared with Frazier Hunt, also from the Hearst stable of journalism. Edward, the never-to-be monarchical champion of the people, faded from view, but not the Duke's anger that Baldwin had not agreed to include a reference to Mrs. Simpson's willingness to do anything possible to prevent the abdication in his speech to Parliament. The Duke stood on safer ground when he vehemently denied the rumour, which may have sprung from remarks by Baldwin, that he had abdicated because he did not wish to be king.

The Duke further rearranged historical fact in his self-portrait as would-be avid peacemaker. Actually, becoming King had interrupted the work for peace he had undertaken as Prince of Wales, presumably such as his notorious 'hand of friendship' speech to the British Legion at the Albert Hall which had enraged his father and the government. The Duke's visit to Hitler in 1937 was spun as an extension of this quest with an insinuation that if he had gone there as king – as he had told the Nazi Duke of Saxe-Coburg he would – he could have saved peace. The one individual who came into the Duke's sights as a threat to peace was Anthony Eden, Foreign Secretary during his reign. Eden had drawn his ire for moves that would have offended Fascist Italy such as allowing Hailie Selassie, recently deposed as emperor of Ethiopia by the Italian invasion of his country, into Britain against Edward's wishes and even asking for him to be received at Buckingham Palace. He had forced on the King the discomfort and inconvenience of travelling through Yugoslavia to board the *Nahlin*, whilst taking the easy route via Venice would have made a friendly gesture to Mussolini as well. At the time of the interview Eden was still working his way back to the political top table after being cast into the wilderness for his opposition to appeasement by Neville Chamberlain so the Duke was on relatively safe ground in depicting himself as Eden's adversary in a battle that would resound through history.

The Duchess's oversensitivity on trivial points shines through in the space devoted to dealing with criticism of her having flown a hairdresser in from New York. Rogers St. Johns wrote up the supposedly innocent explanation for this in such an incoherent and confusing, and naturally unconvincing, way that it is tempting to suppose that the journalist intentionally sabotaged an exercise in self-justification for something that would have been better ignored.

21

A Rope of Sand

Neither the Duke nor the Duchess had relished their time in the Bahamas during the Second World War and were positively delighted when his tenure as governor came to an end. The wartime expedient of public service had, however, aroused his hopes that the British government might be willing to give him some permanent official job. This could give the couple the status he craved as consequential individuals and not merely as newsworthy celebrity fixtures in the higher echelons of French society with nothing but past status as their claim to attention. His sights had dropped from becoming some kind of official older brother to King George VI that he had set out to Adela Rogers St. Johns. The kind of task he had in mind was to be officially attached to the British embassy in Washington, representing the country outside the normal diplomatic machinery. Washington society might just have been flattered to be graced by the permanent presence of British ex-royalty, but the new British Labour government gave the proposal a distinctly chilly reception. Winston Churchill, now in opposition, curtly told the Duke that he was in no position to help.

Stung by the prospect of returning to the limbo of insignificance that had followed his abdication, the Duke turned his thoughts to doing something about this. He might not have been able to create a position for himself in the current affairs of the world but he could begin to shape his place in history. He thought the moment had come to dispel 'doubt and conjecture' and to feed the appetite for material on 'a subject of such historical political interest [as] the lone hand I had to play throughout the negotiations with the politicians, both of church and state'.[1] From the outset the ex-king was to be depicted as the hero of an epic struggle between an individual and the massed forces of the state. Unlike the Duke's pre-war literary projects to restore his reputation, this one would carry his signature, but the vulgar work of actually organizing words on paper could be left to someone else.

The Duke's choice as lineal successor to Charlie Murphy and Philip Guedalla was Charles J. V. 'Charlie' Murphy, a prominent US journalist with strong ties to magazine publisher Henry Luce. Murphy had contributed to the huge and inflated popular standing of the polar explorer Admiral Richard Byrd and had come to the Duke's attention through an evanescent book he had produced about Winston Churchill. From the start the project was essentially an American one and not a British one. Murphy's employer, Time-Life magazines, was an obvious publisher for the fruit of their collaboration. With a near-guaranteed big seller in the offing, Time-Life was also in a position to pay the Duke a great deal of money and his ghostwriter was going to receive a healthy cut, 21 per cent, of gross royalties. The publishers would milk the project to the utmost with a series of lavishly illustrated articles in *Life* magazine to be followed by a full-scale book. The memoirs would bolster both the Duke's reputation and his bank balance. The Duke was turning his face against British culture and society in favour of America so it was a positive advantage that Murphy was an American. To begin with Murphy succumbed to the Duke's charm and it seemed that he might take the place of the Duke's literary friend and companion that had been occupied by Philip Guedalla.

The Duke did not entirely cut himself off from his British circle and tried to recruit Walter Monckton to help in the project.[2] After a series of high-level government appointments during the Second World War, Monckton had returned to his legal work as adviser to an Indian prince defending his interests as the country moved towards independence. If the Duke had thought that Monckton would be an enthusiastic partner in the project, he was to be sadly mistaken. Monckton willingly revived his role during the crisis and its aftermath as liaison officer between Edward and the establishment, but once again his loyalties lay far more closely with government and court than the ex-king. From the start his goal was to prevent the book ever appearing and, if he failed in this, to censor it radically.[3] Monckton was a true man of the establishment and he knew by instinct what the upper echelons of Britain would find especially distasteful if it were mentioned in the Duke's book. He would use all the tact and discretion that he had honed with Edward during the abdication crisis to keep as much of its ugly side – and there was little else – hidden from the public gaze. He certainly professed to have the Duke's interests at heart too, but his vision of the risks that the Duke was running by publishing frank memoirs was deeply coloured by the considerations of the establishment. Once again, he would oil the wheels of discretion.

Monckton discreetly flagged an interest in the events of the abdication to the royal household without disclosing the precise reason for this. It would not take much guesswork to work it out. He had opened a channel of communication with the people who had a similar interest and instincts to his own and who would be deeply interested in what emerged. He stopped short of sending the Palace copies of the draft for their direct comments, but he was well enough attuned to their concerns to try to censor on their behalf.

The Duke was deaf to the strong advice from both Monckton and his wife Biddy not to write the book at all, but he provided one crumb of comfort for advocates of discretion. The Duke had made a firm decision to end the narrative when he left Britain on 11 December 1936 and would not refer to his family's part in the crisis or, more valuable, its ugly aftermath.[4] His memoir would thus not be covering the questions of the financial settlement he made with his brother or the tale of how he came to retain the rank of a Royal Highness but how Mrs. Simpson was not allowed to share this rank when she became his wife. These were only the two most rancorous post-abdication episodes but they were far from all and few would be happy to see them aired again. It was a matter of public record that none of his family or anyone prominent in society had attended the wedding at Candé but the inner story of this estrangement was too intimate to bear close examination. Even less to the taste of anyone in Britain would be a close examination of the protracted process by which Mrs. Simpson obtained the second and final part of her divorce.

Leaving the royal family out of the story fell on the credit side of the ledger but trouble lay ahead on the political side of the narrative. Monckton was confronted by the possibility that the memoir project might become even more of a menace to the decencies of the establishment. The Duke mentioned the project to Churchill and Beaverbrook, who were in the South of France with him in the autumn of 1948. Churchill had his lustre as wartime prime minister to preserve from unhappy memories of his politically suicidal attempt to shield Edward in 1936 and was 'cagey', but Beaverbrook was, ominously, 'more than cooperative'.[5] He shared his already substantial trove of material with the Duke. The memoir was now open to the influence and agenda of the man whose attitude during the crisis had been the most dangerously irresponsible as the de facto leader of the King's Party. Beaverbrook had been desperate to split the country over the issue of the King's marriage to Mrs. Simpson; there was no reason to suppose that his approach would in any way have improved now that it was a question of writing the record of the crisis.

Caught in the middle of all of this was Murphy, the Duke's ghostwriter, now in a deeply uncomfortable position. The initial happy glow of the relationship had worn off rapidly as the journalist was confronted with the grinding reality of collaboration with the Duke, who proved unable or unwilling to operate steadily or consistently. He would excuse himself and disappear for hours, sometimes days. Everything had to be fitted around the couple's travel plans, themselves subject to change at whim. Within months, Time-Life were complaining at the lack of copy and Murphy had to confess that 'Operation Belvedere [was] at a point of special crisis'.[6] He blamed the Windsors, whom he was coming to detest. Murphy complained of the 'slow geological workings of the royal brain' and the difficulty of dealing with a couple who 'both live so far apart from reality'.[7] Murphy put the Duke's attention span at a maximum of two and a half minutes. Over a champagne-fuelled dinner with Monckton in London his disenchantment had reached such a pitch that he let his emotions take charge.[8] Murphy accused the Duchess of active hostility and sabotage because the book touched on the Duke's life that had been happy even before she entered it.[9] If she dragged the Duke to a nightclub until dawn this would destroy any hope of progress the following day. It would have been bad enough if the memoir had been a single, uncontroversial piece of writing for a single client but Murphy found himself called on to 'restring the pearl necklace' as Monckton worked on the Duke to amend the text.[10] Beaverbrook was also claiming his share of the project. The Duke's memoirs were a literary task from hell. Murphy described it as trying to weave a 'rope of sand'.

22

This Wretched Publication

By the middle of 1949 the Duke and his ghostwriter had assembled the draft of a complete book which was sent to Monckton and George Allen, the Duke's solicitor, for their comments. They disliked it immensely. Allen even questioned whether the Duke had actually had a hand in writing the book because it was so bad. He foretold it would do the Duke 'untold injury' if it appeared.[1] Monckton did not even think it made a good presentation of the Duke's case and anyway contained 'much that was not worthy of him' and 'cheap petty criticism of individuals'. Throughout the abdication crisis Edward had struggled to disentangle substantial reasons for complaining about someone from aspects of the behaviour or personality that irritated him. Baldwin was a particular target of the Duke's dislike for his mannerisms and style of talking. On one crucial point Monckton threatened to use the nuclear option and to 'disassociate' himself from the book and treat it as purely the work of the Duke, giving a clear implication that he disagreed with it. The Duke was opening the Pandora's box of complaining in public of the way the politicians had handled the crisis. As Allen noted, the draft practically accused Baldwin of forcing Edward to abdicate so as to improve his own flagging political fortunes. This would be almost guaranteed to provoke a huge public controversy with Baldwin's relatives and friends openly challenging the book in a full-blooded refight of the abdication crisis, tearing open the old wounds.

The draft opened legal pitfalls as well. It was dangerously frank about the relationship between Edward and Mrs. Simpson in a way that offended the morality of the day, clearly expressed in the law that had governed Mrs. Simpson's divorce, which worked on the assumption that a divorce could only be granted if all the fault lay on one side. Having an affair with a married person was tantamount to breaking up their marriage and to harming the partner who was not involved. If, as the draft rather indicated, Edward and Mrs. Simpson had decided to marry before the divorce, the divorce itself could be seen as illegal. Had there been any evidence pointing this way at the time, the King's Proctor would have been duty-bound to intervene formally and to block the finalization of the divorce and the issue of a decree absolute.

The Duke's legal friends were looking through the drafts hoping to eliminate controversial material, but at the same time Beaverbrook was looking through the drafts with a quite different eye. He wanted the book to put over his own version of the abdication crisis and that would provoke an even worse furore than Allen feared from the Duke's own efforts. Somehow Beaverbrook had got Charlie Murphy onto his side and had opened a back channel of communication that bypassed the Duke entirely. Beaverbrook insisted that this was to be kept hidden from him.[2] The ghostwriter was supplying him with material and passing Beaverbrook's comments onto the Duke as though they were objective criticism. Beaverbrook wanted to prove that he and the King would have won out in a direct confrontation with the government. Beaverbrook applied a peculiar piece of analysis to demonstrate that the King had had public support behind him and through Murphy provided him with the material to support the argument. Beaverbrook had totalled the circulation figures for the newspapers supporting the King over the morganatic proposal during the crisis – mainly his own and the Harmsworth papers – and compared them to those of the newspapers ranged against him, chiefly the establishment journals such as *The Times*.[3] The balance was in favour of the King: 12,500,000, against 8,500,000 but even leaving aside this highly questionable approach to assessing democratic opinion, the figures looked like calculations of troop strength in a civil war. Beaverbrook had had no qualms about splitting the country. Whilst Edward turned down Beaverbrook's desire to launch this fight during the crisis, the figures found their way into the published book.

Beaverbrook lost himself so far in his conviction that only he was qualified to tell the story of the abdication that he claimed Edward 'never grasped the meaning of his own crisis'.[4] Fortified by this piece of historical megalomania, Beaverbrook took the programme of duplicity that he had begun with his concealed dialogue with Murphy one very large step further. He went behind the back of both the Duke and the ghostwriter directly to the Duke's publisher, Harry Luce, of Time-Life. He presented Luce with his own versions of the three chapters covering the abdication crisis that he had written himself even whilst he was working on Murphy's draft. He wanted Luce to abandon Murphy's efforts and just to use his own.

Beaverbrook's chapters are passionate and highly readable, but it is baffling that he imagined that anyone would have thought for a second that the Duke could have been the author, even using a ghostwriter. They are dominated by a highly slanted political analysis in which Baldwin was fighting for his political life and thought that overthrowing the King was a way he could restore his fortunes. At no point did Beaverbrook square this claim with the fact that Baldwin voluntarily resigned as prime minister less than six months after the abdication. He also accused the government of blatantly exploiting the legal process to put pressure on the King. Beaverbrook went far further than the Duke's unarguable and objective claim that intervention by the King's Proctor might have left Mrs. Simpson trapped in her marriage, unable to marry the ex-king who would thus have abdicated to no purpose. The short-lived but conspicuous plan to couple the abdication bill with one expediting Mrs. Simpson's divorce was designed solely to protect the couple from this risk, however slight it might have been. Beaverbrook added a far deeper layer of menace by putting into the Duke's mouth a complaint of brutal and oppressive behaviour by Baldwin, accusing him of using the threat of intervention by the King's Proctor to demoralize and pressurize Mrs. Simpson. Beaverbrook was unable to come up with any evidence for this claim beyond a letter from Sir John Simon discussing the various scenarios for intervention which was shown to George Allen, the King's solicitor, presumably with the intention that it would be shown to the King. If there is any sinister aspect to this letter, it was to insinuate that the King could reduce the danger of intervention by abdicating as quickly as possible.[5] Nonetheless Beaverbrook built the threat of intervention up as a key part of his own narrative of the crisis.

Predictably Luce turned down Beaverbrook's proposals and instead gave him the opportunity to write a piece under his own name, which would be positioned as a tail-piece to the memoirs. Beaverbrook did not take up the offer but the seed had been sown. If Beaverbrook was going to put over his own version of the story of the abdication crisis, he would have to do it himself.

The articles in *Life* appeared in the spring of 1950 and the book under the title *A King's Story* was published early in 1951 after another year of agonized discussion. Monckton and Allen had succeeded in softening the tone compared to earlier drafts but far from decisively. Moreover, the book's references to Baldwin were sharper than in the articles that had appeared. The prime minister was no longer accused of having forced the abdication to improve his political fortunes but is presented as 'an astute intriguer disloyal to his master'. He and his ministers are cast as the front men for a campaign of social conservatism masterminded by the Archbishop of Canterbury. From the word go Baldwin is depicted as the King's opponent in a 'one-sided' struggle. He deals a series of 'crushing blows' against the King designed to put pressure on him. Hardinge's letter is a 'big pistol' aimed at the King by Baldwin. Baldwin is castigated for confronting the King with a choice between marriage to Mrs. Simpson and the throne, even though the Duke admitted to having told him spontaneously and unprompted that if he could not marry her he was prepared to step down. The book sneers at Baldwin's claim to speak for public opinion with the pretension to being a 'Gallup poll incarnate' and sets against this the claim of the King's own (unnamed) supporters that he would have been able to 'rally a vast majority' around him. He quoted Beaverbrook's figures for the circulation of favourable and unfavourable newspapers with the qualification that they did not represent public opinion in themselves, but he wanted both to have his cake and to eat it. He claimed that the circulation numbers reflected the size of the public that could have been mobilized on his behalf had he been willing to split the country.

There is no single favourable word about Baldwin, who is described as arrogant and determined to force his King into the 'iron bed of convention'. On a personal level, Baldwin is derided as cowardly and mocked for travelling slowly in a small car, the 'black beetle'. The dominant figures in the government are painted as the front men for conservatives in the church, at court and in Whitehall, who were scared that the young king would change a comfortable, established order. The Duke even allowed himself a dig at one of his brothers, the Duke of Gloucester, for being afraid that abdication would increase his own royal workload and compromise his career as an army officer.

The book is replete with refighting of old battles, both important and trivial. As these happened almost all in private it is impossible to judge the scale of the criticisms that the Duke of Windsor was attempting to rebut, but it provides a useful guide to episodes that still rankled with him. Prominent is his first audience with the Cosmo Gordon Lang, the Archbishop of Canterbury, which provided fodder for the book's portrayal of an imaginary conservative conspiracy against him orchestrated by the Church of England. His resentment at Anthony Eden, the foreign secretary, (and his desire to appear witty and forthright) trumped any fear of revealing the depths of his enthusiasm for appeasement, which had been far more clearly on show in his interview with Adela Rogers St. Johns in the Bahamas. When Eden told him that it would be popular for him to receive Haile Selassie, who had just been expelled from his throne by Mussolini's invasion of Ethiopia, *A King's Story* has him replying, 'Popular with whom? … certainly not the Italians.'[6] Edward was notably short of self-awareness as the book makes painfully obvious. He devotes two pages to the story of his set-to with the Royal Mint over which direction his profile should face, but immediately claims that he did not take this or other such things seriously. As well as lengthy self-justifications for his behaviour toward the Privileged Bodies and summarily curtailing a presentation of debutantes at Buckingham Palace when it rained, he trotted out the umbrella tale, unaware of the self-contradiction in deriding the supposed criticism for using the royal Daimler whilst he mocked Baldwin for choosing a small, inconspicuous car, the 'black beetle'.

Beaverbrook did not have it all his own way in *A King's Story*. The Duke did disclose Beaverbrook's leading role in the 'conspiracy' to persuade Mrs. Simpson to renounce him. In his own chapters Beaverbrook had written himself out of the conspiracy which appeared as the work of Monckton and Allen who recruited Lord Brownlow to do their work. The Duke gave the most positive spin possible to Beaverbrook's involvement, which was supposedly motivated by thoughts of the King's best interests and not a desire to 'destroy his happiness'. *A King's Story* even quoted Beaverbrook's ostensible reasoning that renunciation by Mrs. Simpson would kill off 'Mr. Baldwin's crisis' and allow the question of marriage to be re-opened at the King's leisure. It speaks much for Beaverbrook's ability to find limitless narratives to fit his prejudice that he could also be arguing almost simultaneously that Baldwin had tried to force Mrs. Simpson to renounce the King by the threat of intervention by the King's Proctor.*

---

* See p. 144.

The Palace knew that Monckton and Allen had tried their utmost to reduce the damage from a book that none of them had wanted to appear at all. The best that they could claim was to 'have succeeded in doing, by the most drastic attacks, has been to make what was horrible and [sic] a little less so'.[7] George VI's private secretary Sir Alan "Tommy" Lascelles, who was acting as linkman between the Palace and the two advisers, thanked them on behalf of the whole Royal family for having 'done all that mortal men could do to make this wretched publication as decent as possible'.[8] Lascelles dismissed the Duke's efforts as little better than mining his private life to produce near pornography for money, 'It is obscene to write gainfully [i.e. for payment] about one's own love affairs; but like most obscenity it won't do any real harm to anybody else.'[9] Not only was the book an aberration but everyone on the court side from King George VI down believed it would do more harm to the Duke than to anyone else.[10] The genie was out of the bottle, never to be put back, and a precedent had been set for royals openly to engage in public discussion of controversial aspects of their lives. The Duke, his publishers and his ghostwriters could enjoy the financial rewards of a highly successful launch; 80,000 copies were sold in the United Kingdom alone in the first month.[11] This set a tempting benchmark for the commercial potential of insider books on British royalty which is powerful to this day.

23

The Beaverbrook Car Service

The Duke of Windsor had fallen far short of Beaverbrook's hopes that he would act as an obedient ally in his literary campaign against the memory of Stanley Baldwin. The Duke's memoirs had been severely critical of the prime minister but he had not written them as though removing Baldwin from office should have ranked high in his priorities. Crucially, the Duke did not treat the failure to launch a full-scale press war against the government as an error. He had been willing to recycle Beaverbrook's calculation of the newspaper readerships that each side might have been able to address in the public controversy Beaverbrook hoped to stoke. In Beaverbrook's mind this was the great missed opportunity of the crisis which might have mobilized public sentiment in favour of the King and against Baldwin. The Duke had qualified the importance of the circulation figures and had frankly admitted that an open controversy would have damaged the nation.[1] He claimed that the idea of splitting the nation was repugnant to him.[2] The Duke's retrospective surge of public spiritedness deserves to be treated with scepticism in view of his enthusiasm to broadcast his case to the nation which would have been equally divisive, but there is no doubt he held Beaverbrook back. This ran against the belief in Beaverbrook's mind that anything that could have served to throw Baldwin out of Downing Street was not only acceptable but in the nation's best interests and so actively desirable. If Beaverbrook wanted his own version of the story to appear it would have to do so under his own name, and not that of some pliant dummy. Beaverbrook set to work to gather details from the other players in the crisis.

Baldwin himself had died in 1948 and his closest ministerial colleague at the time of the crisis, then Chancellor of the Exchequer Neville Chamberlain, had died in 1940. Beaverbrook thus began his quest for damaging material with Sir John Simon, Home Secretary at the time of the abdication and one of the highest-profile figures in Baldwin's government. Moreover, Simon was closely tied to what Beaverbrook saw as a ruthless government stratagem against Edward both before and after the abdication, which Beaverbrook had tried unavailingly to make the Duke of Windsor feature prominently in his memoirs. In Beaverbrook's eyes the government had manipulated the legal process of the day by exploiting the power of the King's Proctor to intervene in Mrs. Simpson's divorce (as he could in any divorce proceedings) as a weapon to brutalize the couple into submission to its wishes.

The Duke of Windsor had put into Beaverbrook's hands a letter that pointed to a sudden and sinister reversal of government thinking with regard to intervention by the King's Proctor which he could follow up in his quest for dubious behaviour. It looked a perfect piece of evidence. Until a week before the abdication no one in government had been worried about the prospect of intervention. Esmond Harmsworth had told Beaverbrook that the solicitor general, Terence O'Connor, believed that 'if the King remained on his throne, the King's Proctor or any private complainant would in law find it quite impossible to raise objections to the progress of the divorce case' but that this would become possible if the King stepped down.[3] O'Connor's reasoning has not survived, but he may have assumed that the only scenario he needed to address was one in which the King would be accused of adultery with Mrs. Simpson and would not be 'justiciable' in his own court. Even this looks dubious. Beaverbrook had taken O'Connor's assessment to be the opinion of all the government's law officers advisers, so that when he discovered that Simon, admittedly not a law officer but a lawyer nonetheless, had changed the advice he was giving to the prime minister, he scented that the government was trying to move the legal goalposts. Beaverbrook did not have the full facts. Simon too had been confident that there would be no intervention but this was because of what he calculated that people would do, not on a legal opinion. He believed that abdication would actually reduce the risk of intervention by removing 'patriotic' grounds for private intervention. Simon did not believe that there was any prospect of action by the King's Proctor unless 'new and glaring evidence of collusion [in Mrs. Simpson's divorce] was forthcoming'.[4] Insofar as anything from Simon could be seen as sinister, it was his stated belief that the abdication would practically eliminate the danger of action by someone from the public, which could be seen as an attempt to jog the king off the throne.[5]

Simon's prophesy turned out to be wrong; a member of the public, Francis Stephenson, did make a personal intervention claiming collusion which set off the King's Proctor's own involvement. When Simon got wind of this three days after his first letter, he wrote to Baldwin changing his advice and revising his analysis of the considerations that the government would face over intervention by the King's Proctor. He made the unarguable point that abdication would not affect the legal process; Mrs. Simpson's divorce case was merely an action between two private citizens. Mrs. Simpson would just have to face the ordinary perils of the law. Simon's confidence that abdication would practically remove the danger of intervention had evaporated. All this proves is that Simon's letter shows that it might have been in the government's short-term interest for Stephenson to intervene, but it fell a long way short of giving reason to suspect the government of being behind his move, which admittedly remains mysterious to this day. Simon also did not address what might happen if the King's Proctor ultimately blocked Mrs. Simpson's divorce. This would have been a nightmare for all concerned: the abdication would have become motiveless because the marriage for which the King sacrificed his throne would have become impossible.

Beaverbrook was also falling into the journalists' trap of making a single piece of evidence into a broader story which ignored its context in a fast-moving and often confused flow of events. Baldwin had been willing to short-circuit the King's Proctor's legal authority by accelerating Mrs. Simpson's divorce under the 'two bills' scheme; it was only the opposition of his Cabinet colleagues who saw more clearly the political objections to the 'two bills' that stymied the plan. Fear of the King's Proctor certainly helped keep the couple quiet and docile ahead of George VI's coronation but the dominant force on the government was respect for the legal system and practice. It would have exposed itself to severe criticism if it had not let the legal process run its due course.

None of this was going to be allowed to stand in the way of a good story. Beaverbrook mapped out a tale in which the government suddenly swung from O'Connor's optimistic analysis to one in which intervention was an immediate danger. Beaverbrook dreamed up a scenario in which it would be to Baldwin's advantage to force the King to stay on the throne, 'pledged not to marry Wallis.' Baldwin would enjoy the kudos of having been 'a wise and fatherly guide who had guided the King through an

acute emotional crisis and brought him back to the path of duty'.[6] Simon's
second letter was the tool that was used to exert unequivocal pressure on
the King.

Beaverbrook's opening move was to confront Simon with a copy of his
second letter together with a draft paragraph from his proposed book on
the abdication that implied that Baldwin had not been frank with the
public and that Simon's letter had been used to terrorize the King.

He [Baldwin] did not tell the House that on Monday 7th December,
the King was deeply shaken by a letter written by Sir John Simon.
This letter declared that there was danger of intervention in the
divorce case on the basis of alleged collusion between Mr. and Mrs.
Simpson.[7]

Beaverbrook wanted Simon's permission to quote the letter itself. He
did open the prospect of amending his text, implicitly to something less
slanted against Simon, but stated bluntly that he would mention that
Simon had been a member of the inner Cabinet around Baldwin through
the crisis together with Chamberlain and Hoare. Beaverbrook claimed
this point was of 'no consequence', whilst of course it tarred Simon with
any misdeeds by the government. He invited Simon and his wife to lunch,
offering to send a car to drive him the six miles between their houses in
Surrey. To round it all off, he reminded Simon that he still enjoyed the
favour of Churchill, who was poised to re-enter Downing Street, and that
he had been summoned to Chartwell, implicitly for consultation about
the upcoming election campaign.

Beaverbrook might have been forgiven for being nonplussed when
he received a hand-written, genially worded and prompt reply from
Simon accepting the invitation.[8] He might also have bridled at Simon's
liberal extension of Beaverbrook's offer of transport. Simon booked
Beaverbrook's driver to collect him from his flat in Westminster, a distance
of twenty-five miles rather than just from the next village. He pulled
Beaverbrook up over an error in his dates but did dangle the prospect of
hitherto unpublished details of the abdication in front of him. However,
he braced Beaverbrook to prepare for disappointment over whether he
would permit him to publish a 'secret' letter.

Sadly, no account has come down of the conversation that followed so it is a matter of speculation how Simon was able to comprehensively flatten the press baron. He would have had ample material to use against his host. As Home Secretary during the crisis, he had access to the police files detailing the 1935 investigation which had thrown up the story that Mrs. Simpson was conducting an affair with car salesman Guy Trundle behind the backs of both her husband and the then Prince of Wales. Simon had personally authorized the wiretap on the King at the height of the crisis. As part of the inner Cabinet, it is a near certainty that he would have known of the other intelligence linking Mrs. Simpson to the US press magnate William Randolph Hearst and the plots of the King's Party. Simon might also have been drawing on the material used to smear the Duchess of Windsor after the abdication, the stories of her Chinese lovers. Whatever Simon might have used, it probably referred to the Windsors or to Churchill. It took a fortnight after the lunch for Beaverbrook to write back to Simon, which would have given time for him to write to the Duke in France and for the Duke to have replied. Beaverbrook told Simon that he had discussed the matter 'with some of my friends' so might also have had to consult Churchill too.

Whatever buttons Simon might have been able to punch directly on Beaverbrook and indirectly on the Windsors, they were enough for Beaverbrook to promise not to mention the King's Proctor at all in his account and he proposed a severely altered draft.[9] The description of Simon as a member of the inner Cabinet went too. But any material that Simon fielded that could be used to pressurize the Windsors or Churchill held no terrors for Beaverbrook himself and his proposed revisions still left a suitably provocative account. Beaverbrook could rely on supporting evidence from Lord Brownlow to quote an anecdote of a 'characteristically devious' intervention by Baldwin in which Simon assured Brownlow that phones in Britain were not tapped and tried to warn him off taking legal action against the Archbishop of Canterbury for his derogatory remarks on the ex-king's social circle in his radio broadcast immediately after the abdication. Beaverbrook next tried to introduce a claim that Dawson, Lord Halifax and Simon had conspired together during the crisis at All Souls, Oxford, the intellectual heart of the establishment. Here again, Beaverbrook faced disappointment. Simon squashed his Oxford tale with a magisterial, 'At All Souls we talk about everything – but we don't plot!'[10]

Beaverbrook was baulked in his desire to use the King's Proctor story as a bludgeon on Baldwin and the passage of arms with Simon appears to have taken the impetus out of Beaverbrook's direct literary ambitions. He did continue to accumulate material on the abdication assiduously and he envisioned incorporating the story into a sweeping history that would destroy the reputation of his *bête noire* under the title *The Age of Baldwin* but it was never written and his account of the abdication was not published in his lifetime. The celebrated gadfly historian A. J. P. Taylor fell under Beaverbrook's spell and anointed himself the keeper of the press baron's reputation after his death. As a precursor to his largely uncritical biography of his mentor, Taylor edited Beaverbrook's draft into a book that was published as *The Abdication of King Edward VIII* a few years after he died. Taylor presented Beaverbrook's work as a sparkling piece, worthy of attention in its own right and as what would have been a chapter in his projected masterwork assailing every aspect of Baldwin's career. It might have been better for Beaverbrook's reputation if Taylor had held his hand. The book is self-contradictory, fragmented and disjointed; it is all too obviously intended principally if not exclusively as an assault on Baldwin (and tangentially on Geoffrey Dawson). It makes plain that Beaverbrook saw the crisis purely as a means of removing Baldwin from office. Some of its judgements are so weird as to be positively delusional; Beaverbrook's musing that he could have installed Sir Archibald Sinclair, leader of the opposition Liberals, in Downing Street, comes over as that of a megalomaniac living in a world of his own.

The book's most flagrant piece of self-contradiction comes over the attempts to persuade Mrs. Simpson to give up the King. Beaverbrook came up with a convoluted narrative which allowed him to have his cake and eat it. He admitted that the King's aide in the crisis tried to make Mrs. Simpson give up the King, but fails to mention that he organized the attempt using his servant Lord Brownlow as his tool. He was not trying to break up the relationship permanently but simply to create breathing space to build public support for the King. The King would have stayed on the throne and Baldwin, 'would find that his seemingly impregnable position had been overturned'. Implicitly, Baldwin's goal had been to remove the King and if he failed, the King's Party and the King would surge to power. But Beaverbrook went on to claim that Baldwin also wanted Mrs. Simpson to step back. Beaverbrook presented the last-minute journey to Cannes by her solicitor Theodore Goddard as part of a government conspiracy. In it Baldwin sent Goddard to procure Mrs. Simpson's withdrawal so as to get him off the hook of having promised to resign if the 'Two bills scheme' was rejected. In Beaverbrook's version, Baldwin had staked his political future on the 'Two bills scheme' and would otherwise be doomed. Quite how the two scenarios of Mrs. Simpson renouncing the King could be reconciled was left unsaid. Beaverbrook accused Baldwin of hypocrisy in his attitude to renunciation and gave as proof for this the fact that Baldwin afterwards told Brownlow that he would have been put in the Tower if he had succeeded.[11] Readers were left to assume that Beaverbrook was motivated by the highest considerations in his attempt to persuade Mrs. Simpson to stage a token and temporary withdrawal.

24

The Beaverbrook Broadcasting Service

Whilst Beaverbrook mounted his remorseless, but only partly successful, campaign to transform the Duke of Windsor's memoir into a tract against the men he saw as the villains of the abdication crisis, he was enjoying a far smoother time steering another book in the direction he wanted. The principal target was Geoffrey Dawson, the editor of *The Times*, and Beaverbrook's efforts were conducted in almost total secrecy.

He had become firm friends with a distinguished typographer, Stanley Morison, whom he had met in 1948 on the liner *Queen Mary* sailing between Britain and the US, his accustomed route between the continents. Beaverbrook entertained Morison regularly in the Bahamas and the South of France and according to Beaverbrook's friend and biographer, A. J. P. Taylor, was his closest friend after the Second World War.[1] Morison's best-known achievement was as typography adviser to *The Times* newspaper which he persuaded to ditch its antique and dreary presentation in favour of the Times New Roman font, which Morison invented and which remains one of the most popular standard printing fonts to this day. Morison's interests went far beyond the mechanics of typography. Early in his career Morison had become fascinated by the political power of the press which he made the subject of lectures to Cambridge University. He somehow managed to combine firm Roman Catholicism with Communism in a balancing act that speaks volumes for his intellectual flexibility. He had begun as a supporter of *The Times*'s stridently pro-appeasement line in the 1930s but after the Barbarossa invasion of the Soviet Union he had swung to a militant line in favour of Stalin. Similarly, Beaverbrook himself had migrated from his pre-war isolationist and anti-Communist standpoint to positioning himself as the champion of the Soviet Union's war efforts in the British government. Beaverbrook's stance here was opportunistic but nonetheless vehement.

Morison had been commissioned to edit the official history of *The Times* in 1935. He wrote most of the text but his work was anonymous in keeping with *The Times*'s then practice with its journalists. This suited Beaverbrook perfectly as the last thing he would have wanted was for his hand to be visible in the work. Morison had begun by spontaneously contacting Beaverbrook for assistance on one chapter of the fourth and final volume of the history which covered the London press broadly. Their collaboration soon widened and Beaverbrook appears to have provided much of the material in an appendix to the fourth volume that covered the abdication crisis. It may have been kept out of the main narrative as *The Times*'s direct involvement – like that of most other newspapers – was brief and rated barely a paragraph in the main text. Perhaps Morison felt the need to ring-fence a part of the book that he had not authored fully and with which he was not entirely comfortable. The appendix gave a detailed narrative of the doings of Dawson and his deputy Robin Barrington-Ward through the crisis. These included Dawson's contacts with the prime minister and others of the mighty in the land, including the King's private secretary Alec Hardinge, as he tried to position himself as a privileged counsellor of state. The fact of Dawson's conversations with Baldwin gave some credence to Beaverbrook's depiction of Baldwin and Dawson working as a duo to push the King off the throne. Some of Morison's statements all too obviously came from the Duke of Windsor via Beaverbrook: the King's reported belief that the unfavourable press coverage had been 'organized' by Baldwin, the Archbishop of Canterbury and Dawson; the King's fear that *The Times* would head a concerted press attack on Mrs. Simpson under Dawson's malignant leadership.[2] Morison also claimed that Dawson suppressed the publication of readers' letters to *The Times* which were initially favourable to the King. As we have already noted, Beaverbrook appears to have been entirely unaware that Baldwin's favoured press proprietor and de facto mouthpiece was Berry of *The Daily Telegraph* and that Dawson's actions were driven by what he believed was in the interests of the establishment and not by Baldwin's reading of the political battle.

When the fourth volume of *The History of The Times* with the abdication appendix was published in 1952, it might have escaped wide attention as an in-house history, subject to the customary restraints on controversial material or criticism of its subject; all the more so as Beaverbrook's effective contribution was tucked away at the back. However, Beaverbrook was presented with a perfect platform to publicize the book and to put a gloss on its contents that supported his agenda of revising the history of the abdication by showcasing the appendix. He was given slots by the BBC on both radio and the quite new and exciting medium of television to review the history. He did not disclose his friendship with Morison or his influence on the book and hijacked the talks to deliver a stinging criticism of Dawson as though this was the book's main subject. He distorted freely Morison's writing.

In his talks Beaverbrook claimed preposterously that he was 'not taking up any partisan attitude in this matter. Nor do I desire to rake over the dead embers of this controversy'.[3] This was the diametric opposite of what he attempted to do. Beaverbrook admitted that he 'put a different interpretation [to Morison's] upon some of these events, but the accuracy of the narrative cannot be disputed'. The core of his case was that the abdication appendix was the unarguable truth. In practice he had manufactured his own source material and was going to milk this to the full.

Beaverbrook began by complaining that the episode had been consigned to an appendix and not 'boldly brought out' like the treatment of *The Times*'s important part in the Munich crisis. Beaverbrook claimed that the book set out as fact:

(1) That the editor of The Times, Geoffrey Dawson, was the most important factor – with the sole exception of the Prime Minister, Stanley Baldwin – in compelling the King to abdicate.
(2) That he did it by methods which many would condemn.
(3) That he pursued his quest with a vigour that seemed more like venom.[4]

Much of Beaverbrook's talk was simply wrong: 'Dawson was more important than any of the Prime Minister's Cabinet colleagues … Dawson was almost invariably consulted first.' Beaverbrook conjured into existence an imaginary press duel between himself and Dawson. Dawson supposedly 'was intimidating the King in code. He succeeded in terrifying his Majesty'. Beaverbrook described the King as being 'in terror' of Dawson as Dawson prepared to attack him personally in print, as a means of 'block[ing] any help that I might be able to give'. Beaverbrook awarded himself the credit for wringing out an assurance from Dawson that *The Times* would not publish an editorial attacking Mrs. Simpson. No trace of any such editorial has emerged, but down the years the Duke of Windsor and Beaverbrook fed each other's belief that one existed.

Towards the end of Beaverbrook's rant against Dawson was one piece of information and Beaverbrook's interpretation of it which appears to have – undeservedly – escaped notice at the time and still does not get the attention it merits. Breaking away from his aggressive distortion of the text, he cited something from his own files. Ulick Alexander, a friend and courtier who had accompanied the Duke of Windsor on the destroyer HMS *Fury* on the voyage to Boulogne, the first stage in his journey into exile, quoted him as saying walking down the gangway: 'I *always* [author italics] thought I could get away with a morganatic marriage.'[5] Rather more plausibly than his comments on Dawson, Beaverbrook took this to mean that 'it had been his [the King's] intention to barter the threat of abdication against government acknowledgement of the morganatic marriage'.

This raises the intriguing possibility that the King had a morganatic marriage in mind from the very beginning as a fall-back position if the government objected to his making Mrs. Simpson his queen. This would have shown unusual flexibility and pragmatism as it contradicts what he told his brother the Duke of Kent after the crucial audience with Baldwin on 16 November: that he wanted to have Mrs. Simpson as his queen in the fullest sense. There was widespread gossip that he might marry Mrs. Simpson morganatically from an early stage. Esmond Harmsworth's later account of having persuaded Mrs. Simpson of the scheme's merits might thus have been part of a charade.

Moreover, there is much to support the belief that the King wrongly thought that his popular status gave him the whip hand over the government and that the threat of abdication would force Baldwin to climb down, over a full or a morganatic marriage. In the welter of Beaverbrook's near-delusional denunciation of Dawson to fit his own narrative of the crisis, Beaverbrook had let slip evidence that gave a simple and persuasive explanation of the crisis that was quite at variance to his conspiracy theory, one where the arrogance and misjudgement of the King himself had proved to be his undoing, when Baldwin in practice called his bluff with the fateful phrase, 'Sir, that is most grievous news.'

Beaverbrook's broadcasts were great technical successes, especially the television broadcast where he spoke directly to camera rather than being interviewed as was the practice then. He was using a technique that was to be adopted equally successfully by the historian A. J. P. Taylor who was to become his last major and most vigorous apologist. Taylor built a stellar television career on his own broadcasts. The response from the establishment was not so welcoming and Beaverbrook was accused of inaccuracy. He responded by preparing a booklet which quoted the appendix to *The Times* history as a definitive proof of the truth of what he had said, albeit concealing again his role as a source for Morison's work. He also devoted almost as much space in the booklet to the text of his broadcasts as to excerpts from mostly flattering newspaper reviews of his performances. Perhaps Beaverbrook spotted that this might leave him vulnerable to a (justified) charge of vanity and the booklet was never published.

Beaverbrook had brought coverage of the royal family into the television age with a blend of features that it has never shaken off since: professional slickness masking insubstantial content flawed by the determination to promote one agenda, combined with complete nonchalance towards the dangers of self-contradiction.

25

A Novice Lost on the Cresta Run

N ot content with trying to trash the reputation of Stanley Baldwin, who had worsted him in the battle over the abdication, Beaverbrook moved onto another target, whom he also held responsible for his disappointment. At the height of the abdication crisis, he had been desperate to unleash the full power of his newspapers against Baldwin and in favour of the King's marriage plans, but the King had refused to let him launch the offensive. By Beaverbrook's reckoning, his newspapers combined with those of the Harmsworths would have addressed a far greater readership than the establishment newspapers backing the government's line and he had been confident of winning the battle. Beaverbrook was perfectly happy to divide the nation over the issue of the King's marriage and believed that his side would win, which would mean the downfall of Baldwin. To Beaverbrook the overriding aim was to displace Baldwin from 10 Downing Street; his obsessional hatred for the prime minister blinded him to any other consideration.

But the King had refused Beaverbrook's schemes. His priority was to shield Mrs. Simpson from the publicity that she detested and feared. Beaverbrook recognized that she was the dominant partner in the relationship and blamed her for the King's unwillingness to back a full-scale newspaper campaign in favour of the marriage. In Beaverbrook's deluded eyes she had wrecked a golden opportunity to rid the country of the incubus of Baldwin and he was not going to let this go unpunished. He had met her as the crisis was getting under way and had not liked her, although all he admitted openly was that he disliked her hairstyle.[1] From his point of view there was nothing to be lost by offending the Duke of Windsor by attacking her. The Duke's memoirs had fallen well short of the anti-Baldwin tract that he had hoped for so he had little more to expect from that quarter. He could afford to compromise whatever store of goodwill he held with the Windsors.

Beaverbrook's chosen assassin was a journalist and author still under the age of thirty. Geoffrey Bocca had been commissioned to write a book on the new queen, Elizabeth and her husband, which gave him some sort of authority as a commentator on the affairs of the house of Windsor, but he could be counted on to be sufficiently pliable to obey Beaverbrook. Bocca began his work on the biography in late 1952. He was under no illusions that he was anything other than a member of Beaverbrook's stable of 'whizz-kids', some of whose number could be seen as walking wounded in Fleet Street, the British literary world or politics, occasionally prematurely aged by their experiences. Bocca knew full well that there was a price to pay for succumbing to 'Beaverbrook's siren song of gold, glamorous parties, transatlantic voyages in the *Queen Mary* and exotic travels to the Caribbean and the Riviera'. Bocca frequently felt like 'a novice lost on the Cresta Run' but knew that he could not resist the temptation. Bocca was set to work on an unauthorized biography of the Duchess of Windsor to the fury of her and her husband. This mattered not a jot to Beaverbrook and it provided Bocca with an opportunity to make his mark in the literary world.

The project was as much Beaverbrook's as Bocca's. Bocca was a far less challenging quasi-amanuensis than the Duke or Charlie Murphy, his ghostwriter. There was no pretence that this was anything other than a joint project. The book was published by Express Books and he was to all intents and purposes Beaverbrook's employee. Beaverbrook stopped short of outright dictation to Bocca but they discussed the work extensively and Beaverbrook reviewed at least one draft. Beaverbrook gave Bocca sight of extensive papers and gave him many introductions to prominent figures whose doors might normally have stayed closed to an unknown journalist. Beaverbrook could even dictate the title, although the libel lawyers blocked his choice of *The Woman Who Would Be Queen*, an echo of the Rudyard Kipling novel title. This would have showcased Beaverbrook's belief that Mrs. Simpson actively wanted to become queen with the support of the King and that both had worked diligently to achieve this end. Beaverbrook had to settle for the biography's eventual title, *She Might Have Been Queen*, and Bocca's preferred choice of *The Iron Duchess* came nowhere. Lawyerly prudence did not, though, stop Bocca stating in the book's text that the couple schemed to make her queen. The book also magnified Beaverbrook's direct influence on what had happened. It gave prominence to Beaverbrook's story that Mrs. Simpson had fled to France via Fort Belvedere when a brick was thrown through the window of the house in Cumberland Terrace off Regent's Park and that this had precipitated the last act in the crisis. In reality, the brick was probably thrown after Mrs. Simpson had left for Fort Belvedere – it is not mentioned in either her memoirs or any government documents – but the incident featured conspicuously in Beaverbrook's version of the crisis. Churchill believed that Beaverbrook had instigated it as part of a scheme to frighten Mrs. Simpson out of the country.[2] Beaverbrook denied the direct allegation but did admit that the attack might have been carried out by someone from the *Daily Express*, which seems to be a distinction without a difference. Beaverbrook relished the idea of having been closely involved in something that affected the course of history, however dishonourable or thuggish his actions might have been.

At least at the outset Bocca did not intend to write a hatchet job on Mrs. Simpson. He was pleased to come across favourable references to the Duchess from her time in the Bahamas, to which her husband had been exiled as British governor during the war. This would be 'needed to keep the work fair and balanced as it is obviously going to be all too easy to get the other kind of story'.[3] He knew that the Windsors were furious at an unauthorized biography, but did not want to produce a mere exercise in vindictiveness.[4] He had his future as an author to nurture. His book, though, was anything but uncritical of the Windsors, whom he described as 'confused and ingenuous'.[5] It opened with a picture of their insubstantial social life in America featuring Jimmy Donahue, the gruesome playboy who dominated the Duchess of Windsor's life for five years in the 1950s and might even have made an exception to his usual sexual tastes by becoming her lover.

Bocca did not pull punches on the couple's politically dubious friends either, with an account of how Joachim von Ribentropp, the Nazi German foreign affairs 'expert', had cultivated her as a supposed tool to swing British foreign policy into a pro-German direction and the activities of Charles Bedaux, the Franco-American business efficiency guru, who lent them his château in France for their wedding and organized their catastrophic tour of Nazi Germany. Bocca noted that Bedaux was facing treason charges in the US when he killed himself in 1943. He delved into the vexed question of the Duke of Windsor's finances and pointed out that he had ended up far wealthier than his brother, George VI. Bocca made one of the first public mentions of the 'dossier' of information on Mrs. Simpson available to Baldwin when he had to confront the scandal of her relationship with the then Prince of Wales. It is today usually referred to as 'the China dossier' as a source on her sexual proclivities, but the intelligence on which Baldwin was working may also have included her closeness to the Nazis.

On at least one point it worked against Bocca's interests – and perversely the Windsors' – to be writing an unauthorized book. Beaverbrook had put Bocca in touch with the distinguished lawyer Sir William Jowitt, who had given advice to the Duke of Windsor supporting his belief that the Duchess of Windsor had been illegally deprived of the status of Royal Highness. It would have been possible to slant Jowitt's testimony further in favour of the Windsors by disclosing that he had spoken to Alan Lascelles, George VI's private secretary and intimate adviser, which could have been made to suggest that the royal family was prepared to give serious consideration to the Duke of Windsor's claims. In the event, Jowitt learned that the Duke of Windsor was not behind Bocca's book and developed severe cold feet over his involvement in the project, demanding that the mention of his discussion with Lascelles be withdrawn.[6] The source would have been all too obvious.

When the Duke of Windsor got wind of Bocca's project he tried to get advance sight of the draft so that he would be able to censor it, presumably with lawyerly assistance. He failed and was confronted with a fait accompli when the book was published. Perhaps fortunately for Beaverbrook, the Duke never learned that *She Might Have Been Queen* was as much Beaverbrook's project as Bocca's and read nothing more into the fact that it was published by Express Books than, 'Old Max Beaverbrook certainly has reached an all time high in unpredictability by publishing that lousy Bocca book about the Duchess'.[7]

Unsurprisingly the relationship between Beaverbrook and Bocca soured. Beaverbrook was still able to keep him on a tight lead by dangling in front of him the prospect of another book project that might prove even more sensational than the Duchess of Windsor book.[8] Between the wars Beaverbrook had employed an Irish peer called Castlerosse as a gossip-writer whose wife was a top-flight courtesan. Her lovers included Randolph Churchill and, quite possibly, his father. Winston Churchill and Doris Castlerosse became very close during a difficult period in his marriage to Clementine. Bocca found that the Beaverbrook Cresta Run did not lead him to a glittering literary career. His biography of the Duchess of Windsor, *She Might Have Been Queen*, enjoyed only modest commercial success; the Castlerosse book never materialized and Bocca eventually switched to writing fiction including Nazi sadomasochistic erotic novels. Nor, despite its insider access, did the biography enter the canon of historians' sources on the Windsors and has practically vanished from view.

26

Garnished With Malice

Beaverbrook might not have told Bocca precisely what to write but on one point he did give him explicit instructions. As well as settling Beaverbrook's score with the Duchess of Windsor, Bocca was to be used as an unwitting pawn in one of Beaverbrook's top-level political manoeuvres. The opportunity had presented itself to Beaverbrook to use the Duke of Windsor and his doings as a lever to keep himself seated firmly at the top table of decision-making, or maybe just to make large-scale mischief. With Beaverbrook the two goals could often merge. With his humiliation at the hands of Sir John Simon in 1951 a fresh memory, Beaverbrook had good motive to reassert his credentials to top-level consideration as a major player in the abdication crisis. Moreover, his patron Churchill was once again installed at 10 Downing Street.

Bocca became a fringe player in the long-running and tangled affair of the Marburg documents. This was a cache of high-level German foreign office papers, evacuated to safety from Allied bombing and the Soviet advance towards Berlin in Marburg, a quiet town north of Frankfurt, and discovered by US Army units at the close of the Second World War. Churchill was still prime minister at this point before his defeat in the Labour landslide election victory of July 1945 and he recognized the extreme sensitivity of some of the material when the Americans alerted their British allies. It included communications between the foreign ministry in Berlin and the Nazi German embassies in Spain and Portugal during the period when the Duke and Duchess of Windsor had fled there from France as resistance to the German invasion collapsed in June 1940. Both sets of diplomats reported extensively on contacts between the Duke of Windsor and nationals of the two countries who were friendly to the German cause. They were feeding the appetite of Joachim von Ribbentrop, the Nazi foreign minister, who had tried assiduously to cultivate Edward from his time as the Nazis' roving international negotiator and then as ambassador to London between 1936 and 1938. He believed correctly that Edward was well disposed towards Germany and, more debatably, that he might swing British policy to a more favourable stance.

The abdication had come as a severe disappointment to von Ribbentrop but with a German invasion of Britain in the offing, he thought that the former king might once again feature in the Nazi programme. In von Ribbentrop's deluded view of the world, the Duke, once freed from the oppressive surveillance by the British secret service, would happily settle in Switzerland and for the modest sum of 50 million Swiss francs, publicly dissociate himself from the actions of his family.[1] The German embassies in Madrid and Lisbon assiduously harvested anything that the Duke said to various Spaniards and Portuguese friendly to the Nazi cause which might support von Ribbentrop's analysis. Foremost amongst these was the Portuguese banker Ricardo Espirito Santo who lent his house to the Duke during his time in Portugal. The diplomats' efforts were translated into a series of telegrams to Berlin relaying defeatist remarks by the Duke. Von Ribbentrop was blindly convinced that it would take little effort to swing the Duke into outright support for Germany and persuaded Hitler to invest time and effort in the project. One of Germany's most adroit intelligence/special operations officers, Walter Schellenberg, was sent to Portugal in case the opportunity arose to grab the Duke and put him into German hands. A few months before, Schellenberg had humiliated the British intelligence service by luring two of its officers to the Dutch-German border with a concocted tale of dissenting Wehrmacht generals and snatching them into captivity.

Churchill's immediate reaction to the news of the documents' discovery was to try to have them destroyed. He feared that the Soviets could exploit them to support propaganda that the British had never been wholeheartedly committed to fighting Nazism. However unfairly, they would embarrass the British royal family with proof of the aberrant behaviour of its black sheep. Unstated by Churchill but obvious was that they would give the world reasons for questioning his judgement in supporting the King's stance during the abdication crisis less than four years before the conversations they reported. As the triumphant leader of Britain's war effort against Nazism, he had little desire for the public to be reminded that he had put his political career on the line to support a man now shown to have been sympathetic to Germany before the war. Even had the Americans supported Churchill's instincts, it was too late;

the documents had been copied and knowledge of them had spread far enough for *Newsweek* magazine to leak their existence in November 1946. The position was further complicated by the agreement reached in June 1946 between the US and Britain to publish a collection of important German documents in Allied hands. The government of the newly created democratic Federal Republic of Germany was also seeking the return of the original documents. In July 1947 the British, by-then Labour, government and the royal household bowed to the inevitable and accepted that the documents would ultimately be published; the Duke of Windsor and Churchill would be given advance warning, but that was all.[2]

It was practically inevitable that the documents would appear publicly at some stage but Churchill was taking an unduly alarmist view of the danger, doubtless fed by his personal exposure. The documents were potentially embarrassing but far from conclusive when exposed to objective examination.

> The German reports are not clear-cut enough to make a good news story for the Press generally – although of course they could be cooked up and garnished with malice. Nor would the ordinary reader regard these despatches as really damaging to the Duke – after all, the authority for them is simply that of German diplomats who were trying to show their chiefs that they were exploring every avenue, hopefully but apparently without success.[3]

Moreover, all of the conversations relayed at second-hand were with Spaniards or Portuguese who could be regarded as German agents, with the exception of one with the Spanish foreign minister. This added an extra layer of reason to treat them with considerable caution.

There the matter rested until 1953 when the pending publication of the documents, expected in the following year, gave the matter topical urgency. At this point Bocca came on the scene and proceeded to stir things up. In April, he met a man called Boyd of the Foreign Office claiming to be researching articles for Beaverbrook's *Daily Express* and asking for information on the documents. The government was being confronted by the prospect that the documents might become public knowledge in Britain. According to the Foreign Office's notes on the conversation, Bocca said that Beaverbrook had told him of the existence of the Marburg documents but almost immediately regretted doing so. Once again, the government was fighting a rear-guard action and Beaverbrook rapidly offered to help the government in its predicament by using what he presented as his domination over Bocca to prevent anything being published.[4] This had probably been what he had hoped for when he unleashed Bocca in the first place. If Beaverbrook's goal had been to buy his way back onto the top table of decisions on the Duke of Windsor, he had succeeded.

At this point a discordant note entered the relationship between Bocca and Beaverbrook. The writer found himself providing cover for the press baron against any accusations that he might have been indiscreet in disclosing knowledge of the Marburg documents outside the charméd and discreet circle of the establishment at its top level. Bocca wrote a letter giving a quite different account of his conversation at the Foreign Office to the one that official had noted at the time.[5] He claimed that he had told Boyd that he knew of the documents from the *Newsweek* article, common gossip in Washington and, mysteriously, something written by Compton Mackenzie.* He did admit to having spoken to Beaverbrook, but that he 'gave me no information on the matter, and that blame must be attached only to me for introducing your name improperly into a conversation'. It would seem that at some point in the six-week gap between Bocca's visit to the Foreign Office and his letter, Beaverbrook had been criticized for his indiscretion about the Marburg documents and had persuaded his underling to exonerate him.

Behind the front of cooperatively offering to keep a muzzle firmly on Bocca, Beaverbrook used him to sniff out material far more damaging to the Duke of Windsor than the Marburg documents on their own. He despatched Bocca to Lisbon to speak to Espirito Santo, or as he translated with relish, the 'Holy Ghost'.[6] Bocca was astonished to be told that von Hoyingen-Hühne, the German ambassador to Lisbon, had suggested to the Duke of Windsor that he should return to Britain once it was conquered by the Germans as a *Friedenskönig* or 'peace king', with Lloyd George replicating Marshal Pétain's role in France

---

* The author has not been able to trace anything matching the description and Mackenzie is anyway an unlikely source for material damaging to his idol, the Duke of Windsor.

as collaborationist prime minister. Lloyd George, who visited Hitler in 1936, had given ample reason for suspicions in this direction. What truly amazed Bocca was that Espirito Santo then showed him a note in the Duke of Windsor's own hand hoping that he would stay in touch with von Hoyingen-Hühne. Unlike the second- or third-hand gossip conveyed by the German telegrams, this was proof that that the Duke knew he was talking (indirectly) to the Nazis. Even though Bocca saw instantly the libel considerations against publishing the Duke's note, he was aware of Beaverbrook's insatiable appetite for this kind of material and that he would be happy to spend heavily to obtain it. Bocca suspected that it had been Beaverbrook's intention all along to flush out something like the note. All he asked of Beaverbrook was that anything his mentor did to help him get hold of the note would not prejudice his right to publish the story.[7] Beaverbrook, though, was more interested in the top-level political manoeuvres over the Duke of Windsor's reputation and told the government that Espirito Santo had (unspecified) documents of interest.[8]

From then on, the note of tension between Bocca and his master deepened. Bocca was peeved when information on his Espirito Santo scoop became known and he saw it as an extension of the leaks that had begun with his conversation with the Foreign Office.[9] He seems to have been blind to the fact that Beaverbrook had considerations that went well beyond those of mere publisher. He was not to know that Churchill had finally briefed Beaverbrook fully on the Marburg documents in September; Churchill was still set against their publication, even if this was a quite unrealistic goal, and needed all the allies he could get. This might explain a strange tailpiece to Bocca's tale in which Ricardo Espirito Santo backed away from what he had passed on to Bocca. A few months after they had met in Portugal, Espirito Santo asked Bocca urgently to dine in Paris. In a state of obvious agitation, he told the writer that the note was a fake and not written by the Duke, and please would he not use it. Bocca was puzzled but admitted, 'As my long years with Beaverbrook taught me, the labyrinthine mental processes of the high and mighty are too much for the likes of little us.'[10] The best guess as to what had happened is that Beaverbrook had told Churchill of the note, perhaps when Churchill briefed him on the Marburg documents, and Churchill had reacted by telling Beaverbrook to make sure that it was discredited.

When Bocca's biography of the Duchess of Windsor was finally published in 1955, there was not a trace of his Espirito Santo scoop and the tale of German intentions towards the Duke was softened to the point of near invisibility. This is hardly surprising as the libel reader assigned to check the initial draft had found it vulnerable to attempts by the Duke and Duchess of Windsor to obtain an injunction preventing its publication.[11] The published version described the 'peace king' plan as fantastic. It claimed that the only communication between the Duke and the Germans had come from the German side in the form of a message that von Hoyingen-Hühne passed to the Duke via Espirito Santo about the 'prospects for him remaining inside the German circle of communications'.[12] Bocca's teaser that 'the full facts ... still lurk in private notes and in confidential files' primed readers for the publication of the Marburg documents but these would face the same objection that they had faced all along: that they reflected nothing more than German sources. The testimony from Espirito Santo showing that the Duke had been fully aware that Espirito Santo was a channel of communication to the Nazis remained completely secret. By the time the story made it into print in a book of memoir sketches of Beaverbrook, everyone directly involved including Bocca himself had died and it fell through a crack in history.

Both Bocca and Beaverbrook had been trying to operate in a market that was falling against them anyway: Bocca in his attempt to break into the literary big time; Beaverbrook to parlay his potential for mischief into political influence. Interest in the Duke and Duchess of Windsor had been waning since the publication of their memoirs. The publication of some other German documents served to test the water for revelations of Edward's dealings with the Nazis and showed demand for Nazi scandal was ebbing. The indiscretions revealed by the Marburg documents were by no means the Duke's first. Whilst he was serving on the British liaison mission to the French Army in 1940, he had spoken over-freely to someone who was in contact with Count Julius Zech-Burkersroda, the German ambassador to the Netherlands, then still neutral. The Duke had complained of the work he had to do and the personality of Chamberlain as well as talking about Allied war plans, on which his information was incorrect. As his colleagues in Spain and Portugal had done, Zech passed these up the chain of command to Joachim von Ribbentrop.

The telegrams from the Netherlands reporting these exchanges were published in the D Series of Documents on German Foreign Policy in November 1954; Churchill's fears and the lengthy planning for news management and advance damage limitation that different governments had felt they needed for years proved to be unnecessary. The head of the Foreign Office was surprised that not a single question about the Duke of Windsor was asked by any of the journalists at the press conference held for the publication.[13] The government line that the German diplomats' claims about the Duke were 'vague and unsubstantiated' set the tone for press coverage. As had been predicted long before, the fact that the Duke's supposed statements came almost exclusively from German sources set an impossibly high bar for them to be taken seriously. Zech's widow helpfully told British newspapers that she believed that her husband had never met the Duke. The Duke had been entirely unmoved and quite relaxed when he had been shown the documents in advance. No one challenged the Duke's statement that the allegations were without foundation. When the Marburg documents proper appeared, they received a similarly gentle reception.

The top level of politics was also moving on from Churchill's concerns. In 1955 he had been replaced as prime minister by Sir Anthony Eden who had already detected that the public was getting bored by the tales of the Duke when he was still Foreign Secretary.[14] Eden carried none of Churchill's baggage of friendship with the Duke and he had little use for Beaverbrook. As Foreign Secretary in 1936 he had direct experience of the then King's sympathy for Fascist Italy. More ominously for the Duke's reputation in the long term, it was clear that tittle tattle of his defeatist remarks during his exile were only the start and paled into insignificance against earlier material from the German foreign ministry archives that would find their way into the public gaze.[15] The next tranche of documents which would be published as Series C detailed diplomatic contacts with Edward as Prince of Wales and King and one at least was reckoned by the Cabinet Secretary to be 'much more damaging' to him. It was not specified which amongst the various wildly pro-Nazi comments that he made directly to German representatives was intended, but a strong candidate must be what he said to his distant cousin and ardent Nazi, Duke of Saxe-Coburg, at the funeral of George V. The minute of the conversation showed not only that the King made a distinction between Nazi and German interests, which favoured the former, but that he aimed to claw back political influence from the politicians. The judgement of the Series C documents as damning proof of Edward's true political inclinations was correct, but the relatively innocuous gossip from the post-abdication documents had inoculated public interest against stronger material. The tortured governmental discussions as to how to handle it make the post-abdication documents seem far more important than they really are and the vastly more telling pre-abdication documents are almost ignored.[16]

27

The Black Rat and the Jazz-Boy King

S tanley Baldwin was the master of the darkest of political black arts: making ugly things happen without appearing to do anything, committing crimes without leaving fingerprints so as to leave an image of reputable decency untarnished. The process relies on having people around you who understand your mind and anticipate your wishes, without compromising your reputation by asking permission. Often enough, they believe what they are doing is right, justified and efficacious. They are happy to follow their instincts in the certainty that they will never be exposed or punished. A true master of the art can avoid even the appearance of wanting something done, and leave his or her circle to do the deed in the genuine belief that their leader is too prissy or weak to do what is necessary. The more cutouts and intermediaries that can be inserted between the top level and the individuals who actually do the deed, the better. The fainter the trail, the better. Should the move fail, cause unexpected difficulties, or embarrassingly come to anyone's attention, the individuals at the bottom of the pyramid can be sacrificed to protect those more highly placed.

The most famous specimen of this process on Baldwin's watch was the dissemination of the Zinoviev Letter, a forgery that cast the Labour Party as a tool of the Soviets, days before the 1924 general election. In the abdication crisis Baldwin began by distancing himself from the MI5 operation against the King and the men who had organized it, 'S.B. showed signs of his half Highland ancestry by being very suspicious of him [Dugdale, his Parliamentary private secretary] and Horace Wilson, for they did much delving into the gangster side of this affair; the seamy side not politic for the P.M. to know about.'[1] But it was the affair of the Hardinge letter which shows Baldin's full addiction to conjuring up deniable actions. In the days after Mrs. Simpson's divorce hearing, the King was showing no signs of discretion or restraint and Baldwin was groping to find a way to make it unmistakeable to him that his behaviour was not acceptable, to deliver a 'real jolt'. The King had shown he was impervious to gentle advice so something brutal would be needed, but Baldwin wanted at all costs to avoid the appearance of trying to pressurize his sovereign. Here fate had dealt the prime minister a good hand. He was surrounded by men who were convinced that stern measures were needed against the King and were not afraid to take them. In turn there was someone to hand who was willing to fall in with the hard-liners' plans, thinking too that he was doing right without calculating the risks to his reputation.

The man who found himself cast in the role of assassin was Major Alec Hardinge, the King's private secretary. He was already in a difficult position. The King had accepted him for the job as a sop to his mother and the court. He simply wanted a one-way channel to the government; he had not the slightest interest in any advice from Hardinge, which left Hardinge as a powerless spectator whilst his royal master drove remorselessly towards the rocks of confrontation with the government. Hardinge knew that he had extremely limited leverage with the King and his attempts to warn him of the risks from the relationship with Mrs. Simpson had been tentative and ineffectual. Hardinge was painfully aware of the dangers and easy meat when the hard-liners around the prime minister and finally the prime minister himself set to work.[2] Geoffrey Dawson of *The Times* also put in his contribution. Hardinge knew, or thought he knew, that they all shared his fears and they did not hold him back. But the letter that he wrote to the King was his initiative. The most astute and ruthless of the hard-liners was Sir Horace Wilson, the prime minister's personal civil service adviser, and he committed this fact to the record in a secret briefing paper for any government that found itself having to justify what Baldwin had done:

I was present when Major Hardinge saw the Prime Minister. It was pointed out that Major Hardinge was accepting a considerable responsibility in communicating with the King on the lines proposed.[3]

Before sending it to the King, Hardinge showed his letter to Dawson and left Wilson with a copy, but it is unclear whether Baldwin himself read it. The letter reflects an alarmist picture of government thinking, fed to him by the hard-liners that went beyond anything that Baldwin had in mind.[4] To his credit Hardinge was not deterred, unaware that he was being set up not just as assassin, but fall guy as well. The King's furious reaction to the letter triggered the next stage in the crisis, with the King telling Baldwin that he was willing to leave the throne if he were not allowed to marry Mrs. Simpson. The hard-liners had over-egged the pudding. They had manipulated Hardinge into sending a far harsher letter than they could have admitted to themselves, but they had not reckoned on the King seeing through the screens of middlemen and understanding that the ultimate author of the letter was the prime minister. It went far beyond delivering the 'jolt' Baldwin wanted. It was intended as a warning but reads perilously close to an ultimatum.

Hardinge was an easy victim to set up as scapegoat. He was not a man who had the gift of popularity. His successor as private secretary acknowledged Hardinge's practical abilities in the job, but wrote of his 'complete inability to establish friendly, or even civil relations with the great majority of his fellow-men'.[5] Another courtier described him as '[a] tragic figure ... the Gods have withheld too much. A contempt for *servility* had barely left standing-room for *civility*; and what profiteth a man in his position to be irreproachable if he is even more unapproachable?'[6] The King's erstwhile backer and friend of Mrs. Simpson, the MP and socialite 'Chips' Channon, loathed him passionately and referred to him as 'the black rat'.[7] There were few in high circles who would speak up for him. He had also weakened his position by indiscreet criticism of Mrs. Simpson which had reached the King and government circles. In the confidential briefing paper that he prepared on the crisis, Sir Horace Wilson was not restrained by any sense of hypocrisy. He and his notional superior, Sir Warren Fisher, had led the hard-line camp and manipulated Hardinge towards delivering a brutal warning to the King, but in the paper he was depicted as practically a lone wolf and loose cannon. Hardinge's precipitate initiative is depicted as having spoiled a carefully thought-out plan to approach the King after his visit to South Wales had filled his head with appropriately kingly thoughts and thus amenable to a call to his sense of responsibility. Wilson's paper contains almost no personal criticism of individuals, but he made a large exception for Hardinge.

It seems doubtful whether the decision to appoint Major Hardinge to succeed Lord Wigram last summer was a wise one. Even if, had there been more time, Major Hardinge could have gained the confidence of the King (about which there must be considerable doubt) he certainly had not done so by the time the storm broke. His feelings seem to have led him to make remarks that were tactless to say the least of it and some of them were said to have been retailed to the King. And his letter of the 13th November – however well intentioned – may well have made the worst possible impression.[8]

In the immediate aftermath of the crisis Hardinge's role remained concealed. More to sustain an illusion of continuity than anything else, the new King kept him on as private secretary until well into the reign. Hardinge's relationship with George VI went from bad to worse and he eventually resigned in 1943 after a messy row with his subordinate (and successor) Tommy Lascelles. He kept his grace-and-favour apartment in St. James Palace but he had no serious job at court or elsewhere. He inherited his father's peerage in 1944.

The publication of the Duke of Windsor's memoir *A King's Story* in 1951 brought to public notice his letter during the abdication crisis which had not even been disclosed to the Cabinet. It quoted some of the letter. Whilst George VI and Queen Elizabeth, and the rest of the family kept their silence, the disclosure was not well received in the Hardinge household, 'he [the Duke of Windsor] apparently found it necessary, some years later, to exchange a highly coloured and, in my view, one-sided account of his Abdication, for a large cheque.' Just as the bitterness left by the crisis and its aftermath gnawed at the Duke, so it gnawed at the Hardinges that the crisis had placed Alec in an invidious position and that no one seemed to recognize that he had tried to make an honourable attempt to resolve the crisis. He was caught between the Duke of Windsor's depiction of him as the slavish tool of a remorseless government and the far better concealed, but equally poisonous, Whitehall view of him as a poor choice for his job and who had precipitated the crisis by writing his letter to the King.

Discreetly enough the Hardinge family joined in with a very gentle attempt to deliver insiders' criticism of the former king. His wife Helen's *The Path of Kings*, published in 1952, was ostensibly an overview of the British monarchy, but it contained enough references to her husband's time with Edward VIII to make its point. Edward was accused of ignorance of the constitution and ingratitude towards his staff, who had experienced 'suffering and heartbreak' because of his personal life. Instead, he had persisted in self-justification which others were unable to forgive. Mrs. Simpson was mutedly depicted as ambitious and selfish. The book barely caused a ripple, but was a warning that there was more in store.

The accession of Queen Elizabeth II in 1952 brought youth, new energy and optimism to the British monarchy but the shadow of the abdication crisis still hung, albeit barely mentioned. But one brief moment during the coronation ceremony warned the world that it was about to return with a vengeance when the new Queen's sister Princess Margaret brushed fluff off the sleeve of a royal equerry, Group Captain Peter Townsend, a much-decorated wartime fighter pilot. She and Townsend had been conducting a secret romance and Margaret now told her sister that she wanted to marry him. Townsend was divorced so this was exactly what their uncle had been forbidden to do less than ten years before. The nation's sense of morality had moved on, helped by the unsettled years of the war – Anthony Eden, a divorcé, was now Foreign Secretary and prime minister in waiting – but there was still a great risk of appearing to apply double standards. Townsend was also fifteen years older than Margaret and of solidly middle-class family rather than the aristocracy. A great scandal ensued, although the Queen finally relented on condition of her sister losing her position in the line of succession, in practice an even more severe form of morganatic marriage. The nation never had the opportunity to judge whether this would also have been an application of double standards as Margaret decided against marriage and the Queen's offer only became public many years later. This all provided excellent advance publicity for the Duchess's memoir *The Heart Has Its Reasons* which was being written at the time and would be published the following year. The Windsors were set to take another bite out of the financial cherry that had so outraged Lady Hardinge. With another iteration of the Windsors' version of the abdication story about to appear, Hardinge decided to take action and present his side of the story.

Hardinge wrote a letter to *The Times,* a well-established forum for airing such questions, which gave his version of the story. It also gave the full text of his fateful letter to the King, including the warning of the risk that a conflict between the King and government might result in a general election with the King's personal life as the principal issue. As the Duke of Windsor's memoir had insisted that he wanted to avoid splitting the country, this was something that he had suppressed. Hardinge even included for the sake of completeness the Pooterish postscript to his letter in which he informed his master that he was going off for the weekend shooting but could be reached through the local post office.

The contents of Hardinge's letter to *The Times* were sensational, but the way it was delivered fell squarely within the conventions of dignified discourse amongst the members of the British establishment; however, his next move opened the way for the dispute to degenerate into the kind of full-blown public slanging match conducted through barely masked intermediaries that is the stuff of today's royal media coverage. Hardinge struck up a relationship with Robert Sencourt, an established historical writer, albeit one who was far less prominent than Compton Mackenzie or Philip Guedalla had been in their days. He is chiefly known for an indiscreet memoir of T. S. Eliot, which breached the protective wall of confidentiality that the poet had erected around himself. Sencourt was invited to stay with the Hardinges and he was fully briefed on their version of the abdication crisis and their unflattering view of Edward. Sencourt also interviewed two of Baldwin's intimates: his parliamentary private secretary, Tommy Dugdale and his personal civil service adviser, Sir Horace Wilson, who could give a picture of the crisis from the heart of government that was unsparing of the King's behaviour and personality. Dugdale and Wilson hoped to restore Baldwin's reputation. Baldwin had been hugely praised for his handling of the abdication crisis and his speech to Parliament giving his narrative, but he knew politics too well to believe that this lustre would last. He had told one MP that the pattern of the General Strike in 1926 would repeat itself when his handling had been at first admired, but 'within six weeks all were damning him'.[9] Few criticized his handling of the abdication but any favourable view of his premiership as a whole was swamped by the uncontradicted savagery directed against his foreign policy, enthusiastically fostered by Churchill and Beaverbrook. Dugdale and Wilson were amongst the handful of people willing to try to rescue Baldwin's reputation by reminding the world of the difficulties that he overcame to prevent the abdication crisis doing more damage than it had to the nation. Everything was set for

Sencourt to publish a book that would in his words 'redress the balance' with a savage assault on the Duke and Duchess of Windsor.[10]

Sencourt overreached himself. He followed up Hardinge's suggestion that he contact Sir Walter Monckton, with whom he had a slight acquaintance at pre-First World War Oxford. This cut no ice with Monckton who had enjoyed a far higher place in the pecking order at university and a far, far higher one in the post-Second World War establishment, which rested to a great extent on his success in the near-impossible task of keeping Edward as close as possible to the straight-and-narrow path appropriate for a king and ex-king. Sencourt mentioned his contact with Dugdale and Wilson to Monckton but this proved no more of a validation. All it did was to establish that Sencourt was firmly in the Baldwin camp. Just as he had recognized with Mackenzie's project twenty years before and the Duke's own memoirs, Monckton saw that Sencourt's book could re-open old wounds and revive old conflicts.

The sample material that Sencourt sent Monckton for comment was enough for him to reply with a barely veiled threat of legal action as well denouncing the book as 'biased against them' (the Duke and Duchess) and riddled with innuendo and misunderstanding. He told the author that it was 'offensive in tone form and substance. That it is defamatory of both of them there can be no doubt'.[11] He flatly refused Sencourt's repeated requests to help him with documents or comments. He even refused to write a tribute to the Duke as counterweight to Sencourt's abuse as he judged that any kind of contribution would 'lend weight' to a work written from 'a hostile angle' which he was just as keen should never see the light of day as he had been with Mackenzie's biography.

Monckton appeared to have achieved his goal a few months later when Kimber, Sencourt's publisher, asked for his advice. Monckton showed him the letter that he had sent to Sencourt to alert him to the risks he was running.[12] The opinion of a well-placed lawyer that Sencourt's draft was potentially libellous was a clear warning to any publisher, especially with the fate of Geoffrey Dennis and Heinemann to alert him to the Duke's litigious instincts. Monckton had in fact been in constant touch with Philpotts, now the Duke of Windsor's solicitors, about possible libel action against Sencourt's book. Whether for fear of writ for libel or other reasons, Kimber vanished from the scene and there was a three-year hiatus before Sencourt's project resurfaced.

In the meanwhile, Hardinge himself had died in 1960 and Sencourt had to content himself with help from his widow and his son, to whom he sent a new draft of the book. The third Lord Hardinge was much more in sympathy with Monckton's approach. Even though he was a publisher himself, he declined to offer 'literary criticism to a writer as experienced as yourself' but did recommend that Sencourt remove any statement for which he could not quote a firm source.[13] As much of Sencourt's research had been done on a non-attributable basis, this would have shorn the book of much of its worthwhile content. Crucially, he asked Sencourt to tone down the author's 'emphasis on [Hardinge] as the prime source of your information'. The younger Hardinge had no desire to appear to be carrying the fight on to the next generation. When he alerted Monckton to what Sencourt was up to, Monckton reminded him of the danger of legal action.[14]

Monckton was pushing at an open door. Lord Hardinge wanted to defend his father's reputation as much as anyone, but saw that Sencourt's work was not an effective way of doing this. He rated Sencourt's second attempt as a great improvement on his first, but this is not necessarily saying much. He told Monckton bluntly that it was 'indifferent' and 'isn't really much good'.[15] The lapse of time had also blunted its edge. The memoirs of the Duke and Duchess were fading from memory. The publication of the German wartime documents which disclosed the Duke's indiscretions with German agents in Spain and Portugal was four years in the past and had, anyway, failed to excite much interest. Sencourt's disclosures that the surveillance operation on Mrs. Simpson and her flight to France had been inspired by her supposed closeness to the Nazis, above all the German ambassador Joachim von Ribbentrop, had little impact. Sencourt had found a new source in Lord Brownlow, Mrs. Simpson's companion on the flight to France, but he added little beyond inconsequential detail.

As Hardinge spotted, the book was badly flawed. It now barely features in the canon of sources for the abdication even though Sencourt had access to some of the crisis's best-informed insiders. They did feed him some pearls, such as the use of intelligence services to investigate Mrs. Simpson's links to the Nazis but these failed to make the impact they deserved. Long, irrelevant pronouncements on European foreign affairs are typical of its structural weaknesses. There is no subtlety in its criticism of Edward and his poor level of education or of Mrs. Simpson. Intriguingly, one of the book's notable features is the cultural assault on Edward, which might reflect the views of Hardinge or the wider court. The crisis is depicted as a struggle between American and British values.[16] Sencourt's criticism of Edward reflects a positively quaint, if not antique edition of a blast from the culture wars of the late 1950s. He denounces Edward for 'dancing in the new restless negroid style' and labelled him as the 'Jazz-boy prince'.[17] Sencourt's assault on the supposedly foreign influences on Edward echoes the denunciation of 'alien' values in the Archbishop of Canterbury's broadcast immediately after the abdication. The book mentions that Hardinge visited the Archbishop two days before the broadcast without hinting what they discussed, but an informed reader could easily have made the connection and picked up the implication that Lang was expressing the view of the royal court as well as his own.[18]

28

Palace Persecution

The Duke of Windsor's decision to exclude the events that followed his abdication and his family's part in the crisis from his memoirs extended a self-denying ordinance that he had applied to his collaboration with Guedalla. He was anxious to vent his growing fury with what he saw as his unfair treatment by the government, under the moralistic influence of the Archbishop of Canterbury, but he was willing to keep quiet about the more intimate side to the affair, which was even more painful to him. He held to the choice for the rest of his life, letting the unhappiness fester in private. He complained bitterly and openly that the title of Royal Highness was withheld from the Duchess but was otherwise discreet. Just as he was working on his memoirs, though, he was confronted by the danger that one of the most sensitive features of the world about which he was still being discreet would be held up to public gaze and the threat came from a quite unexpected quarter.

The abdication was the turning point in the strained and distant relationship between Mrs. Simpson and the Duchess of York, who became queen when her husband succeeded his brother as George VI. Although they had no direct contact after the abdication, a venomous personal feud developed between them. The Duchess of York had enjoyed a happy relationship with her glamorous brother-in-law until his relationship with Mrs. Simpson got under way, cutting Edward off from the rest of his family. Mrs. Simpson had never hidden her contempt for 'Cookie', as she called the then Duchess of York, whose plain tastes were the diametric opposite of her metropolitan chic. The Duke of York and his wife were perfectly happy with the relatively quiet family life that they could have and neither had relished the prospect of becoming king and queen. Both, though, followed their duty in accepting the accession which the new queen blamed on Mrs. Simpson.

There is little reason to doubt that she drove the ostracism of the Duchess of Windsor by the royal family. Her personal hurt magnified a belief that the Duchess of Windsor was simply not fit to be accepted into the family. This ostracism was the source of immense bitterness. The Duke of Windsor had naïvely imagined that the Duchess of Windsor would be welcomed into his family like any new bride, multiplied many times over by his deluded belief that she was a paragon of all virtues and that this would be obvious to anyone who met her. For the rest of his life, he would try obsessively to secure proper 'recognition' for his wife.

Withholding the title of Royal Highness from the Duchess had provided a specific cause for complaint and the Duke made his unhappiness plain, notably in his interview with Adela Rogers St. Johns in Nassau in 1940, but the more venomous substance to the dispute was masked. Both sides were happy to keep this poison out of the public gaze until a wholly unexpected development dragged it partially into the daylight. The affair of the memoirs written by Marion 'Crawfie' Crawford, the former governess to the 'little princesses', the future Queen Elizabeth II and Princess Margaret, is chiefly remembered as the first major breach in the *omertà* surrounding the royal household but it also threatened to expose the battle between Queen Elizabeth and the Duchess of Windsor to public scrutiny. Under the harmful influence of her new husband and a couple of unscrupulous American journalists, Mr. and Mrs. Gould, Crawford had accepted a lucrative proposal to write an account of her time in the royal household. Queen Elizabeth II was given advance sight of the draft and demanded a number of changes, although the American journalists later put in changes of their own without anyone's agreement. Most of the content was entirely bland and calculated to present American readers with an attractive portrait of the royal household; it was the principle of breach of confidence that rankled with the Queen and led to Crawford being ostracized. There seems to have been a genuine misunderstanding as to whether the articles and book would appear over Crawford's signature. Almost the only exception to the unchallenging nature of the narrative was a candid and unflattering picture of Mrs. Simpson's irruption onto the royal scene, notably a visit that she and the King paid on the Duke and Duchess of York at their home Royal Lodge, which is still widely quoted as evidence of the difficulties that she created for the family. It is unclear whether this was consciously left uncensored by the Queen or was part of the Goulds' additions.

The picture Crawford painted of Mrs. Simpson was critical from the start:

> She was a smart, attractive woman, already middle-aged but with that immediate friendliness American women have.* She appeared entirely at her ease; if anything, rather too much so ... She had a distinctly proprietary way of speaking to the new King ... I have never admired the Duke and Duchess [of York] more than on that afternoon. With quiet and charming dignity, they made the best of this awkward occasion and gave no sign of their feelings. But the atmosphere was not a comfortable one ... No one alluded to that visit when we met again later that evening ... nothing whatever was said, though I suppose most of us had the subject in our minds. Maybe the general hope was still that, if nothing was said, the whole business would blow over.[1]

Crawford's book fell just short of stating explicitly that the Queen Mother, as she had become, loathed her future sister-in-law, but here was a well-informed intimate source on the royal household apparently reporting her manifestly unhappy 'feelings'. It was perilously close to a declaration of war.

Fortunately, the Duke of Windsor's ever-vigilant legal team saw no more than a standard question of defamation and reacted accordingly and prepared to fire off letters. Extracts had been serialized in a British magazine so they could make full use of a law that was heavily slanted in favour of the subject of unfavourable comment. As well as the unflattering view of Mrs. Simpson in Queen Elizabeth's eyes as relayed by Crawford, they objected to the almost unarguable statement that 'Uncle David had fallen in love with someone England could not accept as Queen because she had been married before and her husband [sic] was still living' and (more debatably) to 'Britain would have none of her'.[2] The lawyers contemplated demanding a full and humiliating surrender with the issue of an abject apology and the withdrawal of the magazines from circulation. Only afterwards did the Duchess's lawyers learn that Queen Elizabeth had extensively censored Crawford's drafts or that the

---

* This would have been a decidedly double-edged comment in 1950s Britain.

Goulds had added material of their own.[3] Alan Lascelles, the lawyer's liaison with the royal household, gave further reason to stop short of an all-out assault on Crawford's writing. Lascelles no more approved of the publication than his royal masters, but took a shrewdly pragmatic approach to the problem:

> I have always felt that any outward interference would be a grave error of policy, though I believe it w/d. be legally possible to restrain publication of certain letters. But anything wh. could be represented − as it undoubtedly wd. be in certain newspapers − as "Palace persecution" wd. be unwise.[4]

The Duchess's lawyers had to swallow the appearance of the offending comment in what they disdainfully referred to as an 'ephemeral' publication but did succeed in keeping it out of the book edition in the UK.

29

Transference of Responsibility

I n 1954 the Duchess of Windsor decided to complement her husband's efforts with memoirs of her own. The process proved to be similarly complicated and packed with event, albeit less agonizing than the writing of *A King's Story*.

Just as had happened with Philip Guedalla, the Duke of Windsor's legal team featured in the choice of the Duchess's ghostwriter. They urged her successfully to appoint Charlie Murphy, who had undergone a tortuous two years writing *A King's Story* and discovering at first hand the couple's glittering but empty lifestyle and the Duke's unfocused approach to work. After *A King's Story*, Murphy had had a brief stint as a US Air Force staff officer before returning to *Fortune* magazine. At least to begin with, he feared the Duchess would be no better than her husband, but the terms of her contracts with her publishers provided the funds to make this a lucrative assignment. One of the magazines lined up to publish the story was *McCall's*, still edited by her tame journalist from the days of the abdication crisis, Otis Wiese. The Duchess was to receive a minimum of $700,000. Murphy took on the job subject to three conditions: that the Duchess's divorce from her second husband would be presented straightforwardly, that the Duke's flirtations with the Nazis would not be suppressed and finally, in what was manifestly the work of Sir Walter Monckton and George Allen, the Duke's solicitor, that the book would not attack the royal family. Work began in November 1954.

The Duchess began the project as she meant to go on: putting the responsibility for potentially embarrassing choices on other people's shoulders. She wanted her ex-husband's help to write the book and wrote to him that it was Allen who had forced her into the 'uncomfortable position' of writing her memoirs, so that 'a bit of truth should be forced to the top'.[1] Given the time and energy that the Duke's legal advisers had invested in trying to stop him writing his memoirs, this is patently ludicrous. Similarly, the notion that she was putting the book out against her better inclinations is preposterous. It beggars belief that Allen could have wanted a follow-up to *A King's Story*, but the fact that she should have claimed his approval of the project opens an intriguing possibility. For the rest of his life Ernest Simpson showed iron discretion over his second marriage and divorce, which the Duchess of Windsor was hoping to weaken. Claiming that Allen was sponsoring the book as a means of breaking this wall of silence suggests that the Duchess was aware that Allen was playing some part in keeping Ernest Simpson quiet; that it was more than gentlemanly reticence on Ernest's part that explained his silence. Ernest did eventually provide some help on the book, but he disapproved of his ex-wife's attempt at self-justification, 'he had been accused of every possible thing, but the truth lay at the bottom of a well, and so far as he was concerned, anyone who wished to dig for it was welcome to do so.'[2]

The Duchess's work habits proved to be far less challenging for the ghostwriter than her husband's. She talked easily and freely. By the middle of 1955 two-thirds of the book was written and Murphy had high hopes of meeting the deadline of October, but the optimism was not to last. The Duchess and Murphy began to fall out over her growing desire for the book to present her as an ever-youthful leader of international society. Murphy also made a poor job of concealing his scepticism at her 'more improbable "recollections"'.[3] More dangerously, she began to backslide on the promise given to Murphy when he agreed to the work by proposing that the book be used to present her own unflattering picture of the royal family. This would have been a declaration of all-out war between the Windsors (1917 vintage*) and the Windsors (1936 vintage). She sacked Murphy but his replacement, another American journalist, Cleveland Amory, quickly spotted that he had been hired to whitewash the Duchess and he too was sacked after five months' work. He responded with a number of hostile newspaper interviews, describing the 'psychic wounds' from his 'battle of wills' with the Duchess, who had tried 'to impose worrisome conditions of servitude upon him'.[4] He had been supposed to promote her claim to high social status and the fiction that the couple were now 'happy and busy people'. He also bridled at

---

* King George V had changed the name of both the family and the dynasty from Saxe-Coburg-Gotha in response to anti-German sentiment.

being asked to attack the royal family's 'mean' treatment of her. Amory presented himself as dedicated to facts and accused the Duchess of wanting a 'soap opera'. He insisted that reality would prevail, 'The facts of life are very stubborn things ... You can't make the Duchess of Windsor into Rebecca of Sunnybrook Farm.'*[5]

The publishers insisted that Murphy be brought back and it was the Duke who was given the humiliating task of calling Murphy with the summons. By dint of working at high pressure with minimal reworking, the manuscript was completed on time and the memoirs appeared as *The Heart Has Its Reasons* in 1956. It proved to be as great a publishing success as her husband's. The Duchess was allowed to indulge in a modest amount of hostility towards the royal family, but it was suitably muted. In her account of her visit to the Yorks at Royal Lodge with the King, which had featured prominently in Crawfie's depiction of the tension between the couple, she went no further than coyly noting that whilst the King had convinced the Duke of York of the merits of an American station wagon (or estate car in British parlance), 'the Duchess was not sold on David's other American interest'.[6]

The Duchess was more direct in describing her pariah status following the abdication. Bluntly and probably accurately, she wrote that she did not exist as far as the royal family was concerned.[7] She repeated the Duke's analogy that the family had lifted the 'drawbridge' against them.[8] She also complained of the decision to allow the Duke to continue using the style 'His Royal Highness' but that she was not to be permitted. She practically blamed this on 'strong pressure' on George VI, implicitly from his wife, and called it 'humiliating' and a 'gratuitous thrust' that hurt the Duke more than anything else in the aftermath of the abdication and was a standing bar to any reconciliation for him.[9] Her memoir also questioned whether it was even legal, quoting the opinion of Sir William Jowitt, the eminent lawyer who had been consulted by the Duke. Fortunately, *The Heart Has Its Reasons* did not open a campaign to reverse the decision or, more broadly, to obtain for the Duchess the 'recognition' that the Duke claimed was her right. The Duchess of Windsor even slipped in the tale of how the Duke's mother, Queen Mary, responded to a message that she sent through an intermediary, expressing sadness at having caused

---

* A character from children's fiction, a byword for sentimentalism.

the estrangement from her son with a faint but gentle acknowledgement of her existence. The book cannot have improved relations but its impact on the royal family was muted. Even Michael Thornton's *Royal Feud*, which was written from the royal family's standpoint and with their gentle assistance, mentioned only that Queen Elizabeth II had disliked a double-edged reference to her mother.[10]

The Heart Has Its Reasons followed a consistent pattern of transferring responsibility for problematic or unpleasant decisions from the Duchess's own shoulders. This does little for the book's credibility, but it provides a handy guide to things about which she was sensitive. She presented the HRH title question as one of indifference to her, albeit deeply wounding to the Duke. With the benefit of three years in which to observe her in action, the ghostwriter Murphy thought she was not 'altogether candid' on the point and assessed that, 'More likely, it meant everything [to her]'.[11] On the crucial question of who had been the driving force behind her marriage to Edward, she admitted to no more than that the idea of marriage had been only 'a pleasant daydream' and ascribed all the practical steps to the King. She stopped short of admitting that her divorce action was at the King's behest, but blamed it on Ernest's affair with another woman. She contradicted her husband's version of her flight to France when the press silence broke given in *A King's Story*. In *The Heart Has Its Reasons* she goes because the King judged that she was no longer safe, whilst the Duke puts it down to her initiative. One draft of *A King's Story* stated that she fled because she was terrified of mob violence against her and wanted to get away from oppressive newspaper publicity.[12] The Duchess's unwillingness to take responsibility extended to the relatively trivial: Edward's bursting into a room at St. James's Palace to observe his own proclamation as King – scandalous in the arbitrary and bizarre traditions of British royalty – is laid at his door. The decision to invite her friends, the Rogers, for the fateful stay at Balmoral is recounted in a guiltily passive voice.

The book attempts to mislead the reader on the damning point of her connection to the Nazis for which she had been severely criticized and on which she still felt vulnerable. She repeats the fiction that the Duke merely wanted to observe Nazi work on housing developments when the couple went to Germany in 1937 and not as an attempt to re-establish himself as a significant world figure. She makes much of the fact that the first part of the journey was under the auspices of a relatively junior (and deeply unimpressive) Nazi leader, Robert Ley. In her detailed account of the visit, she presents the Duke's meeting with Hitler at his mountain retreat, the Berghof, as something that was suddenly sprung on the couple at the last minute.[13] In reality the Duke had first approached the Führer directly about the project, emphasizing how pleased he would be if he could meet Hitler in person for a discussion.[14] Hitler had superintended the arrangements throughout.

30

A Forlorn Thermos of Tea

As the 1950s drew on the Duke of Windsor had to cope with the threat of alternative and authoritative narratives of the abdication appearing from a dangerous quarter that might undermine his own or his wife's accounts. It has become an established practice when a British monarch dies for an official biography to be commissioned by his or her successor, whose author enjoys full access to royal (but not necessarily government) archives. These books respect the conventions that surround the royal family of tact, discretion and the avoidance of controversy, but cannot entirely ignore difficult episodes in the lives of their subjects. To a greater or lesser extent, the reign of King Edward VIII and his abdication would feature. The combination of such high-level access combined with the imperative to produce a definitive record means that it is practically impossible to dismiss them as motivated by base motives or marred by slipshod work.

The Duke might have permitted himself a sigh of relief when the official biography of his father, George V, was finally published in 1952. The disruption of the war years and their aftermath had delayed the work an unusually long time after the subject's death. The author, Sir Harold Nicolson, had known the Duke well as Prince of Wales and had observed the abdication closely. The long gap between George V's death and Nicolson's biography might have softened the need for discretion over the King's increasingly strained relationship with his heir. In the event, this was skated over completely and no mention was made of George V's forebodings for what would happen when his son succeeded him. The Duke of Windsor can have entertained no such hopes that the official biography of his brother, George VI, would apply the same level of blanket silence on his own reign and the circumstances in which it ended. Here the timing fell back into a more usual pattern and John Wheeler-Bennett was commissioned to write the biography in 1952. Wheeler-Bennett had made his reputation as an expert on Germany and by coincidence had headed the British team working on the German documents that included the Marburg papers.

Wheeler-Bennett inevitably consulted the Duke about his brother, who shared with him tales of how the boys had teased their pompous, and self-righteous tutor, Mr. Hansell, among other boyhood memories.[1] Wheeler-Bennett discreetly left these out of the biography in favour of excerpts from Hansell's reports to their father. The contact does not appear to have been very fruitful; neither the Duke nor his papers are acknowledged as a source. Wheeler-Bennett found himself having to fend off the Duke and Duchess's importunate desire to talk about the 'time-worn grievances of the abdication', which would have meant being exposed to a potentially unwelcome narrative.[2] Wheeler-Bennett steered the conversation firmly onto safer ground. He does not seem to have liked the Duke and referred to a 'flurry of sentimentality' when he died.[3]

As Wheeler-Bennett set down to write, the Duke began by asking him directly for advance sight of the passages that concerned him with the exaggerated claim that 'you are actually writing part of the official history of a living former Sovereign'.[4] When Wheeler-Bennett referred the question to Queen Elizabeth II as the sovereign who had commissioned his work, she claimed the final say over what should be shown to any other member of the family. This threw the Duke into a paroxysm of fury which predictably enough involved an imaginary conspiracy against him by a disloyal former courtier:

> Obviously that evil snake Lascelles and others have been working on Wheeler-Bennett to set my brother on a pedestal and to present me in as bad a light as possible ... I am incensed over this latest display of rudeness towards me from the Palace, and am determined that, unless my niece has the common courtesy to give me an opportunity of reading all references to myself in Wheeler Bennett's official biography of my late brother, then no mention of me whatsoever shall appear therein.[5]

The Duke had come see "Tommy" Lascelles as an implacable enemy at court. They had known each other since the early 1920s when Lascelles had been his private secretary, but he had become disillusioned with the then-Prince of Wales's personality and resigned in 1929. He returned to royal service as assistant private secretary to George V and his two successors, although he barely features in accounts of the reign of Edward VIII. He had a happy and successful relationship with George VI, becoming his private secretary in 1943 and went on to be a close advisor to Elizabeth II. He took a particular interest in the official biographies of royal family members. Lascelles was the epitome of court conservatism.

The Duke of Windsor was eventually granted sight of a proof copy of the book but found no more than two minor points on which he could ask for changes.[6] Wheeler-Bennett's biography is broadly neutral towards the record of the Duke of Windsor and makes no open criticism, although much was written in light code. The abdication is simply referred to as the 'tragic climax' of his reign and Wheeler-Bennett described the prime minister's shock and dismay at the news that Edward was willing to go and, without drawing attention to the contrast, observed that the King himself suffered no such qualms. The picture of the then Duke of York is favourable, beginning with his unhappiness at the unilateral measures that Edward as king took to reduce the costs of running Balmoral. This carried an implicit statement that the relationship between the two brothers had deteriorated from earlier in the reign when the King had commissioned the then Duke of York to investigate the running costs of Sandringham.[7] Wheeler-Bennett described the Duke of York as having been left feeling 'shut off from his brother, neglected, ignored, unwanted', but willing to follow his duty and take over from his brother with deep reluctance.

Wheeler-Bennett gave the Duke of Windsor credit for his stance over the abdication and cited the 'dignity and willingness with which King Edward VIII accepted the constitutional position' as a factor in making the outcome of the abdication as smooth as possible. However, Wheeler-Bennett did make the first unambiguous mention on the royal family's part in the key specific cause of the friction between them and the Duke. He reported that the Duke had been 'bitterly incensed' that the Duchess was refused the style Royal Highness by the Letters Patent* of 28 May 1937 and 'had not hesitated to make his views known with some vehemence'.[8] Wheeler-Bennett's biography was respectfully received, but many reviewers found the deferential tone grating. Possibly to the Duke's

---

* And thus George VI's own act.

relief there was practically no mention of how it treated the preceding reign or how it ended.

The Duke of Windsor was placed at double jeopardy of appearing in an unfavourable light from a similar quarter when his niece decided to commission an official biography of his mother Queen Mary after she died in 1953. Queen Victoria had commissioned the first official biography of a royal spouse with the official life of Prince Albert and the practice has more recently been extended with an official life of Queen Elizabeth, the Queen Mother. Queen Mary's unhappiness at her son's affair with Mrs. Simpson and obvious misery at his abdication could have easily been presented as severe criticism of the Duke.

Two years after his unhappy dealings over Wheeler-Bennett's biography of his brother, the Duke came into contact with his mother's official biographer. He was to have a quite different and far more happy experience. The writer chosen to do the work was James Pope-Hennessy, a young but recognized writer whose life of the Liberal statesman Lord Crewe had caught the Palace's eye. Pope-Hennessy came with impeccable establishment credentials. His father was a distinguished public servant and he had been educated at the prestigious Catholic public school Downside and Oxford. Professionally, he was personable, discreet and charming; his work was thorough, perfectly structured and well written. 'Tommy' Lascelles had a hand in choosing him and provided invaluable support and advice throughout the Queen Mary biography project. He thoroughly approved the result and had given it a healthy boost as an authoritative source with a piece of glowing advance publicity.[9] Pope-Hennessy was witty and perceptive. His private life presented a rather different picture. He had a penchant for rough trade sexual encounters and a growing fondness for drink; the former led to his miserable death in 1974.

Pope-Hennessy was invited to stay with the Windsors in November 1958 and he went to Le Moulin de la Tuilerie, their home in the country near Paris, only the second house that the Duke ever owned. He was not blind to their faults but he was hugely taken with them and their exotic lifestyle, 'they are like people after a cataclysm or a revolution, valiantly making the best of infinite luxury. I am delighted by them.'[10] He thought the Duke was intellectually superior to other royals and detected the void left in his life by twenty years without a serious occupation. Unlike

Wheeler-Bennett he was willing to engage with the Windsors on the subject of the abdication and its aftermath. He was taken aback at the Duchess's icy contempt for the Queen Mother, but did not let that spoil the relationship.

The warm feelings were reciprocated and on the Windsors' side and these were not limited to purely social considerations. They glimpsed the prospect of bringing into their camp a writer who carried the validation of being an official royal biographer. If Pope-Hennessy could be persuaded to put his pen at the Windsors' disposal this would give them a far more powerful channel than Mackenzie or Guedalla in their long battle to present themselves as members of the royal family in the full sense as well as putting over their own version of the story. Wisely they opened with a relatively uncontroversial writing project, but unwisely the Duchess attempted an all-out frontal assault with a phone call at midnight.[11] The project would be both 'dignified' (one of her favourite words of approbation) and 'financially rewarding'. As well as trying to persuade Pope-Hennessy to fly over the following day to discuss the matter, she subjected him to a twenty-minute harangue of flattery from an American lawyer. It also appeared that Beaverbrook's Express group would be involved, which was no recommendation to Pope-Hennessy. A less raucous phone call from the Duke the following morning, in which he made clear that Pope-Hennessy's name would not be used, overcame the resistance his wife had instilled in Pope-Hennessy and he agreed to take the idea further. He would be ghostwriting articles for the Duke, setting out his influence on men's fashions since the 1920s.

Pope-Hennessy did not demur when it emerged that Beaverbrook's organization would indeed be the publisher, but he took fright when he went to discuss details with Beaverbrook's nephew. He detected both a strong advertising aspect and a political agenda in which the Duke would denounce ill-informed 'Socialist' police uniforms. Pleading hostility towards Beaverbrook newspapers, Pope-Hennessy withdrew. He also declined another project which appears to have come to him along the same lines. The American film director Jack Le Vien had pioneered the docudrama format with *The Valiant Years*, lauding Britain's war effort, which had helped him become friends with Winston Churchill. He moved on to a far more sensitive project, a documentary about the Windsors. Pope-Hennessy was to have been historical adviser, which would have given the programme considerable, cachet but he declined.

Le Vien's *A King's Story* was not especially controversial although the nod towards the Duke's memoir is clear and the programme had footage of the Duke reading out his abdication speech – a prospect that had appalled the Palace when it was first mooted.[12]

Pope-Hennessy did not join the ranks of the Windsor literary army as fully paid-up soldier, but they could still be grateful of his support. When his biography of Queen Mary appeared, he opened his chapter on the abdication by referring readers firstly to the couple's memoirs. He contrasted their versions which he felt set out motives and the 'emotional climate', with George VI's 'precise and careful chronicle' that had appeared in Wheeler-Bennett's despised official biography.[13] Pope-Hennessy's book focused on the anguish that Queen Mary suffered but he passed no judgement on the actions that caused it. On one point he swung fully behind the Duke's hostile analysis of the way his family had behaved over the abdication. When they were talking at the Moulin, the Duke had shown 'disgust' to Pope-Hennessy when he told him that Queen Mary had written trying to dissuade him from broadcasting after the abdication.[14] When Pope-Hennessy retold the episode in his biography, it became an illustration of how unsupportive she had been to her son by trying to prevent something to which he 'attached the highest importance ... his first opportunity to ... speak candidly to the nation and explain personally and publicly the reasons for his action'.[15] By the discreet rules of official royal biography, Pope-Hennessy went a long way to endorse the Duke's sentiments.

Pope-Hennessy had mixed feelings about becoming immersed in the Royal world – 'the tiniest smut of royalty on one's name ruins life, don't it?' – but delivered a spectacular blow in the fight over the Duke's reputation in 1964 as he approached his seventieth birthday.[16] By then Pope-Hennessy was clearly marked as a royal insider. He had been made a Commander of the Royal Victorian Order (CVO), one step down from a knighthood, which is awarded for personal service to the monarch, for writing *Queen Mary*. Headlined 'James Pope-Hennessy Suggests a 70th Birthday Present for the Duke of Windsor', an article in *The Sunday Times* oozed with praise for the Duke of Windsor and his achievements as 'Ambassador of Empire' during his world tours, which Pope-Hennessy believed might overshadow the abdication in future history. Pope-Hennessy dismissed Queen Mary's feeling that giving up

Mrs. Simpson would have been a lesser sacrifice than that made by so many of the Duke's countrymen in the First World War as 'feminine irrelevance'. He argued that as a birthday present the Duke should be 'welcomed back into this country, granted a grace and favour residence and asked to play a part in British public life'.[17] With somewhat dubious logic he claimed that as the Duchess's two former husbands had died, she need no longer be classed as a divorcee. The article appalled his patron in the royal household, Lascelles. He warned Pope-Hennessy that he was being accused of being 'a stooge of the Windsors' and of trying to dictate the Queen's social programme to her.[18]

Quite unintentionally Pope-Hennessy did an immense service to future historians and defenders of the Duchess's reputation in one of the other interviews he conducted for his Queen Mary biography. It was almost a pure exercise in completeness that made him speak to the current head of the trivial royal house Württemberg, from which Queen Mary was descended, and his brother.[19] The conversations provided as good as no hard information on Queen Mary but gave an unequalled insight into the tastes and interests of the brother, a Benedictine monk under the name Dom Odo, formerly Prince Carl Alexander of Württemberg. He chatted happily to Pope-Hennessy about the supposed sexual peculiarities of every German and Austrian royal family, including a princess who had a bestial relationship with a goat and a prince who had an incestuous relationship with his daughter. Afterwards Pope-Hennessy bemoaned the fact that he had not been able to remember more of this stuff. Dom Odo claimed that the Duke of Windsor had demanded that he be made Commander-in-Chief of the British armies in France and that the Duchess become 'the First Princess of Great Britain'. This all gives a telling guide to the filthy-mindedness and general reliability as a witness of Dom Odo, who was the sole source for the story that Mrs. Simpson slept seventeen times with Joachim von Ribbentrop, who then sent her bunches containing the same number of carnations as mementoes. Dom Odo thought that Mrs. Simpson had been 'the only woman who had been able to satisfactorily gratify the Duke's sexual desires'. The Duke of Windsor had reduced himself to the gutter (*s'encanailler*). The fantasy about Ribbentrop was recorded by an FBI interrogator which has lent it a spurious air of authenticity and it is still repeated as though it might have a grain of truth. Like the 'China dossier' story it is too spicy not to be given an outing, *se non è vero, è ben trovato* (even if it's not true, it's a good story).

Pope-Hennessy's call to rehabilitate the Duke was disregarded and nothing came of a rumoured project for him to write a full biography of the Duke. The Windsors had to drop their sights in their search for their next literary champion. The ultimate successor to Compton Mackenzie and Philip Guedalla was Patrick Balfour, Lord Kinross, a socially distinguished, well-established travel writer and something of an authority on modern Turkey, with a well-regarded biography of Kemal Atatürk under his belt, but no one would have described him as a first-rank figure in the world of books or particularly qualified to comment on the royal family. By the late 1950s he was associated with the humorous magazine *Punch* under the editorship of his friend Malcom Muggeridge. Nor was the project on which he worked with the Windsors at the cutting edge of publishing. *The Windsor Years* was a workaday coffee-table book filled with brief text around its grainy and dull photographs. It was in marked contrast to the sharp and glossy illustrations of his *Life* magazine articles. Muggeridge describes the Duke and his last ghostwriter 'sharing a forlorn Thermos of tea' on the steps of Fort Belvedere, once his beloved Eden, now in sore need of restoration after lying empty for almost twenty years.[20] The book's text was little more than an abbreviated rehash of *A King's Story* and in a notable piece of inattention, the Duke allowed it to repeat his version of the story of Mrs. Simpson's flight to France which contradicted hers in *The Heart Has Its Reasons* by saying that the initiative had come from her. It was not a great publishing success.

31

The End of Discretion

Wen William Randolph Hearst was confronting his failure to put Wallis Simpson on the throne of Britain, he delivered what might be the definitive verdict on the abdication crisis in the media together with a very accurate prophesy, "'The Woman I Love" is news now and of course she always will, even as a has-been, and so will he. But over the years, the American Queen would have been bigger.'[1] His focus on the Duchess, and not on her husband, as the object of future media attention was perceptive and it was to prove doubly so following the Duke's death from throat cancer in 1972.

Beaverbrook had died in 1964 so the heart finally went out of the long campaign that he and the Duke had fought to persuade the world that the Duke had been forced off the throne in a ruthless plot by a conservative establishment. Up to a point the Duke of Windsor and Beaverbrook had succeeded by putting before the world stridently and emphatically their belief that two institutions of the conservative British establishment, the Church of England under Archbishop Cosmo Gordon Lang and *The Times* newspaper under its editor Geoffrey Dawson, had been major forces in this conspiracy. It is now firmly embedded in the national consciousness that they were major players in the crisis. The Duke and Beaverbrook did far less well in pinning blame on their political opponent, the prime minister Stanley Baldwin. His deft handling of the crisis combined with his politician's ability to keep his fingerprints off anything incriminating made him a far more difficult target.

The crisis had played out in the arid world of the corridors of power between politicians, bureaucrats and lawyers but now the human interest could take over. The way was clear for the human, family aspect to take first place in people's attention. This fell into two parts. First came the fascinating mystery of how a woman could be so attractive that a king would give up his throne for her. Beside this the alternative question of how a king could be so misguided and irresponsible as to threaten his country with a huge crisis and leave his monarchy gravely weakened because he could see no option other than marrying the woman he loved seems dull and judgemental.

Secondly came the saga of how the Duchess had been ostracized by the royal family. Part of this had been on public show since their marriage. The Duke had never concealed his fury that his wife was not accepted as a Royal Highness and he lobbied long and hard in private to reverse the decision. Occasionally it bubbled to the surface as in his 1940 Nassau interviews but the Royal Highness dispute was noticeably absent from his memoir *A King's Story*, although his wife was less restrained in hers, *A Heart Has Its Reasons*. Less visible though, was the personal hostility between the Duchess and her sister-in-law Queen Elizabeth.

It would never have been possible to keep the Duke and Duchess's conflict with his family after the abdication entirely out of the public gaze. It is something of a miracle that the wall of discretion around it remained intact for so long. The basic facts of the ostracism of the Windsors by the royal family and the Windsors' resentment at this were plain to see, but the story was one-sided, mostly presented from their standpoint.

The first major chink to be opened in the wall came in 1967 when Alec Hardinge's widow Helen published a memoir of him, *Loyal to Three Kings*. Hardinge had become a whipping-boy for the Duke and a scapegoat for the government side of the crisis, and had been side-lined by the royal court so his family had an axe to grind with everyone. After Hardinge's death the need for utter discretion had softened and Lady Hardinge set out far more directly what had only been faintly hinted at in her earlier book: how the powers that be had manipulated her husband in the run-up to writing the letter to the King which took the crisis into its final stage. She also gave an insider's picture of the growing estrangement between Edward and the rest of his family.

Unlike the press's wall of silence that had surrounded Edward's affair with Mrs. Simpson, the screen that hid the hatred between the royal family and the Windsors was intentionally demolished. The wrecking ball was swung by the royal family in its first active move in the whole saga. Queen Elizabeth, the Queen Mother, authorized her entourage to talk freely to a friendly journalist, Michael Thornton.[2] The result was the best-selling *Royal Feud* which was published in 1985 and laid bare the royal family's side of the poisoned relationship with the Windsors.

The acknowledgements section was entirely frank that the project had had royal assistance. As its title made plain, the book was all about the enmity between the Duchess of Windsor and the Queen Mother. It gave a frank account of how the feud had begun properly when Mrs. Simspon was invited to Balmoral in September 1936, including an unattributed account of the infamous dinner at Balmoral Castle when the Duchess of York, as she then was, snubbed Mrs. Simpson's presumptuous attempt to position herself as the hostess. Thornton described the Duchess of York's resentment at Edward lumbering her husband with the task of opening the new Aberdeen Infirmary, when he insultingly preferred to fetch Mrs. Simpson from the railway station. The bitterness plumbed its depths after George VI died and Elizabeth referred to her sister-in-law as 'the woman who killed my husband'.[3] The book made abundantly clear that the Queen Mother saw the Duchess as entirely unfit to be a member of the royal family. Even had the Duke's blackmail from Spain in 1940 forced the King to show some form of recognition to the Duchess, his wife would have refused to receive her.[4] She was adamantly opposed to giving the Duchess a seat in the royal box for her daughter's coronation as Elizabeth II and neither the Duke nor the Duchess was even invited.[5] Nor was the trivia of family relations forgotten. The royal family were handed the opportunity to repay Mrs. Simpson for her mockery when the Duke and Duchess commissioned a picture for their first Christmas card in 1937 as a married couple which showed her towering over him.[6] It was christened 'David and the giantess' in the royal family.

The Duchess herself was in no position to respond directly and her literary champion was inept in the extreme. Her health had begun to deteriorate severely soon after her husband's death. Her life fell increasingly under the influence of the French lawyer Maître Suzanne Blum who eliminated all her rivals. The Duchess's descent into bedbound senility and Blum's takeover advanced hand in hand until, at the end, Blum was the sole spokesperson for a helpless invalid. Blum had a strong view of how the Duchess should be presented to the world and gave numerous press interviews in which she promoted this. The Duchess was a person of radiant goodness in every respect, who had not had a sexual relationship with Edward before they were married. The abdication had been forced by a conspiracy between Tommy Lascelles and Alec Hardinge, under pressure from the Church, 'the Establishment' and *The*

Times.[7] It was not the stuff of penetrating history. Blum made one attempt at commissioning a historian to write a story to her taste, but as we have already mentioned, Alain Decaux proved to be a disappointment, perhaps because he was willing to accept that the couple might have had a sexual relationship before they married. Blum's influence on the Windsor story was essentially negative. Her greater preoccupation was to suppress any comment on the Duke and Duchess or their story that did not emanate directly from her. Her chief tool was loud threat of legal action, which was hardly ever followed up. She never appears to have entered into anything approaching dialogue with writers or broadcasters to influence their version of the story.

Blum's highest card was that she controlled much of the Duchess's correspondence, above all the letters that the couple had exchanged before their marriage. These would give unrivalled insights into the characters of the Duke and Duchess and the progress of their affair. Just as the Duchess was dying, this correspondence was published in edited but extensive form. It put on display the venomous hatred between the Windsors and the royal family, but rather than putting their side of the tale effectively, it probably did them more damage than good. Edward's letters show him as cloying and infantile; hers as self-obsessed and manipulative.

The war is still being fought today and rightly so. Who needs the preposterous fictions of Netflix's *The Crown* when the true drama of the abdication crisis and the fight to control its memory are there for all?

Notes

1. The House of Windsor Enters the Age of Media
1. www.james-gillray.org/pop/fashionable.html accessed 12 January 2022
2. Brendon & Whitehead *The Windsors* p64

2. No Minister Will Dare to Go Against This Force
1. Hunt *One American and His Attempt at Education* p126
2. St John Rogers *The Honeycomb* p435
3. Ziegler *King Edward VIII* p185
4. *The Neville Chamberlain Diary Letters* to Hilda 24 March 1934
5. Hunt *The Bachelor Prince* pp 235f
6. The Duke of Windsor *A King's Story* p255
7. DGFP Series C Vol IV p331
8. Andrew *The Defence of the Realm* p199
9. NA FO800/847 Grandi report 7 May 1936
10. DGFP Series C Vol. IV p1063. Edward's official biographer, Philip Ziegler, does not believe he could have been so indiscreet and quotes a letter from John Julius Norwich Cooper's son in which he challenged Saxe-Coburg's account of his father's views given in the same despatch. He derided Saxe-Coburg's veracity because the published English language version of the despatch can be read as claiming he was an Eton contemporary of Duff Cooper, Anthony Eden and Neville Chamberlain. In the original he only claimed unambiguously to have overlapped with Duff Cooper. He may simply have meant that the other two were also Etonians, incorrectly in Chamberlain's case. Even if Saxe-Coburg misreported the conversations with Edward, von Ribbentrop subsequently viewed him as pro-Nazi and politically ambitious.
11. Hunt *The Bachelor Prince* p8

3. Unnatural Silence
1. *The Times* 2 & 4 March 1936
2. Baldwin papers 3/3/B(iii) Windham Baldwin A KING'S STORY 27 August 1950
3. Vickers *The Quest for Queen Mary* pp261f
4. *The Times* 6 March 1936
5. Brooks journal p175

4. Friday's Job
1. Monckton papers, Goddard narrative
2. Bruce Lockhart diaries 1 September 1928 pp70–1
3. Beaverbrook *The Abdication of King Edward VIII* pp19–20
4. Beaverbrook *The Abdication of King Edward VIII* p30
5. Beaverbrook *The Abdication of King Edward VIII* p30fn

6. Mrs Simpson to King 15 October 1936 [misdated as 14 in *Wallis and Edward*]
7. Beaverbrook *The Abdication of King Edward VIII* p30
8. Jones *A Diary with Letters* p277
9. *The Neville Chamberlain Diary Letters* to Ida 13 April 1936
10. Ramsden, *The Age of Balfour and Baldwin 1902–1940* pp297f & 306–12; Searle, *Corruption in British Politics, 1895–1930*, pp399–404 & 409ff
11. Phillips 'Chronicle of a conspiracy foretold' in *Journal of Conservative History* Vol II Issue 5

5. Furnishing an American Queen

1. Lawrence '"You furnish the pictures, and I'll furnish the war": argues for its truth but does give a narrative of how the story developed
2. Rogers St Johns *The Honeycomb* p435
3. Coblentz papers Hearst to Coblentz February 3 1936
4. Crawford *The Times We Had* p128
5. Crawford *The Times We Had* p150. Hearst already knew at this point but it is possible that Davies muddled her timing and was thinking of an incident on an earlier European journey
6. Rogers St Johns *The Honeycomb* p434
7. Rogers St Johns *The Honeycomb* p457
8. Rogers St Johns *The Honeycomb* p458
9. Belloc Lowndes *Diaries and Letters* p150
10. Owen & Thompson *His Was the Kingdom* p42
11. Beaverbrook papers BBK G/6/27
12. Leeds *The Cards the Windsors Hold* p147
13. Crathorne papers, Dugdale diary
14. NA CAB301/101
15. NAA M104 Bruce memorandum 15 November 1936
16. Sitwell *Rat Week* pp35–6
17. Crathorne papers, Dugdale diary
18. Hearst papers Universal Service despatch 11 November 1936
19. Hearst papers Berkson to Willicombe 17 November 1936
20. Hearst papers Simpson Symposium of British dominions 17 November 1936
21. Hearst papers Berkson to Willicombe 11 & 17 November 1936
22. Hearst papers Hillman to Hearst via Berkson 15 November 1936
23. Rogers St Johns *The Honeycomb* p472
24. Rogers St Johns *The Honeycomb* p479
25. Head *It Could Never Have Happened* pp222f
26. Rogers St Johns quoted in Swanberg *Citizen Hearst* p568
27. Hearst papers Duke of Windsor (through secretary) to Hearst 1 November 1937

6. Editors as Statesmen

1. Neville Chamberlain papers diary 2 November 1936
2. Wrench *Geoffrey Dawson and Our Times* p344
3. NA PREM 1/466
4. NA PREM 1/466
5. K. Gwynne Wilson, 'Howell Arthur (1865–1950), journalist' in *Oxford Dictionary of National Biography*. Retrieved 21 January 2022, from www.oxforddnb.com/view/10.1093/ref:odnb/9780198614128.001.0001/odnb-9780198614128-e-33622.

6. NA PREM 1/466 Gwynne to Baldwin
7. Phillips *The King Who Had to Go* pp99–100
8. Deedes *Dear Bill* p41
9. Morison *The History of the Times* Vol IV p1029
10. Jones *A Diary with Letters* 21 October p277
11. Wrench *Geoffrey Dawson and Our Times* p358
12. Wrench *Geoffrey Dawson and Our Times* p344
13. Wrench *Geoffrey Dawson and Our Times* pp341, 346
14. NA PREM 1/463 Simon to Dawson November 19 1936

7. The Jolt
1. Phillips *The King Who Had to Go* pp93-105
2. Hansard 11 December 1936
3. Monckton trustees 22 Sir Edward Peacock's notes

8. King Edward's Contribution to Democratic Government
1. *The Times* 19 November 1936
2. Hunt *The Bachelor Prince* p235
3. DGFP Series C Vol IV p331
4. *Daily Mail* 23 November 1936
5. Jones *A Diary with Letters* p288

9. The Filthy Newspaper and the Mind of the English People
1. The Duchess of Windsor *The Heart Has Its Reasons* p269
2. The Duke of Windsor *A King's Story* p342
3. NA CAB 23/68
4. Crathorne papers Dugdale diary
5. Windham Baldwin papers, 11/1/1 Monica Baldwin AN UNPUBLISHED PAGE OF ENGLISH HISTORY
6. Windham Baldwin papers, 11/1/1 Monica Baldwin AN UNPUBLISHED PAGE OF ENGLISH HISTORY
7. NA CAB 23/68
8. NA CAB 23/68
9. NA PREM 1/466
10. Hart-Davis *The House the Berrys Built* pp69f, 84
11. Neville Chamberlain papers, diary 30 November 1936

10. Round Trip to New York
1. *The Times* 'Shipping and Mails' 27 November 1936
2. Vickers *The Quest for Queen Mary* p215
3. Duke of Windsor *A King's Story* p384f

11. The Dam Bursts
1. Hansard 17 November 1936
2. Bloch *Wallis and Edward: Letters, 1931–37* p209
3. Martin *Editor* pp194f
4. The Duke of Windsor *A King's Story* p349
5. The *Birmingham Post* December 1 1936

6. NA PREM 1/446 Attitude of the British Press
7. NA PREM 1/446 Attitude of the British Press

12. A Friend on Fleet Street
1. Bryan & Murphy *The Windsor Story* p245
2. Monckton papers Monckton ADDITIONAL NOTE MADE ON THE 13 August 1940
3. Bloch ed. *Wallis and Edward: Letters, 1931–37* p121
4. Bloch ed. *Wallis and Edward: Letters, 1931–37* p128
5. The Duke of Windsor *A King's Story* p373; John Entwistle, www.thebaron.info/archives/ultra-british-editor-who-lovedamerica-took-royal-s
6. Bloch ed. *Wallis and Edward: Letters, 1931–37*, Duke of Windsor to Mrs. Simpson 2 April
7. NA WO 339/37027
8. NA WO 339/37027
9. NA WO 339/37027 Rickatson-Hatt to War Office 24 June & 19 September 1923, Reuters archives Rickatson-Hatt memorandum 17 February 1930
10. Hesse *Das Spiel Um Deutschland* p81
11. www.thebaron.info/archives/ultra-british-editor-who-loved-america-took-royal-bribes
12. Bank of England Archive Montagu Norman diary 8 April 1941
13. Elizabeth Hennessy *A Domestic History of the Bank of England 1930–1960* p378
14. Reuters archive memo 26 January 1967, *The Times* 25 January 1967

13. A Powerful Propaganda Agency
1. The Duke of Windsor *A King's Story* p359
2. Cudlipp *Publish and Be Damned* p93
3. Beaverbrook *The Abdication of King Edward VIII* p69
4. Beaverbrook papers BBK G/6/19
5. Beaverbrook *The Abdication of King Edward VIII* pp78f
6. Beaverbrook papers BBK G/6/19
7. Brooks journal 5 December 1936
8. NA PREM 1/446
9. Amery diary 4 December 1936
10. NA PREM 1/446 CONSTITUTIONAL CRISIS: Attitude of the British Press, Bruce Lockhart diaries 4 December pp359–60
11. Beaverbrook *The Abdication of King Edward VIII* p72
12. NA PREM 1/446 CONSTITUTIONAL CRISIS: Attitude of the British Press
13. Beaverbrook *The Abdication of King Edward VIII* p95
14. Rhodes Davis *Memoirs of a Conservative* pp414f
15. NA PREM 1/446 CONSTITUTIONAL CRISIS: Attitude of the British Press

14. A Fireside Chat
1. *Birmingham News* 16 December 1936
2. The Duchess of Windsor *The Heart Has Its Reasons* p272; The Duke of Windsor *A King's Story* pp356–7
3. NA CAB 23/68
4. Neville Chamberlain papers diary 2 December 1936
5. Reith diaries 3 December 1936

6. Reith diaries 3 December 1936, NA PREM 1/466
7. NA PREM 1/466
8. Beaverbrook *The Abdication of King Edward VIII* p70
9. NA CAB 23/68
10. Crathorne papers, Dugdale diary
11. Crathorne papers, Dugdale diary
12. NA CAB 23/68
13. NA CAB 23/68
14. Reith diaries 3 December 1936
15. NA CAB 23/68
16. Duff Cooper diaries 2 December 1936
17. NA CAB21/4100, King's proposed broadcast
18. Neville Chamberlain papers, diary 4 December 1936
19. The Duke of Windsor *A King's Story* p361
20. NA CAB 21/4100
21. www.bbc.com/historyofthebbc/anniversaries/december/edward-viii-abdication-speech/ accessed 13 November 2022
22. Williamson & Baldwin *The Baldwin Papers* Baldwin to Lang 14 December 1936
23. *The Times* 14 December 1936
24. Reith diaries 13 December 1936
25. Williamson & Baldwin *The Baldwin Papers* p388
26. Windham Baldwin papers 3/3/B(iii) A KING'S STORY. Baldwin did not say where or when the conversation took place but there is no realistic alternative to the Sunday afternoon conversation at Downing Street.
27. Williamson & Baldwin *The Baldwin Papers* pp415f
28. De Courcy papers 'The Windsor Papers'
29. Sencourt *The Reign of Edward VIII* p189
30. Joseph Kennedy diary 13 June 1938
31. De Courcy papers memorandum on Killbritain Newspapers paper n.d
32. NA PREM 1/466, Attlee *As It Happened* p102
33. Williamson & Baldwin *The Baldwin Papers* p462

15. A Thoroughly Efficient Horse-Whipping

1. Monckton papers Allen to Monckton 22 December 1936
2. *Daily News* 19 December 1936
3. *Time* 18 January 1937
4. Dennis *Coronation Commentary* p272
5. *The Times* 'Law Report' 22 November 1937
6. Bruce Lockhart *The Diaries of Sir Robert Bruce Lockhart* p372
7. Blackwood *The Last of the Duchess* p41; Vickers *Behind Closed Doors* p146
8. Gordon Lennox *The Tiddly Quid & After* p128
9. Decaux *L'abdication* p91
10. Monckton papers Allen to Heinemann (draft) 26 January 1938
11. Monckton papers extract of letter from the Duke of Windsor to Allen 1 December 1938
12. Baxter *Westminster Watchtower* p86
13. Baxter *Westminster Watchtower* pp90f

16. The Brand of Unfitness

1. Bryan & Murphy *The Windsor Story* p341
2. NA HO 144/22945 Wigram to Simon 11 March 1937
3. NA HO 144/22945 note of conference 6 April 1937
4. NA PREM 1/448 Simon to Baldwin 24 April 1937
5. NA HO 144/22945 Monckton to Simon 24 May 1937
6. Neville Chamberlain papers, diary 23 May 1937; H. Montgomery Hyde letter to *The Times* 20 September 1972
7. NA HO144/22945 minute 'Style & title of "Royal Highness"' 1 June 1937
8. Aldgate *Cinema and History* pp138f
9. Aldgate, *Cinema and History* pp138–41
10. Phillips *The King Who Had to Go* p167
11. www.youtube.com/watch?v=pGpmkqA0Bbo
12. Briggs *The Golden Age of Wireless* p611
13. Hearst papers Willicombe to Berkson or West 12 November 1938
14. Joseph Kennedy diary for 14 April 1939 in *Hostage to Fortune* p326 & fn

17. The Behaviour of Those in Power

1. Gardiner *The Thirties* pp 462–4, Graves & Hodge *The Long Weekend* pp362f, Pugh *We Danced All* Night pp383–5,
2. Linklater *Compton Mackenzie* p253
3. Mackenzie *Octave Seven* p248
4. *Gramophone* January 1937
5. Monckton papers Gardiner to Monckton 13 April 1938
6. Monckton papers Trustees 15 fol 284 'The Truth about the Duke of Windsor's Biography'
7. Monckton papers Note on Compton Mackenzie's book project 19 October 1937
8. Monckton papers Monckton to Wilson 19 October 1937
9. Monckton papers Monckton memorandum Note on Compton Mackenzie's book project 19 October, Duke of Windsor to Mackenzie 31 October 1937 quoted in Allen and Overy to Metcalfe, Copeman and Pettefar 18 January 1938,
10. Monckton papers Gardiner to Monckton 13 April 1938
11. NA PREM 1/466 Monckton to Wilson 9 June 1938
12. NA KV 2/1271
13. NA PREM 1/466 Monckton to Wilson 9 June 1938

18. Careful and Delicate Handling

1. Coote *Editorial* p31
2. Bloch 'Philip Guedalla Defends the Duke' in *History Today* 12 December 1979
3. Monckton papers Monckton to the Duke of Windsor 19 November 1937
4. Monckton papers Trustees 15 fol 276 Monckton to Wilson 19 October 1937
5. Guedalla *The Hundredth Year* p82
6. Guedalla *The Hundredth Year* p173
7. Guedalla *The Hundredth Year* p175
8. Guedalla *The Hundredth Year* p252

19. Interlude

1. Minney *The Private Papers of Hore-Belisha* p239
2. Ziegler *King Edward VIII* p415

3. DGFP Series D Vol VIII pp513 & 789
4. Sebba *That Woman* pp229f

20. Despatches from St Helena
1. Rogers St Johns *The Honeycomb* Chapter 37
2. Duke of Windsor to Guedalla 15 October 1940 reproduced in Bloch 'Philip Guedalla Defends the Duke in *History Today* 12 December 1979
3. St Johns's articles appeared in many US newspapers 17–26 November 1940. The following were examined: *Richmond Times-Dispatch*, *The Times-Tribune*, Scranton PA, *Lexington Herald* and *Indianapolis Star*

21. A Rope of Sand
1. Monckton papers the Duke of Windsor to Monckton 31 May 1946
2. Monckton papers the Duke of Windsor to Monckton 31 May 1946
3. Monckton papers Monckton to Phillips 17 December 1948
4. Monckton papers Allen to Monckton 1 September 1948
5. Monckton papers the Duke of Windsor to Monckton 2 October 1948
6. Monckton papers Mackenzie to Monckton 23 April 1949
7. Monckton papers Mackenzie to Monckton 15 July 1949, Murphy to Allen 4 April 1950
8. Monckton papers Mackenzie to Monckton 5 October 1949
9. Bryan & Murphy *The Windsor Story* pp464f
10. Monckton papers the Duke of Windsor to Monckton 24 October 1949

22. This Wretched Publication
1. Monckton papers Allen to Monckton 13 October 1949
2. Beaverbrook papers, BBK G/6/23 Beaverbrook to Murphy 19 August 1949
3. Beaverbrook papers, BBK G/6/23 Beaverbrook to Murphy 3 September 1949
4. Beaverbrook papers, BBK G/6/23 Beaverbrook to Luce 13 September 1949
5. Baldwin papers Simon to Baldwin 3 December 1936
6. The Duke of Windsor *A King's Story* p298
7. Monckton papers Trustees 20 fol 205 Monckton to Lascelles 5 May 1950
8. Monckton papers Lascelles to Monckton 10 May 1950
9. Monckton papers Lascelles to Monckton 18 March 1950
10. Monckton papers Monckton to Lascelles 5 May 1950
11. Ziegler *King Edward VIII* p527

23. The Beaverbrook Car Service
1. Duke of Windsor *A King's Story* p372n
2. Duke of Windsor *A King's Story* p384f
3. Beaverbrook papers BBK G/6/6 Beaverbrook to Monckton 4 December 1936
4. Baldwin papers Simon to Baldwin 3 December 1936
5. Baldwin papers Simon to Baldwin 3 December 1936
6. Beaverbrook papers BBK G/6/24
7. Beaverbrook papers BBK G/6/13 Beaverbrook to Simon 21 September 1951
8. Beaverbrook papers BBK G/6/13 Simon to Beaverbrook 24 September 1951
9. Beaverbrook papers BBK G/6/13 Beaverbrook to Simon 17 October 1951
10. Beaverbrook papers BBK G/6/13 Simon to Beaverbrook 24 October 1951
11. Beaverbrook *The Abdication of King Edward* p93

24. The Beaverbrook Broadcasting Service
1. Taylor *Beaverbrook* p316
2. Morison *The History of the Times* Vol IV p1036
3. Beaverbrook papers BBK/G/6/17 Lord Beaverbrook on the Abdication p29
4. Beaverbrook papers BBK/G/6/17 Lord Beaverbrook on the Abdication pp29f
5. Beaverbrook papers BBK/G/6/3 Transcripts of handwritten notes and memoranda

25. A Novice Lost on the Cresta Run
1. Beaverbrook *The Abdication of King Edward VIII* p34
2. Colville *The Fringes of Power* p667
3. Beaverbrook papers BBK C/46 Bocca to Beaverbrook 25 November 1952
4. Bocca 'Mentor and Tormentor' in *The Beaverbrook I Knew* ed. Logan Gourlay p173
5. Bocca *She Might Have Been Queen* p181
6. Beaverbrook papers BBK G/6/13 Jowitt to Beaverbrook 26 March 1954
7. Ziegler *King Edward VIII* pp552f
8. Beaverbrook papers BBK C/46 Bocca to Beaverbrook 13 October 1953

26. Garnished With Malice
1. Schellenberg memoirs p68
2. NA PREM 11/5209 Foreign Office memorandum 7 May 1953
3. NA PREM 11/5210 JCC to Churchill 27 May 1954
4. NA PREM 11/5209 Colville to Strang 5 June 1953
5. Beaverbrook papers BBK C/46 Bocca to Beaverbrook 8 June 1953
6. Bocca 'Mentor and Tormentor' in *The Beaverbrook I Knew* ed. Logan Gourlay pp173f
7. Beaverbrook papers BBK C/46 Bocca to Beaverbrook 5 July 1953
8. NA PREM 11/5209 Colville to Churchill with manuscript note by Churchill 10 July 1953
9. Beaverbrook papers BBK C/46 Bocca to Beaverbrook 10 September 1953
10. Bocca 'Mentor and Tormentor' in *The Beaverbrook I Knew* ed. Logan Gourlay p174
11. Beaverbrook papers BBK C/46 unsigned, undated 'Copy report on THE WOMAN WHO WOULD BE QUEEN'
12. Bocca *She Might Have Been Queen* p198
13. NA PREM 11/5210 Kilpatrick memorandum 10 November 1954
14. NA PREM 11/5210 Rumbold to Colville 23 October 1953
15. NA PREM 11/5210 Brook to Eden 9 July 1957
16. Morton *17 Carnations* passim

27. The Black Rat and the Jazz-Boy King
1. Crathorne papers, Dugdale Diary
2. Phillips *The King Who Had to Go*
3. NA PREM 1/466
4. Phillips *The King Who Had to Go* pp95–9
5. Lascelles *King's Counsellor* p138
6. Lascelles *King's Counsellor* p142
7. Channon diaries 6 May 1940 and subsequent entries. On 18 March 1941 he changed this to 'the red rat' when he fancied that Hardinge had become a communist.
8. NA PREM 1/466

9. Blanche Dugdale diary 13 December 1936
10. Monckton papers Monckton to Sencourt 12 July 1957
11. Monckton papers Monckton to Sencourt 12 July 1957
12. Monckton papers Note of conversation with Kimber 8 December 1958
13. Monckton papers Third Lord Hardinge to Sencourt 6 July 1961
14. Monckton papers Monckton to third Lord Hardinge 13 July 1961
15. Monckton papers Third Lord Hardinge to Monckon 24 July 1961
16. Sencourt *The Reign of Edward VIII* p11
17. Sencourt *The Reign of Edward VIII* p168
18. Sencourt *The Reign of Edward VIII* p189

28. Palace Persecution
1. Crawford *The Little Princesses* pp72f
2. Monckton papers draft 2 May 1950
3. Monckton papers Allen to Monckton 9 May 1950
4. Monckton papers Lascelles to Monckton 10 May 1950

29. Transference of Responsibility
1. Quoted at Sebba *That Woman* p260
2. Vickers *The Quest for Queen Mary* p334n
3. Bryan & Murphy *The Windsor Story* p517
4. *Time* 17 October 1955
5. Vickers *The Quest for Queen Mary* p268
6. The Duchess of Windsor *The Heart Has Its Reasons* p243
7. The Duchess of Windsor *The Heart Has Its Reasons* p312
8. The Duchess of Windsor *The Heart Has Its Reasons* pp313 & 317
9. The Duchess of Windsor *The Heart Has Its Reasons* pp323f
10. Thornton *Royal Feud* p275
11. Bryan & Murphy The Windsor Story pp518f
12. Phillips *The King Who Had to Go* pp165f
13. The Duchess of Windsor *The Heart Has Its Reasons* p333
14. DGFP Series C Vol VI p1032

30. A Forlorn Thermos of Tea
1. Wheeler-Bennett *Friends, Enemies and Sovereigns* p146
2. Schofield *Witness to History* p199
3. Wheeler-Bennett *Friends, Enemies and Sovereigns* p167
4. Ziegler *King Edward VIII* p553
5. The Duke of Windsor to Allen quoted in Bloch *The Secret File on the Duke of Windsor* p347
6. Ziegler *King Edward VIII* p553. According to Bloch *The Secret File on the Duke of Windsor*, which appeared before Ziegler's biography, the Duke threated legal action and was able to remove 'a number of damaging inaccuracies.'
7. Wheeler-Bennett *King George VI: His Life and Reign* p273
8. Wheeler-Bennett *King George VI: His Life and Reign* pp300 and 416
9. 'A New School of Royal Biography' in *The Sunday Times* 14 June 1959
10. Vickers *Behind Closed Doors* p355; Vickers *The Quest For Queen Mary* p246
11. Vickers *Behind Closed Doors* p354

12. Vickers *Behind Closed Doors* p357
13. Pope-Hennessy *Queen Mary* p573
14. Vickers *The Quest for Queen Mary* pp260f
15. Pope-Hennessy *Queen Mary* p580
16. Pope-Hennessy *A Lonely Occupation* p110
17. *The Sunday Times* 21 June 1964
18. Vickers *Behind Closed Doors* pp358f
19. Vickers *The Quest for Queen Mary* Chapter 27
20. Muggeridge *The Infernal Grove* p57

31. The End of Discretion

1. Rogers St Johns *The Honeycomb* p480
2. 'Royal Wives at War' in *The Daily Telegraph* 17 February 2016
3. Thornton *Royal Feud* p259
4. Thornton *Royal Feud* p205
5. Thornton *Royal Feud* p267
6. Thornton *Royal Feud* p178
7. *Point de Vue* 2 May 1986 p10

Bibliography

Government Archives
National Archives, NA
National Archives of Australia, NAA

Other Unpublished Material and Archives
Baldwin, Stanley, Papers, University Library, Cambridge
Baldwin, Windham, Papers, University Library, Cambridge
Beaverbrook, Lord, Papers (BBK), Parliamentary Archives
Chamberlain, Neville, Papers, University of Birmingham Special Collections Neville Chamberlain papers
Churchill, Sir Winston, Churchill Archives Centre, Cambridge
Coblentz, Edmond, Papers, Bancroft Library, University of California, Berkeley
Davidson, J. C. C., Papers, Parliamentary Archives
de Courcy, Kenneth, Papers, Hoover Institution Archives, University of Stanford (microfilm)
Duff Cooper, Churchill Archives Centre, Cambridge
Crathorne Papers, private hands
Hardinge, Helen, The Hon. Lady Murray Papers, private hands
Hearst, William Randolph, Papers, Bancroft Library, University of California, Berkeley
Hesse, Fritz, Nachlaß Hesse (papers), Bundesarchiv, Koblenz
Hoare, Sir Samuel, Templewood Papers, University Library, Cambridge
Monckton, Walter, Papers, Balliol College, Oxford
Reith, Sir John, BBC Written Archives, Caversham,
Rickatson Hatt, Bernard, Papers, Thomson Reuters Archive

Published Collections of Documents
Bloch, Michael (ed.), *Wallis & Edward: Letters 1931–1937*, Weidenfeld & Nicolson 1986
Davenport-Hines, Richard & Sisman, Adam (eds.), *One Hundred Letters from Hugh Trevor-Roper*, Oxford University Press 2014
Documents on German Foreign Policy, HMSO 1957–83 (DGFP)
Hitler, Adolph, *Hitler's Table Talk His Private Conversations, 1941–44*, Weidenfeld & Nicolson 1953
Hore-Belisha, *The Private Papers of Hore-Belisha* J. Minney (ed.) Collins 1960
Jones, Thomas, *A Diary with Letters 1931–1950*, Oxford University Press 1954
Lowndes, Susan (ed.), Belloc Lowndes, Marie, *Diaries and Letters of Marie Belloc Lowndes 1911–1947*, Chatto & Windus 1971
Nicolson, Harold, *Diaries and Letters 1930–39*, Collins 1966
Rhodes James, Robert (ed.), *Memoirs of a Conservative: J. C. C. Davidson Memoirs and Papers 1910–37*, Weidenfeld & Nicolson 1969

Self, Robert (ed.), *The Neville Chamberlain Diary Letters* (references given as Chamberlain to Ida or Hilda respectively), Ashgate 2005

Smith, Amanda (ed.), *Hostage to Fortune: The Letters of Joseph P. Kennedy*, Viking 2001

Williamson, Philip & Baldwin, Edward, *Baldwin Papers*, Cambridge University Press 2004

Newspapers
Birmingham News (Birmingham Alabama)
Daily Mail
Daily News (New York)
Evening News (Harrisburg)
Lexington Herald
Richmond Times-Dispatch (Richmond Virginia)
Sunday Pictorial (London)
The Birmingham Post (Birmingham UK)
The Daily Telegraph (London)
The Sunday Times (London)
The Times (London)
The Times-Tribune (Scranton PA)
The Yorkshire Post (Leeds)

Periodicals
Hansard
History Today
The Gramophone
Time
Life
Women's Own

Published Diaries and Letters
Amery, Leo, Barnes, John & Nicolson, David (eds.) *The Empire at Bay: The Leo Amery Diaries 1929-1945,* Hutchinson 1988

Brooks, Collin & Crowson, N.J. (ed.), *Fleet Street, Press Barons and Politics: The Journals of Collin Brooks, 1932–1940*, Cambridge University Press 1998

Bruce Lockhart, Robert & Young, Kenneth (ed.), *The Diaries of Sir Robert Bruce Lockhart 1915–1938*, Macmillan 1973

Channon, Chips & Heffer, Simon (ed.), *The Diaries: 1918–38*, Hutchinson 2021

Channon, Chips & Heffer, Simon (ed.), *The Diaries: 1938–43*, Hutchinson 2021

Colville, John, *The Fringes of Power: Downing Street Diaries 1939-1955* (revised edition), Weidenfeld & Nicolson 2004

Crawford, Earl of Vincent, John (ed.), *The Crawford Papers: The Journals of David Lindsay, Twenty-Seventh Earl of Crawford and Tenth Earl of Balcarres 1871–1940 During the Years 1892–1940*, Manchester University Press 1984

Dugdale, Blanche Rose, N. A. (ed.), *Baffy: The Diaries of Blanche Dugdale 1936–1947*, Valentine Mitchell 1973

Jones, Thomas & Middlemas, Keith (ed.), *Whitehall Diary Volume II 1926/1930*, Oxford University Press 1969

Duff Cooper Norwich, John Julius (ed.), John, *The Duff Cooper Diaries*, Norwich, Weidenfeld & Nicolson 2005

Lascelles, Alan, *In Royal Service*, Hamish Hamilton 1989

Lascelles, Alan, *King's Counsellor*, Weidenfeld & Nicolson 2006

Maisky, Ivan, Lee, John & Gorodetsky, Gabriel (ed.), *The Maisky Diaries: Red Ambassador to the Court of St James's 1932–1943*, Yale University Press 2015

Pope-Hennessy, James, *A Lonely Business*, Weidenfeld & Nicolson 1981

Reith, Lord & Stuart, Charles (ed.), *The Reith Diaries*, William Collins 1975

Streat, Raymond Dupree, Marguerite (ed), *Lancashire and Whitehall: The Diary of Sir Raymond Streat*, Manchester University Press 1987

Sylvester, A. J., *Life with Lloyd George: The Diary of A. J. Sylvester 1931–45*, Macmillan 1975

Memoirs

Attlee, C. R., *As It Happened*, Odhams (n.d.)

Avon, Earl of, *The Eden Memoirs: Facing the Dictators*, Cassell 1962

Baillie, Hugh, *High Tension: The Recollections of Hugh Baillie*, Laurie 1960

Beaverbrook, Lord & Taylor, A. J. P (ed.), *The Abdication of King Edward VIII*, Atheneum 1965

Boothby, Bob, *Recollections of a Rebel*, Hutchinson 1978

Butler, Lord, *The Art of the Possible*, Hamish Hamilton 1971

Citrine, Lord, *Men and Work*, Hutchinson 1964

Cooper, Duff, *Old Men Forget*, Rupert Hart-Davis 1955

Coote, Colin R., *Editorial*, Eyre & Spottiswoode 1965

Crawford, Marion, *The Little Princesses*, Cassell 1950

Davies, Marion, *The Times We Had*, Bobbs Merrill 1975

Deedes, William, *Dear Bill*, Macmillan 1997

Hardinge, Helen, *Loyal to Three Kings*, William Kimber 1967

Head, Alice, *It Could Never Have Happened*, Heinemann 1939

Hesse, Fritz, *Das Spiel um Deutschland*, Paul List 1953

Home, Lord, *The Way the Wind Blows*, William Collins 1976

Gordon Lennox, Nicholas, *The Tiddly Quid & After*, The Book Guild 2006

Hunt, Frazier, *One American and His Attempt at Education*, Simon & Schuster 1938

MacDonald, Malcolm, *People & Places*, Collins 1969

Macmillan, Harold, *Winds of Change 1914–1939*, Macmillan 1966

Mackenzie, Compton, *My Life, Octave Seven 1931–38*, Chatto & Windus 1968

Martin, Kingsley *Editor*, Hutchinson 1968

Massey, Vincent, *What's Past Is Prologue: The Memoirs of the Rt. Hon. Vincent Massey*, Macmillan 1963

Muggeridge, Malcolm, *The Infernal Grove*, Collins 1973

Reith, J. C. W., *Into the Wind*, Hodder & Stoughton 1949

Rogers St. Johns, Adela, *The Honeycomb*, New American Library 1970

Schmidt, Paul, *Statist auf Diplomatischer Bühne 1923–45*, Athenäum 1949

Schellenberg, Walter, *Schellenberg*, Mayflower 1965

Shaughnessy, Alfred, *Both Ends of the Candle*, Peter Owen 1978

Sitwell, Osbert, *Rat Week*, Joseph 1986

Stuart, Viscount, *Within the Fringe*, The Bodley Head 1967

Templewood, Viscount (Sir Samuel Hoare), *Nine Troubled Years*, Collins 1954

Ustinov, Peter, *Dear Me*, Heinemann 1977

Wheeler-Bennett, John *Friends Enemies and Sovereigns*, Palgrave Macmillan 1976

Windsor, Duchess of, *The Heart Has Its Reasons*, Michael Joseph 1969 (page references to Tandem paperback edition 1974)
Windsor, Duke of, *A King's Story*, Putnam 1951
Woolton, Earl of, *Memoirs*, Cassell 1959

Works by Contemporaries or Drawn Essentially from Contemporary Sources
Baldwin, Windham, *My Father: The True Story*, Allen & Unwin 1956
Baxter, Beverley, *Westminster Watchtower*, Collins 1938
Birkenhead, Lord, *Walter Monckton*, Weidenfeld & Nicolson 1969
Blackwood, Caroline, *The Last of The Duchess*, Macmillan 1995
Bocca, Geoffrey, *She Might Have Been Queen*, Express Books 1955
Bryan & Murphy, *The Windsor Story*, Granada 1979
Colvin, Ian, *Vansittart in Office*, Gollancz 1965
Cudlipp, Hugh, *Publish and Be Damned*, Andrew Dakers 1953
Feiling, Keith, *Life of Neville Chamberlain*, Macmillan 1946
Decaux, Alain, *L'Abdication*, Perrin 1995
Dennis, Geoffrey *Coronation Commentary*, Dodd Mead 1937
Gibbs, Philip, *Ordeal in England*, Heinemann 1937
Gourlay, Logan (ed), *The Beaverbrook I Knew*, Quartet 1984
Guedalla, Philip, *Mr Churchill: A Portrait*, Hodder & Stoughton 1941
Guedalla, Philip, *The Hundredth Year*, Butterworth 1940
Hardinge, Helen, *The Path of Kings*, Blandford 1953
Hunt, Frazier, *The Bachelor Prince*, Harper Brothers 1935
Leeds, Stanton B. *The Cards the Windsors Hold*, Lippincott 1937
Martin, Kingsley, *The Crown and the Establishment*, Hutchinson 1962
Mackenzie, Compton, *The Windsor Tapestry*, Rich & Cowan 1938
Morison, Stanley [uncredited], *The History of The Times: Volume IV The 150th Annniversary and Beyond: Part II: 1921–1948*, 1952
Owen, Frank & Thompson, R. J., *His Was the Kingdom* Arthur Barker 1937
Paterson, Michael, *Personal Accounts of Sir Winston Churchill*, David Charles 2006
Pope-Hennessy, James, *The Quest for Queen Mary*, Zuleika, 2018
Rhodes James, Robert, *Victor Cazalet*, Hamish Hamilton 1976
Roskill, Stephen, *Hankey: Man of Secrets Volume III 1931–63*, William Collins 1974
Sencourt, Robert, *The Reign of Edward VIII*, Anthony Gibbs & Phillips 1962
Stirling, Alfred, *Lord Bruce: The London Years*, Hawthorn 1974
Wrench, Evelyn, *Geoffrey Dawson and Our Times*, Hutchinson 1955
Young, G. M., *Stanley Baldwin*, Rupert Hart-Davis 1952

Secondary Works
Aldgate, Anthony *Cinema and History*, Scolar 1979
Andrew, Christopher, *Defence of the Realm: The Authorized History of MI5*, Allen Lane 2009
Balfour, Patrick (Lord Kinross), *The Windsor Years*, Collins 1967
Beaken, Robert, *Cosmo Lang: Archbishop in War and Crisis*, I.B. Tauris 2012
Brendon, Piers & Whitehead, Philip *The Windsors*, Pimlico 2000
Bloch, Michael, *Operation Willi*, Weidenfeld & Nicolson 1984
Bloch, Michael, *The Reign & Abdication of Edward VIII*, Bantam 1990
Bloch, Michael, *The Secret File on the Duke of Windsor*, Bantam 1988

Bloch, Michael, *Ribbentrop*, Bantam 1994

Bloch, Michael, *The Duchess of Windsor*, Weidenfeld & Nicolson 1996

Bourne, Richard, *Lords of Fleet Street: The Harmsworth Dynasty*, Unwin Hyman 1990

Bradford, Sarah, *George VI*, Weidenfeld & Nicolson 1989

Brendon, *Our Own Dear Queen*, Secker & Warburg 1986

Briggs, Asa, *The Golden Age of Wireless*, Oxford University Press, 1965

Bullock, Alan, *The Life and Times of Ernest Bevin Vol. 1* Heinemann 1969

Campbell, John, *Lloyd George: The Goat in the Wilderness*, Jonathan Cape 1977

Chisholm, Anne & Davie, Michael, *Lord Beaverbrook: A Life*, Knopf 1992

Day, Peter, *The Bedbug*, Biteback 2014

Donaldson, Frances, *Edward VIII*, Weidenfeld & Nicolson 1974

Donaldson, Frances, *A Twentieth Century Life*, Weidenfeld & Nicolson 1992

Dorril, Steven, *MI6: Inside the Covert World of Her Majesty's Secret Intelligence Service*, Fourth Estate 1998

Gardiner, Juliet, *The Thirties*, Harperpress 2010

Graves, Robert & Hodge, Alan, *The Long Weekend*, Hutchinson 1940

Greig, Geordie, *Louis and the Prince*, Hodder & Stoughton 1999

Griffiths, Richard, *Fellow Travellers of the Right: British Enthusiasts for Nazi Germany 1933–39*, Constable 1980

Hardinge, Helen, *Loyal to Three Kings*, William Kimber 1967

Harris, Kenneth, *Attlee*, Weidenfeld & Nicolson 1982

Hart-Davis, Rupert, *The House the Berrys Built: Inside the Telegraph*, Coronet 1991

Hennessy, Elizabeth, *A Domestic History of the Bank of England 1930–1960*, Cambridge University Press 1992

Higham, Charles, *Mrs. Simpson: Secret Lives of the Duchess of Windsor*, Sidgwick & Jackson 1988

Jago, Michael, *Clement Attlee: The Inevitable Prime Minister*, Biteback 2014

Jeffrey, Keith, *MI6: The History of the Secret Intelligence Service 1909–1949*, Bloomsbury 2010

Jenkins, Roy, *Churchill*, Macmillan 2001

Kershaw, Ian, *Making Friends with Hitler: Lord Londonderry and Britain's Road to War*, Allen Lane 2004

Lacey, Robert, *Majesty*, Hutchinson, 1977

Lownie, Andrew, *Traitor King* Blink 2021

Middlemas, Keith & Barnes, John, *Baldwin*, Weidenfeld & Nicolson 1969

Montgomery Hyde, H., ' *Baldwin: The Unexpected Prime Minister*, Hart-Davis MacGibbon 1973

Morton, Andrew, *17 Carnations*, Michael O'Mara 2015

Murphy, Philip, *Alan Lennox-Boyd: A Biography*, I.B. Tauris 1999

Nasaw, David, *The Chief*, Mariner 2000

Nicolson, Harold, *King George the Fifth*, Constable 1952

O'Halpin, Eunan, *Head of the Civil Service: A Study of Sir Warren Fisher*, Routledge 1989

Padfield, Peter, *Hess, Hitler and Churchill: The Real Turning Point of the Second World War: A Secret History*, Icon 2013

Parker, R. A. C., *Churchill and Appeasement*, Macmillan 2000

Phillips, Adrian, *The King Who Had to Go*, Biteback 2016

Pope-Hennessy, James, *Queen Mary*, Allen and Unwin 1959

Procter, Ben H., *William Randolph Hearst*, Oxford University Press 2007

Public Record Office, *The Security Service 1908–1945: The Official History*, Public Record Office 1999

Pugh, Martin, *Hurrah for the Blackshirts*, Pimlico 2006

Pugh, Martin, *We Danced All Night*, Bodley Head 2008

Ramsden, John, *The Age of Balfour and Baldwin 1902–1940*, Longman 1978

Read, Donald, *The Power of News*, Oxford University Press 1992

Rhodes-James, Robert, *A Spirit Undaunted: The Political Role of George VI*, Little, Brown 1998

Rose, Andrew, *The Prince, The Princess and the Perfect Murder*, Coronet 2013

Rose, Kenneth, *King George V*, Weidenfeld & Nicolson 1983

Schofield, Victoria, *Witness to History*, Yale University Press 2012

Searle, G.D., *Corruption in British Politics, 1895–1930*, Clarendon Press 1987

Sebba, Anne, *That Woman*, Weidenfeld & Nicolson 2011 (page references to Phoenix paperback edition 2012)

Shawcross, William, *Queen Elizabeth: The Queen Mother: The Official Biography*, Macmillan 2009

Stewart, Graham, *Burying Caesar: Churchill, Chamberlain and the Battle for the Tory Party*, Weidenfeld & Nicolson 1999

Swanberg, W. A., *Citizen Hearst*, Scribner 1961

Taylor, A. J. P., *Beaverbrook*, Hamish Hamilton 1972

Taylor, S. J., *The Great Outsiders: Northcliffe, Rothermere and the Daily Mail*, Weidenfeld & Nicolson 1996

Thornton, Michael, *Royal Feud*, Michael Joseph 1985

Thorpe, D. R., *Alec Douglas-Home*, Sinclair-Stevenson 1997

Toye, Richard, *Lloyd George & Churchill: Rivals for Greatness*, Macmillan 2007

Vickers, Hugo, *Behind Closed Doors*, Hutchinson 2011

Vickers, Hugo, *Elizabeth: The Queen Mother*, Hutchinson 2005

Wheeler-Bennett, John W., *King George VI: His Life and Reign*, Macmillan 1958

Wiggin, Kate Douglas, *Rebecca of Sunnybrook Farm*, Houghton Mifflin 1903

Williams, Susan, *The People's King*, Allen Lane 2003

Ziegler, Philip, *King Edward VIII*, Collins 1990

Ziegler, Philip, *Mountbatten*, Collins 1985

Articles

Entwistle, John, www.thebaron.info/archives/ultra-british-editor-who-loved-america-took-royal-bribes

Lawrence, Ken '"You furnish the pictures, and I'll furnish the war": The true story of William Randolph Hearst's 1897 cable to Frederic Remington' 2016. Internet published

Phillips, Adrian 'Chronicle of a conspiracy foretold' in *Journal of Conservative History* Vol II Issue 5

Acknowledgements

The staff at the Parliamentary Archives, especially Dr Mari Takayanagi and Annie Pinder, were amazingly tolerant and helpful when confronted by the demands I placed on their time and energies. At Balliol College, Oxford, Stewart Tiley, the Librarian, and Bethany Hamblen at the college archives, were a joy to work with.

Material from the Monckton Papers is reproduced by kind permission of the Master and Fellows of Balliol College. Material from Lord Beaverbrook's papers is reproduced by kind permission of the Parliamentary Archives on behalf of the Beaverbrook Foundation.

I owe special thanks to two people who examined material in American archives for me: Jessica Lage persevered with the mass of material at the Bancroft Library at Berkeley until she finally struck gold. Satu Haase-Webb fruitfully explored the Library of Congress in Washington. research that I undertook for that title and I remain very grateful for all the assistance that was given me then.

The whole team at Pen & Sword – Charles Hewitt, Jonathan Wright, Claire Hopkins, Sarah-Beth Watkins, Laura Wilkins, Lucy May and, of course, my long-suffering editor Chris Cocks – have provided immense support and help for this project from beginning to end.

My biggest thanks go to my wife Sheila, not only for her vital support and advice throughout the project, but also for the countless amounts of practical assistance from research to copy checking.

Index

About the Author

After working as an investment analyst in London and Frankfurt Adrian Phillips returned to university to study history which had been a lifelong passion. His postgraduate thesis looked into the mechanisms of power at the top level of government and how major decisions can be taken far outside the regular democratic political process, hidden from public sight. He has put this understanding to full use in his books on the abdication (*The King Who Had to Go*), appeasement (*Fighting Churchill, Appeasing Hitler*) and rearmament (*Rearming the RAF For The Second World War*). He maintains a popular blog, *Eighty Years Ago This Week*, and regularly contributes on history for TV and radio shows. Adrian is a Fellow of the Royal Historical Society.

Adrian Phillips FRHistS
adrianphillips.co.uk
adriangphillips.blogspot.com
@adriangphillips [Twitter]